DARE NOT BLINK

DARE NOT BLINK

Gerald Gillis

NAVIGATOR BOOKS

SAN DIEGO, CALIFORNIA

DARE NOT BLINK

Copyright © 2012 by Gerald Gillis

Navigator Books

www.navigator-books.com

ISBN-13: 978-0-9852523-4-2

Cover design by Navigator Books

Printed in the United States of America

This book is dedicated to my three children—Jerry Jr., Steve, and Suzanne. I am profoundly grateful for your presence in my life and all the joy you have brought me. You are, and always have been, a source of great pride, in who you are and what you do. I have been blessed with three extraordinarily rich and rewarding relationships, and it remains today a gift that keeps on giving. You have made me better, indeed <u>far</u> better than I would have been otherwise. I can only hope that in some small way I have done the same for you.

Acknowledgements

Dare Not Blink is a work of fiction. It is a story about the business world—its inherent rough-and-tumble, conflict-driven, and often intrigue-filled nature. It is based upon the more than three decades I spent as a managerial element in and observer of the large and complex ecosystem that is corporate America.

There have been many influential friends and colleagues along the way, from Law Engineering Testing Company to Genuine Parts Company to Datex-Ohmeda. I have been truly fortunate to have worked with and learned from many talented and accomplished professionals in the U.S. and around the world. I would especially like to thank Don Spence, President and CEO of Accelent, Inc., for his early critique of my manuscript and his overall insights and encouragement for this project. Don is a valued friend, a gifted and quality individual who makes the business profession better by his presence and example.

— **Gerald Gillis**

At the cycle's center,
They tremble, they walk
Under the tree,
They fall, they are torn,
They rise, they walk again.

—James Dickey,
"The Heaven of Animals"

CHAPTER ONE

The office door was closed, hinting that something was stirring, something big and essential and not widely known—something only for those privileged few who were deemed worthy to hear in advance.

"The Old Man's got cancer, and it's spreading out of control."

Jeff Wylie, president of Atlanta-based Elerbee Engineering, a consulting engineering firm, took an ominously deep breath and exhaled slowly. His two closest associates, anxious and close-mouthed, sat across the big desk from him.

It was April, 2002.

Wylie cleared his throat and took a sip from a plastic water bottle. He looked over each of the two men carefully, deliberately, knowing full well that his own demeanor was likewise being closely scrutinized. He quickly glanced at his open laptop, then at some scribbled notes on a legal pad atop his desk before finally removing his glasses and straightening in his thick leather chair.

"I can't be much more specific than that, except to add that it apparently started in his lungs."

His two associates were dumbstruck. The firm's vigorous, indomitable, sixty-six-year-old founder and chairman, Langdon Elerbee—*the* Elerbee in Elerbee Engineering—had been such a forceful presence for such a long time that the very prospect of his sudden, permanent departure seemed highly implausible. It defied all that was customary and natural, akin to a Federal Reserve proposition to drop the U.S. dollar and adopt the Norwegian kroner as the new monetary standard of value.

"It doesn't look good, gentlemen. The time line's in days and hours, that's how quickly the disease is overtaking him."

"My God!" gasped Jim Ogden, a senior executive and Wylie protégé. "How did you find out?"

Wylie shrugged. "I've known for several weeks that something wasn't right. He'd had some problems, underwent a series of tests, and then his mood changed, almost as if he'd suddenly lost interest in an entire lifetime of work. His coughing was nearly constant, and with his shortness of

1

breath, his arriving late and leaving early, I knew something was up. His wife called last night to tell me he had been hospitalized, that things were serious and that, well, the doctors were now advising things were moving toward a bad outcome."

Don Burroughs, another corporate officer, could only shake his head in disbelief.

Wylie took another sip of water, then fidgeted with a cell phone on his desk. Ogden leaned forward, alternately glancing at his boss and his feet.

Burroughs shook his head again, his face a bright crimson, his shoulders sagging heavily, his mouth forcing a self-conscious half-grin. "What the hell happens *now*?" he asked in a voice unintentionally louder than usual.

Wylie turned and stared out a window to the side. "I think it would be an understatement to say we're in for some challenging days ahead."

Ogden sighed loudly. "No kidding. Who else in the firm knows?"

"Nobody, although Grace Elerbee did ask me to contact Dave Paige and Larry Collier to make sure they understood the severity of the situation."

"Have you done that?"

"No."

"Are you going to?"

Wylie turned and glared at Ogden before sharply replying, "No."

Ogden and Burroughs were suddenly bewildered and unnerved, as much by Wylie's tone and body language as by the news itself.

Wylie reached up and opened the top button of his starched white shirt, loosening his red-striped tie—an uncharacteristic move that hardly slipped the notice of his two hyper-attentive colleagues.

"I should tell you both that I've been planning for and anticipating this very opportunity, which incidentally I've shared with no one else, not even my wife," Wylie added. "Langdon Elerbee had a plan for the continuance of this firm after his eventual retirement, of course, but now his departure seems likely to occur before his final imprint can be put into place. And I should also tell you that my plan differs considerably from Langdon's, especially with regard to the people that he and I see as vital to this firm. He has his preferences, and I certainly have mine."

"But the Board's already approved Langdon's plan to name Dave Paige as Executive Vice President," countered Burroughs after a weighty silence.

Wylie's expression hardened. "I'm well aware of that, thank you. Do you not remember that I sit on that same Board?"

Burroughs swallowed and looked away.

Ogden leaned closer to Wylie's desk. "What the hell's going on here, Jeff?"

"What's going on here is simply that a rare moment of opportunity has arrived, and I don't intend to squander it. Langdon will soon enough pass from the scene, leaving an obvious void at the very top of the firm. I will be elevated to Chairman and C.E.O. by a Board of Directors that I will now lead. I will then proceed to put into place an organizational structure of my own design, and with people of my own choosing."

Wylie hesitated a moment before adding, "Let me say once more: I *do not* intend to let this opportunity pass, gentlemen."

Wylie then sat back and watched. He carefully studied the faces of Ogden and Burroughs as his words were absorbed and comprehended. His two associates were experienced veterans of the intrigue and stealth warfare so common to corporate America, especially at a headquarters level. Wylie's own arrival two years prior had brought with it a sort of ruthless, zero-sum, internecine style that the traditionally conservative Elerbee Engineering had yet to fully emulate or widely embrace. The gentlemanly, consummately professional approach of Langdon Elerbee still remained the behavioral model throughout the vast majority of the company. Wylie understood all too well that his detached and secretive management style was distasteful to most of the old Elerbee hands, but he also knew that many of the firm's top executives could be easily browbeaten with a string of smoking-hot expletives or a strategically arranged display of temper.

Wylie also knew that only one top manager, Dave Paige, could not be so easily cowed. But he would deal with Dave Paige in his new plan, in his own way, and on his own terms.

The reckoning for Paige would come on day one, page one, paragraph one. It was all in the plan. Things would come roaring at Paige like a runaway locomotive, at once so swift and powerful and unexpectedly that an instant replay would be needed to reconstruct exactly what had transpired. Jeff Wylie could not, *would* not tolerate the presence of Dave Paige in Wylie's new order of things. Again, it was all in the plan. And for all practical purposes, it *was* the plan.

That rarest of moments will soon arrive, Wylie now knew, filling his head with a dizzying array of rich possibilities, accelerating his pulse like an astronaut's on the launching pad, triggering his predatory impulses like a tiger stalking its prey. The day would soon be his to win or lose.

And he had every intention of winning.

Wylie suddenly rose, and as he did so he buttoned his collar and straightened the knot of his tie. Ogden and Burroughs also stood, not knowing what else to do.

"Enough of the preliminaries, gentlemen," Wylie said, his hands now resting upon his hips, his words coming faster than usual. "Like myself, you are about to hear a knock on the door. If you are bold enough to answer, you will find yourself face-to-face with a magnificent and unequalled opportunity of a sort that, if you are indeed fortunate, will come along only once or twice over an entire career. If you choose to ignore that knock, you will most likely lose your one and only chance to make some serious noise in this company. And I mean *serious* noise, gents, with all the influence and prestige and remuneration that the term signifies. The decision is yours alone, but the rules are such that you will be required to make it in the next three minutes."

Wylie stopped and stared at his two associates, sensing the shared tension in the deathly silent room, shifting his icy gaze from one man to the other, feeling his own heart rate quickening inside his chest.

"Are you gentlemen hearing me loud and clear?"

Both nodded their understanding, each then cutting a quick glance at the other.

"Good, because you two are the only people in this firm—hell, on the planet earth!—that I've revealed my intentions to. I am going to take control of this organization and drive it to places it never dreamed it could go. There will be new service offerings, new acquisitions, new markets, and unprecedented levels of revenue and profit. I am going to do what I came here to do and overturn the institutional reluctance to take risks and stir up the industry. I am going to reinvent this firm, to change its culture, to put it on a fast track. And I'm going to need a team around me who sees what I see, feels what I feel, wants what I want. And you two are the very first members of that prospective team that I'm approaching. But you must keep silent about this conversation, as I have thus far, for to do otherwise will result in all manner of unpleasantness crashing down upon you. There are those on this executive team who absolutely do not need to hear about this. This has the potential—no, the certainty—that a lot of feelings will be hurt and a lot of careers altered before all is said and done. Be that as it may. I'll do what needs to be done, you can be sure of that. But I will be the only one to make the decisions as to who needs to hear and who doesn't. Am I making myself crystal clear?"

"Yes," they both said in unison.

Wylie then glanced at his watch. "Time is up. I need to know here and now. And then, either way, I will need your silence until I instruct you otherwise. And if you're thinking that I'm asking you first because I value you and want you with me, well, you've guessed correctly. That is why I've called you here. That is why you're hearing this."

Wylie then smiled slightly, sliding his hands into his trouser pockets.

"Gentlemen, your moment has arrived. You've heard the knock. Now you must answer."

Wylie nodded, his slight smile still attached, his eyebrows arched.

"So, are you with me?"

CHAPTER TWO

Dave Paige steered the silver Lexus out of the line of stalled traffic in front of Atlanta's Georgia Dome and out onto a network of idle side streets. They were at least moving, finally, while many others weren't, and soon the city would open up and grant them a quick passage to the interstate. Elton John's concert had been lengthy, if not extravagant, and for the young and not-so-young alike, the old songs had coated them in an almost analgesic-like nostalgia.

"It was okay," conceded Sara Paige, age nineteen, the daughter of the car's driver and one whose musical tastes were decidedly more contemporary. "I'm glad we went. I mean, it was great that we could spend the time together."

Dave Paige gave his daughter a suspicious glance. "I'm glad we went, too," he said, adding, "but it was much better than 'okay,' dearest. It was Elton freakin' John, for crying out loud. Have you no sense of history? Of musical royalty?"

"Dad, the man and his music were definitely awesome in their time," Sara replied matter-of-factly. "But, c'mon, you've got to admit that it does go back to the previous century."

Sara reached over and ran her hand along her father's mostly brown hair, leaning in for a closer look. "Aha! I'm seeing more and more gray. I suppose it's inevitable, and it's completely understandable that you'd still be attracted to Seventies music. Don't be ashamed, Dad. It's just part of who you are."

Paige grinned. "What is it about my insulting, unappreciative, smart-alecky daughter that still makes her my favorite person in the universe?"

"Well, let's see. It couldn't be my money because I never have any. I'm always broke. It's as much a part of the Sara Paige package as my brown eyes or the rose tattoo on my left buttocks."

"The rose *what*? On the left *where*?"

"Dad, I'm just kidding. About the tattoo, that is. But not about the money and the brown eyes."

"And you wouldn't be saying that for my benefit, would you?"

"Of course not."

Paige laughed. "Maybe it's your subtlety that so appeals to me."

"Like father, like daughter."

Paige chuckled. "And you rarely have any money because, when you do, you spread it around like a communicable disease. You can spend money at an award-winning level, kiddo, just like someone else I know."

"Like mother, like daughter."

Paige smiled, inserted a Vivaldi cassette into the car's tape player, and immediately began enjoying *The 4 Seasons*. There was a long pause before he finally asked the question his daughter had been expecting since her arrival in Atlanta earlier in the afternoon.

"So how's your mother?"

Sara swept a handful of her long brown hair behind her ear. "She's good," she answered, staring at the tape player. "Dad, no offense to you and Antonio, but any chance you'd have some John Mayer instead?"

"Some who?"

"Never mind," Sara said, grinning.

"How often do you get home to see your mom?"

"Every few weeks. And we talk on the phone most days."

"She's keeping busy at the gift shop?"

"Yeah. She spends most of her time there. She's even working on getting her entire catalog on her new web site."

Paige nodded, surprised. He was genuinely impressed that his ex-wife had somehow found the entrepreneurial gumption to start her own business. "Tell her to hang in there with the shop. And tell her that I wish her well. Tell her that, uh, tell her—"

"I will, Dad," Sara said softly. "I'll tell her you send your best."

Sara's soothing tone reminded him of Valerie. He momentarily recollected when, in the early Eighties only days before Sara's birth, Valerie and he had stayed up late one cold, wintry Virginia night arguing over a name for the baby; how the freethinking Valerie had joked that a name like Perspicacity or Moonbeam or Fidelity might fit the bill perfectly, boy or girl; and how Marine Lieutenant Paige had countered with Mutually Assured Destruction (nickname Maddie) or Aiming Point (Aimee) or Missile (Missy). And how, in the end, they had settled upon the lovely name of Sara Michelle for their beautiful, bustling bundle in pink.

Sara by now had flowered into a young woman of charm and beauty who, despite her youth and her attachment to each parent, had somehow found the wisdom beyond her years to accept the divorce as one of those unfortunate life experiences over which she had absolutely no control. She had moved to Pittsburgh with her mother immediately afterward, and soon thereafter she had begun her freshman classes at Penn. While she had always been close to her father, she had thus far resisted the temptation to attach blame for the split on one parent or the other. She came to Atlanta as often as she could manage, given her and her father's respective schedules, while Paige managed an occasional detour to Philadelphia, if only long enough to drop by and treat her to dinner at the local pizzeria.

Paige took a deep breath.

It's here again, he thought. And it's always the same: The nagging, unshakeable guilt of leaving a good kid in the rubble of a crashed marriage. It's always there, never very far from the surface; always, the godforsaken guilt. And now it comes with a long-distance dose of that diametrical mix of fatherly pride and worldly horror over his daughter's entry into young adulthood. He had channel-surfed through MTV and VH1 often enough to get a flavor for the way young people dressed, the way they danced, what music they preferred, and his discoveries were at once revealing and disconcerting. He trusted Sara, always had, but he knew from his own not too distant youth that while she was drawing a bead on adulthood, she was still a baby in so many ways, his baby. Or so he thought.

Paige again sighed deeply, having already lost the concert buzz.

Sara reached over and touched her father's hand. "Dad, I meant what I said about being able to spend this time with you. It means a lot. It really does."

Paige smiled and squeezed her hand again. "Same here, sweets. And there's plenty more frequent-flier coupons where this one came from," he said softly, though the truth was that ever since a co-worker's young son had become terribly ill and died a few years ago, he had been giving away many of the free tickets he earned to an Atlanta children's hospital. "Delta is ready when you are."

She giggled. "Good. Now tell me about your love life. I want to hear about all those dozens of girlfriends I'm sure you've got."

Paige laughed out loud. "Yeah, right."

"No, c'mon Dad. Tell me."

"Sara, I've had two dates since the divorce was finalized. That's it. That's the full extent of it. Two dates."

"Are you serious? Just two dates, really?"

"Yes, really. The first one was a blind date where every instinct I possess screamed at me not to do. But I did it anyway. And—surprise, surprise!—it turned out to be a five-hour, stomach-churning, unmitigated disaster. It was such a mismatch that it seemed to cling to me for days, like a cheap-booze hangover. God, what an ordeal. The other involved a lovely, vivacious, otherwise compatible young woman who confessed to me in a moment of absolutely stupefying candor that she had a sexually-transmitted disease, but not to worry because it was certainly nothing that couldn't be properly 'managed,' as she put it."

Sara noticed her father's quick flush of embarrassment, and said, cackling, "Welcome to the real world."

Paige shook his head. "I've been in a time warp, I'm afraid."

"Dad, I'll be happy to review with you the basic tenets of safe sex, if you'd like."

"*I beg your pardon?*"

"From a purely theoretical standpoint, mind you," said Sara, laughing harder still.

"Dammit, Sara!"

"You're *still* blushing, Daddy Paige."

Paige finally grinned, then gave a resigned shrug. "It must be the new role as a single guy, I suppose. I seem to be way out of my element."

"You're right, but I love you anyway."

Little else was said until Sara finally asked, "So how are things at Elerbee Engineering?"

"Things are good. I can't complain."

"And Mr. Elerbee?"

"He's still very much in charge," Paige answered, laughing. "I haven't seen him in a nearly a month because I've been traveling, but I'm sure he's still growling at all the younger lions in the pride. Probably some of the older ones, too."

"So when do you start your new job? Executive Vice President, right?"

"Right. Soon, I think."

Sara gave him an admiring look. "Will he turn it *all* over to you eventually?"

Paige laughed softly and brushed aside a shock of hair. His dark eyes were large and conspicuous, an excellent barometer to his current frame of mind. Sara could see the enthusiasm on his face, in his eyes, but her father resisted any outward display of emotion.

"I'm afraid you'll have to get the Old Man to answer that one, babe."

"Okay," Sara said agreeably. "The next time I see him, I'll ask."

Over a span of forty years, Elerbee Engineering had grown into a $400 million business, with 2,300 employees in 69 locations. The privately-held company provided engineering and environmental consulting services, along with construction consulting. Its founder had liquidated his modest savings and started the firm from scratch while serving as an assistant professor of engineering at Georgia Tech. Its soils and materials engineers were at the very heart of its consulting portfolio, providing clients with services on all phases of a project, from designing to developing to construction management. It was a solid, reputable, profitable firm that was viewed by its clients as an excellent partner, by its employees as an unrivaled place to work, and by new engineering graduates as a highly desirable spot in which to begin a career.

At the age of forty-two, Dave Paige was on a fast track. The Elerbee Engineering Board of Directors had recently confirmed him for promotion to Executive Vice President, a new position created by Langdon Elerbee and scheduled to begin in the coming few months. Presently, Paige was responsible for one of the firm's three geographic regions, and as such, together with his two regional vice president counterparts, along with Elerbee and the firm's president, Jeff Wylie, he was already one of the five members of the top-management club.

It was heady stuff for Paige, the youngster of the group. But it was precisely the kind of environment that fueled his considerable fires, that gave his life a singularity of purpose so tightly focused that virtually everything else in his world ran the considerable risk of becoming, in his own words, merely "background noise."

Sadly, the background noise had included his wife of twenty years, from whom he had been divorced a scant nine months. Valerie's absence now seemed to take up nearly as much room as her presence had—in his head and heart—especially when he returned home to an empty house after a long day. He still missed her, still longed for her at times, and he often wondered if he would ever grow accustomed to living without her.

Yet even the difficult personal circumstances had hardly changed his hard-driving nature. Tall at six-foot two, trim and athletic in bearing, Dave Paige had the look and demeanor of a natural leader. He had begun his career as a staff engineer in the firm's Atlanta Branch, and from there he had progressed to Chief Engineer before an opening had occurred for a branch manager in Pittsburgh. With Langdon Elerbee's blessings and encouragement, young Paige, with his Pittsburgh-born wife and young daughter, had descended upon a struggling Pittsburgh Branch where, within a few short months of previously unknown levels of intensity, he had transformed the old slothful order into an energetic, aggressive, overachieving brotherhood and a virtual money machine of fees and profits. After five ultra-successful years in Pittsburgh, he had transferred to Minneapolis where he had overseen the opening of the Des Moines, Iowa office, along with the forays into Canada. In sixteen years with Elerbee Engineering, Dave Paige had cultivated a wide following in the Elerbee ranks who had watched with interest and awe as he moved from conquest to conquest, always achieving despite the odds, always succeeding beyond expectations, always a bright light of honesty and integrity.

All the while he had hardly gone unnoticed at corporate headquarters. He was a Langdon Elerbee favorite, clearly, but other executives admired his determination and fair-mindedness. Only a handful viewed him as a threat to their own lofty ambitions, that same handful who held him in tight-lipped contempt for what they perceived as his privileged insider status with the Old Man.

Paige didn't seem to mind, though. He stayed far too busy to worry about such frivolity. He spent virtually all of his time driving himself and those around him to higher and higher levels of performance. It was hardly uncommon for the more lethargic associates on his staff to bolt in full retreat once they reached a point of near exhaustion from the hours and the workload. In contrast, Paige's energetic staff members simply adored their boss and the incessant frenzy that seemed to follow and swirl around him like a tropical disturbance. Dave Paige was simply different from the rest. The principle of executive accountability, and specifically *personal* accountability, was a deeply imbedded anchor in the very core of his character. In an on-line, real-time, right-now world where the concept as well as the practice of accountability was talked about incessantly but seen only in the rarest of public or private officials, Paige was an aberration. He never dodged the fallout from a bad personal decision and never ducked the often unpleasant residue that might follow the blunder of a subordinate. He never conveniently folded himself into the creases of the corporate bureaucracy, never made excuses, never sought to avoid or even spread the blame. He had courage; he had character. He sometimes caused Langdon Elerbee to swear, sometimes to marvel, but always to think, *By God, this kid's got balls*!

And with Langdon Elerbee, it meant something to have balls. As a matter of fact, by God, it meant nearly everything.

And so the bond between Dave Paige and Langdon Elerbee was solid, in personal as well as professional terms. Paige was, in many ways, the son Elerbee never had. Over the years, Paige had also come to remind Elerbee of himself, as much for the obvious energy and drive as from the fact that each had grown up with solid Episcopal values in central Illinois and each had matriculated at Purdue University. That Dave Paige was Elerbee's favored young executive was hardly a secret, as was the logical assumption that Paige was destined for even greater responsibility as Langdon Elerbee gradually withdrew from the business over the coming several years.

Meanwhile, Paige was slated to become Executive Vice President. And from there, who knew? Perhaps the presidency. Perhaps more. One man, Jeff Wylie, stood between Paige and Langdon Elerbee on the organization chart. The challenge for Chairman Elerbee was to keep the two men working in harmony, for Elerbee knew all too well that Paige and Wylie cared little for one another. There was a mutual suspicion, a discernible tension between the two men that at times seemed almost to glow from the shared negative energy. It was enough of a problem—Wylie the relative newcomer, forceful and erratic; Paige the dynamic, immensely talented junior—that sometimes just thinking about it had caused the Old Man's ulcer to flare.

"Yep," Sara concluded. "The next time we're together I'll just ask Mr. Elerbee myself when he's going to turn everything over to you."

Paige smiled, certain that Sara would do precisely that as soon as she saw the elder Elerbee again.

Paige felt his stomach rumble. "Feel like getting a bite to eat, sweets?"

"I dunno. What've you got in mind?"

"Well, what do you want?"

"Chili dogs and onion rings."

Paige paused a second, then shrugged. "I might pay a price for it later when it repeats on me, but yeah, we could make that work."

"Then I'm like *definitely* hungry."

"Great," said Paige, suddenly turning onto North Avenue. "I know just the place."

CHAPTER THREE

"Sir, I'm sorry, but you're not allowed in there. I'm afraid that's a private conference. I beg your pardon, sir, but—sir, *sir!*"

Dave Paige winked at the secretary and then proceeded to walk past her, open the door to the large conference room, and step inside. Seven executives from Alsop and Associates, Inc., Houston, Texas, glanced up in unison from the papers, topographic maps, and thick binders that had hitherto commanded their full attention.

It was just past nine o'clock in the morning.

"Good morning, gentlemen. I'm Dave Paige from Elerbee Engineering."

Paige overheard someone mumble, "You gotta be shittin' me," before he nodded a greeting and smiled innocently.

"Mr. Mendelsohn, I tried to tell him that the meeting's private," offered the gray-haired, schoolmarmish secretary in her own defense. "But he just kept right on going."

There was a brief pause before Marshall Mendelsohn, the architectural firm's fifty-seven-year-old president, nodded his absolution to the secretary. "It's all right, Mrs. Sweeny. Mr. Paige may remain as our uninvited but not necessarily unwelcomed guest."

The secretary gave Paige a menacing glance before turning and stepping outside, closing the door behind her.

The slender, silver-haired Mendelsohn, neatly attired in a blue pinstripe suit, took a sip of coffee and sat back in his chair. "This is a bit unusual, Mr. Paige," he said in his thick Texas drawl. "Mind telling me where you get off thinking you can come crashing in on our private meeting and unsettling the hell out of our admin help?"

Paige quickly leaned over and placed his briefcase on the floor. He stood alone at the opposite end of the long table. "I took the red-eye from Atlanta early this morning and I won't stay long, sir, I assure you. But it's my understanding that you and your staff are making a decision today on the engineering firm to work with you on the highway bridge-inspection project throughout the state of Texas."

Mendelsohn glanced around at his colleagues. "This is the team that makes those decisions, yes sir. So, tell me, have we screwed up and left you off the selection committee, Mr. Paige?"

There was chuckling from the others.

Paige smiled softly. "Of course not, Mr. Mendelsohn. I just wanted to make sure that you got the best comparison possible."

"Oh?"

Paige took a deep breath, shifted his feet slowly, and then relaxed with one hand in his suit pocket. "Gentlemen, you're no doubt aware that one of my Elerbee engineers left our firm several weeks ago and joined a new firm that also happens to be competing with us for the chance to work with you on this project."

"And?"

"Anthony Alvarado is a good man, a good engineer. But he's taken our proposal, plagiarized it, undercut our fee schedule, and promised you he'd deliver everything that Elerbee Engineering would bring to the project."

Paige briefly paused to gauge the response of one specific individual in the room, the brother-in-law of his former engineer and now chief rival. The man shifted nervously and avoided Paige's eyes.

"In my professional opinion, he's made a claim that he can't live up to," Paige said, continuing in a non-threatening, matter-of-fact tone. "He's neither staffed nor equipped to give you the kind of quality performance that he's proposing, and if you believe him, my concern is that you'll be disappointed later on."

The brother-in-law winced. "That's just nonsense!"

Paige shrugged. "Anthony's a good engineer. We know; we trained him. And we supported him with a lot of additional resources, both human and materiel. But he doesn't have that depth now. He doesn't have the support structure that he always took for granted when he worked for Elerbee Engineering. And in all honesty I don't think he should be claiming otherwise."

"But at least he's shown an interest," said Mendelsohn. "Your own branch manager doesn't strike me as giving a tinker's damn about our project. Isn't that a bit strange, Mr. Paige?"

"It is," Paige agreed. "I won't deny it. And I'm certainly not pleased about it."

"Why, then, your sudden interest?"

"Only my arrival here this morning is sudden, sir. I assure you that my company's interest has been ongoing. I assisted with the proposal from my Atlanta office, and I'm familiar with all of its technical and financial detail. This is an important project for us. You are an important client. If we've given you the wrong impression, then I sincerely regret it. We want to be your partner on this project, and we'll provide you with everything you've come to expect from us, from our past partnerships. I give you my word on it. "

"Then have you come here to tell us that you'll fire the ole boy if you get the project?"

"No, I have not. I've come here to state my company's interest in and commitment to working closely with you on this and all other projects. I don't think we've made that clear enough to you, and as I've mentioned before, I truly regret it. You'll get the best possible value for your money by hiring us to work with you on this bridge project. Our soils and materials engineers are the best in the business, and our testing labs are fully equipped. I reiterate, we want very badly to be a part of your team."

"What are you going to do with your branch manager, then?" Mendelsohn pressed.

"Respectfully, sir, that's a family matter," Paige said softly but firmly. "I can discuss that only after I've dealt in private with my employee."

"You're taking a helluva big risk crashing in here like this, pal," the brother-in-law commented.

"I recognize that," Paige answered calmly.

"Anthony and his group could easily sue you over such a charge, and win."

"They could easily sue us, yes," Paige replied. "But winning might be a bit more problematic. Our proposal was created when Anthony Alvarado was on our Houston staff. He had no part in formulating it, he would've been too junior to have managed it, but from what I'm told he seems to have used our proposal to develop his own, from cover to cover. I didn't come here to berate Anthony—he's a good man and I remain personally very fond of him—but I won't sit idly by and let him do what I believe he's done with our proposal. My hunch is that the two competing proposals are identical enough in all the right places to validate my argument. But," he said, pausing to notice the brother-in-law swallowing and looking away, "you gentlemen can make that comparison without any further need of me."

Paige reached down for his briefcase. "I hope you'll accept my apology for the disruption, gentlemen. I also hope you and your associates know that Elerbee Engineering stands ready to offer you our very best if we're fortunate enough to be selected. Let me say once more that we value you as a client, greatly, and we would be honored to work with you again. Your firm has been good to us, and we want to be your first choice, now and always. I felt it would be worth the trip over here to stop by and tell you that personally, though I do apologize for barging in like this."

Paige stopped briefly at the large double-doors and looked back at the group. He smiled and nodded. "I wish you gentlemen a pleasant and productive good day."

Paige departed while the others immediately began chuckling. The brother-in-law laughed the loudest and conveyed the greatest incredulity. "Can you believe that guy?" was repeated several times.

Everyone was laughing in the big room. Everyone, that is, except Mendelsohn.

"Gentlemen," he said sharply, quieting the others, "I realize that we'll deviate from our agenda to take up the engineering-consultant selection at this point in the process, but I suggest that we stop now and look at this matter before going on any further."

The others nodded their assent but were otherwise silent.

"So," Mendelsohn said as the group rearranged their materials to get at the two proposal binders, "anybody got any comments?"

The Houston offices of Elerbee Engineering were located west of the city, just off the Katy Freeway and outside the North Loop. Nestled in a modern office complex, the facility housed the labs and offices of the Central Region's largest branch. A contingent of one hundred-twenty engineers, technicians, administrators, and secretaries was busy at work at 10:30 a.m. when Dave Paige arrived.

The marginal financial results from Houston had been a source of ongoing concern. There was an uneven flow of projects coming into the branch, making the utilization of the branch engineers more challenging, along with controlling the branch's overall cost structure. Things were obviously not well, and the man-in-charge in Houston was feeling the heat.

Dave Paige and the Houston Branch Manager, Randall Karsten, faced one another across Karsten's large wooden desk, in the center of the richly appointed office. Paige had slept little the night before, and his appetite had waned. He could sense that his appearance was gradually betraying the cool, calm exterior he was so diligently attempting to maintain. His eyes were puffy and bloodshot, even after what seemed nearly a quart of Visine, and his armpits felt moist and cool. He wanted coffee, desperately, but he declined out of fear that his hands were simply too unsteady. He caught himself glancing at his watch more often than usual, hoping somehow that the whole messy episode would hurry up and end—the same feeling, *exactly*, he had felt as a child as he had waited in the dentist's lobby for his appointment with that dreaded drill.

Randall Karsten fidgeted with a paperclip. He adjusted his glasses, alternately glancing at Paige and the small silver object atop his desk. Karsten's face was full and pockmarked, and his light hair had thinned considerably in the front. He had been in Houston for four years—one as a materials engineer, three as branch manager—after having joined Elerbee from a competitor firm in Indiana. His two hundred-forty pounds on his six-foot frame filled the padded swivel chair, enough so that his paunch drooped over his belt as if it were melting.

Like Paige, Karsten was far from feeling at ease.

Paige felt his cheeks flush. "Okay, Randall. Let's talk about the Houston Branch Manager's position."

"Fine," Karsten said calmly. "Please begin."

"I'm replacing you," Paige said immediately. "I've thought about this for some time. I've looked at it from every angle. I've evaluated the past and how I foresee those results relating to the future. I'm not pleased with what I've seen, and that's not news to you. I wish there were an easier way to say it, but I honestly don't feel that Houston's going to make it with you in charge. And so," Paige said, pausing to draw a breath, "I'm letting you go and moving forward with someone else."

Karsten stared at Paige for a moment, as if to allow his mind to catch up with his ears. "Yeah, so who's it going to be?"

"Lou Thrasher," Paige answered immediately, referring to the branch's Chief Engineer.

Karsten removed his glasses and began rubbing his eyes. "What kind of time frame are you talking?"

"Today, right now. The sooner the better, I think."

Karsten gave a long sigh. "Damn," he said as if all the air had left his lungs. "Is it a clean cut, or is there something to keep me going until I can find something else?"

"Six-months' salary as severance, plus any earned bonuses, plus your medical insurance."

Karsten slid his glasses back into place and stood. He stepped over to a full-length window in the corner of the office where he opened the brown drapes and began staring out at the sunny brightness. "What's going down as the reason?"

"That you've resigned."

"What's the real reason?"

"There are several. You want the full list?"

He turned and looked at Paige. "Yeah, the full and complete list."

Paige nodded. "Fair enough. The chief reason is the branch's failure to hit its fee and profit targets. Not just once or twice, but fourteen consecutive months."

"The last four months we've shown improvement. A few more good projects and we'd be on a roll," Karsten explained, the emotion finally creeping into his voice.

"There wasn't enough progress, Randall. And what little progress there was didn't come until I had outlined for you on at least two separate occasions the seriousness of the situation here. And all the while, your enthusiasm for delivering on what we discussed was approximately nothing."

"But there was progress."

The muscles in Paige's jaw tightened. "Very little, and not nearly enough."

"But there was progress!" Karsten exclaimed, his face reddening.

Their eyes met, and neither turned away.

"Randall," Paige spoke slowly, "I'm sorry, but I'm not here to negotiate this with you. And I'm not going to argue with you over the degree to which this operation improved. It was slight, any way you view it. The fact that we're talking about altogether different forests seems to get lost in your insistence that the trees are similar. I kept waiting, and asking, and delaying the inevitable, and I never saw a plan from you on picking up the tempo. And so I made a decision to let you go and try someone else. And I'll damn well expect this branch to get off dead center and get back in the hunt."

Karsten shifted his gaze back outside, into the distance beyond the building. "What else?" he asked, calmer.

"No new clients were added, and fees were down with the three biggest clients."

"Okay. What else?"

"You let the big Alsop project wither on the vine. That was inexcusable with so much at stake here. Completely unacceptable."

"You don't know the full story there. How can you use that as part of the formula for firing me?"

"I spoke with you enough to know that what you *did* do and what you *could've* done to lock that up and—"

"But you don't have the full picture," Karsten snapped as he turned toward Paige. "How the hell can you come out here from Atlanta and come on to me like you know what's going on here, goddammit?"

Paige's expression softened, as did his tone. "Randall, it's a little late to be using the 'Ivory Tower' thing on me."

Karsten took a long, deep breath and looked away again. "Any others?"

"One other, yes."

"And?"

"I'm aware of how much time you've spent away from the office," Paige said slowly. "And I've got more than a sneaking suspicion that it deals with the landscape business you're operating on the side."

"Is that a fact?" Karsten said mockingly.

"I think it probably is, yes. I'm not sure which is the leading culprit here: Your performance or your outside interests. But be that as it may, you might consider a review of that before you decide to hire on with another company."

Karsten raised his head defiantly, imperiously. "I'll make those decisions without any help from you."

"That's fine. And as to the matter at hand, I think we've discussed it enough. I've given you the full picture as I see it," Paige replied.

Karsten gave a loud sigh. "I've got a few personal things to box up. Mind if I do all of that this morning?"

"Of course not."

"I'll be out of here as quickly as I can pack up and clear out."

"I'm in no particular hurry to have you out of the building, Randall. You can take whatever time you need."

Karsten eventually plopped his large frame back into his chair.

Paige stood. "I'm gonna be with Lou a few minutes. As soon as we're through, I'll send him in and you two can cover any transition issues." Paige reached inside his jacket pocket and produced a folded letter. "Here are the terms of the salary and bonus payments and insurance coverage we discussed. If you have any further questions of me, I'll be around a bit longer."

Paige stepped toward the door but stopped as his hand touched the knob. "I'm sorry it had to come to this, Randall, I truly am. And I appreciate all you've done in the past. I wish you well."

Karsten gave a dismissive wave in acknowledgment before swiveling his chair to the side. Paige then opened the door and stepped out, nodding in the process to the wide-eyed female assistant stationed just outside. He kept walking, turning the corner and proceeding to the entrance of Lou Thrasher's office. Inside, a young staff engineer was discussing a business matter with Thrasher. When the young man noticed Paige in the doorway, he nearly toppled in his haste to stand and leave amid a profusion of embarrassed grins and apologies.

Paige glanced over at Thrasher, who immediately stood and reached his hand toward Paige.

"Got a minute?" asked Paige.

Thrasher smiled. "I think I can work you in, Dave."

Lou Thrasher was a man of modest size, of modest ways, with the perpetually blinking demeanor of one who can't quite adjust to his contact lenses. His office interior was Spartan and lacked the usual oil paintings and framed diplomas that often surrounded others of similar standing. Thrasher was the branch's chief technical consultant, a responsibility he accepted with great skill and care. He was a strict teacher and a demanding supervisor to the branch's many other practitioners, and a respected adviser to the firm's clients in the area. An eighteen-year employee, Thrasher had long ago flown Navy fighters before his eyesight had finally deteriorated and forced him from the cockpit. He was unselfish and dedicated, solid in all respects—the quintessential Elerbee Engineer.

"I don't suppose it's any secret by now," Paige began after closing the door and taking a seat across from Thrasher, "but I've just canned Randall Karsten."

Thrasher displayed no outward signs of emotion. He took a deep breath, then nodded and muttered a soft, "Okay."

"And I'm naming you as his successor, effective immediately."

Thrasher squinted and swallowed hard. "Damn, Dave. You certainly don't mince any words," he finally remarked.

Paige reached inside the coat pocket of his grey suit and produced two envelopes. "The first is the announcement of the change, including your being named as Branch Manager. I'd like it distributed throughout the branch this afternoon, after Randall's departure. The second letter details your compensation program, specifically your new salary and a bonus arrangement related to return-on-investment. Take a minute and look everything over."

Thrasher carefully and deliberately studied the contents of each of the letters. He finally glanced up at Paige and nodded, saying, "They look fine, Dave."

"Anything in either letter bother you?"

"No. I appreciate the opportunity. And I appreciate your generosity."

"Are you surprised at what's happening?"

Thrasher grinned. "At Randall's descent or my ascent?"

"The former."

"Not really. Most of us could see it coming."

"Then what about the latter?"

Thrasher thought for a moment. "I'm a little surprised, yeah."

"You're the man I want in Houston, Lou," Paige said firmly. "You know the clients, you know the way we do business, and you know the strengths and weaknesses of this operation. I know you can make it work, and work better than it's ever worked before. And that's why I'm looking to you. There was never any hesitation, never a second thought. I say again, you're the man I want in charge here."

The truth was evident in Paige's eyes, and that was enough to satisfy Thrasher.

The two proceeded to spend the next twenty minutes discussing many of the details of the changes: Thrasher's replacement; the replacement's replacement; potential changes in service mix; potential cost-cutting measures, including staff reductions; marketing strategies; notification of the changes to the branch's larger clients. There would be much more to cover, but it would have to come later.

"By the way, Lou, we're going to get the Alsop project."

Thrasher stiffened. "No way, Dave. I got the inside scoop from my contact at Alsop that we're thirty percent higher than Alvarado and his bandits. We're dead in the water, what with the brother-in-law bullshit and the big difference in the pricing. Nope, no way we'll get that one."

"We'll get it," said Paige, grinning.

"I wish I could be as optimistic as you, but based on everything I'm hearing, I can't see it happening."

"Lou, believe me, we'll get it. And when we do, I want you to be our main point of contact. Understood?"

"Okay," Thrasher said, acquiescing but still skeptical. "Not a problem."

"And I want you to pay a personal call on Marshall Mendelsohn before this week's out. Tell him what's happened here, what the changes are. He's a good man, and I believe him to be a fair man. And send over a dozen roses and a restaurant gift certificate to a Mrs. Sweeny at Alsop, a secretary. Put a note in with it that says, 'My apologies. Sincerely, Dave Paige of Elerbee Engineering.' Okay?"

Thrasher noted the instructions on his legal pad and then gave Paige another strange look. "Okay," he answered, saying no more.

Paige sat back in the chair and ran his fingers through his hair as Thrasher jotted down a few more notes. Paige was tired, and his fatigue was beginning to numb him.

Thrasher stole a glance at his watch. "How did Randall take it?"

"He's fine," Paige answered flatly. "And I don't think he was surprised."

Thrasher shook his head after considering the situation. "Well then, I suppose it's time to get on with the handling of this crisis."

Paige grinned. "This is no crisis, Lou. This is an aggravation. There's a difference, you know. We used to say in the Marine Corps that an 'aggravation' is a red-hot pimple on your ass the size of a grape, but a 'crisis' is a diagnosis of rectal cancer. Altogether different implications and orders of magnitude. Houston is an aggravation, and you can fix it by popping the damn pimple and washing it off with an antiseptic, by building a team, by doing the absolute best work that a client can find. I don't expect you to pull it off overnight, but I expect you to go like hell like you were intending to have it all fixed by eight o'clock the next morning."

Thrasher nodded enthusiastically. "We'll get there."

"I'm certain of it," Paige said with a wink and a grin.

Thrasher smiled widely. "We'll get Houston off the 'aggravation' list."

Paige stood. "I'm gonna need to make a few calls. Is there an empty office?"

Thrasher opened the door and noticed a message taped to the door's exterior, noting a Jeff Wylie request that Paige call him in Atlanta as soon as possible, that the matter was urgent.

Paige sighed but said nothing. He wondered for a moment why Wylie wouldn't direct that he be interrupted if the matter was indeed urgent.

It was only when he had gone behind the closed doors of an empty office and reached Wylie by phone did he find out the reason behind the call.

Langdon Elerbee was dead.

Paige sat in shocked disbelief for nearly ten minutes after hanging up with Wylie.

The Old Man. Dead.

The news had the effect on Paige of a violent collision, a deceleration so forceful that he thought for a moment that his innards had been ripped loose. His hands were trembling, his mouth dry, his heart racing as if he'd just witnessed a terrorist attack. He was dazed in that particular numbing sort of way that always follows the hot, hard news of an unexpected death. Can this really be happening? he kept thinking, partly in disbelief, partly in denial, as if he had entered that silent world that was motionless and void of color, unreal and ethereal. He then had a sudden urge to weep, to give in if only for a moment to the grief that swept over and crushed him like a Malibu Beach breaker. He drew a deep breath and then just as suddenly remembered who he was, where he was, and the circumstances under which he had arrived. He knew that word of Mr. Elerbee's death may have already surfaced within the Houston operation. He knew that his tearful emergence from the office, after having fired the branch manager only moments before, would undoubtedly serve as the prelude to an even deeper, darker foreboding to those employees who would be looking for some indication—*any* indication—that indeed their top management was in control and that their world wasn't coming apart at the seams.

But Langdon Elerbee dead? It just didn't seem possible.

Paige finally composed himself to the point that he could carry on with the completion of the business at hand in Houston. He took the opportunity before leaving to address the Houston assemblage who had crowded into the cafeteria at Lou Thrasher's request. Paige captivated the group with a twenty-minute talk about adapting to change; about loyalty; about ideals; about professional ethics; about Elerbee Engineering taking care of its clients and in the process taking care of its own. He spoke of the change in the branch management that he had earlier precipitated. He spoke of his full confidence in Lou Thrasher, in all of the Houston employees.

When he began to speak of the Old Man's death, he had to take a moment to sip from a bottle of water. He then spoke of the company that Langdon Elerbee was now leaving in their care, and how they each had a responsibility to build upon an enviable legacy of professionalism and competence. He talked about the founder's familiar Guiding Principles of preeminent technical expertise, unsurpassed service to clients, and absolute integrity in everything the firm touches. The group erupted in much needed laughter when Paige joked that St. Peter would no doubt be at Heaven's gate to offer his welcome to Elerbee, only to present Langdon with a laundry list of "engineering issues" that needed some immediate heavenly attention.

In the end, Paige brilliantly pulled it off and Lou Thrasher thanked him profusely for his words and his presence.

They emerged from the meeting to the news that Elerbee Engineering had been awarded the Alsop contract, a large enough stream of revenue that it would secure the branch's future for nearly a year.

It was over, finally, and Paige immediately left for the airport to catch his flight back to Atlanta. He thought of his firing of Karsten, and even though he had previously terminated employees, dozens perhaps, it was still a tense and uncomfortable experience. He understood the necessities, as well as the realities, that firings were a natural part of the dynamic of running a business. But he had concluded years ago that if the act of terminating the employment of another human being ever became an act of insignificance or emotional neutrality, if ever it became second nature, routine, commonplace—even once—then the message would be clear that he was fast becoming someone completely outside the blueprint of his own self-image. God knows he'd known plenty of managers who actually took pleasure in firing others. But not Paige. He wanted the decision process to evoke enough stress, agony even, that he could be sure that his own sense of fairness and impartiality would be given ample measure.

And even though he attempted to block it from his mind, Langdon Elerbee's death qualified even in Paige's terms as a certifiable crisis. What would happen now? To the firm? To the plans? To the top-management structure as it currently existed?

Paige sat in a window seat near the rear of the plane, looking out but not really seeing the dark landscape beneath him as he fell under the soft, soothing hypnosis of travel. He eventually asked for and received something for his headache from the flight attendant. The questions remained, tumbling through his head and appearing in flashes, like a meteor shower in an otherwise ink-black sky, gathering mass and then dissipating into still other questions.

What the hell happens now? he kept thinking.

With Wylie? With Ogden? With the Executive Vice President position? What the hell would happen *now*?

It was too much, Paige concluded. He couldn't deal with it now. He needed time to think, to distance himself from the sudden emotional jolt. He needed wise counsel, someone experienced in the ways of Elerbee Engineering, someone who could see the truth *and* tell it. Someone like Larry Collier.

He wanted badly to talk it out. The shock; the uncertainty; the vulnerability. He needed to unburden himself, and his mind quickly produced the image of his former wife. Nope, no good, he thought. He and Valerie hadn't communicated in nearly twenty years of marriage, and were she waiting for him on the other end of his trip home, still as his wife, it's just as likely that they *still* wouldn't communicate, even amid such bad tidings. No, he concluded. He needed someone else.

Larry Collier.

Larry could see it. Larry would know. Larry would listen.

Right.

Larry Collier.

CHAPTER FOUR

A brisk, surly wind rushed along the length of Peachtree Street, blowing tiny particles of debris into the eyes of pedestrians and creating its own fanfare among the usual urban cacophony of buses, taxis, horns, and sirens. It was nevertheless warm in Atlanta, the South's flagship city, host to the '96 Olympic Summer Games and the land of the distinct and wholly tolerable Four Seasons. The land of the glass skyscraper; the grueling rush-hour traffic; the luxury auto; the cellular phone; the manicured suburbia and chic shopping enclaves separated by light-years of expectation and ten miles of distance from the hard, foreboding, inner-city housing projects.

Cradled within the majestic confines of Peachtree Center South, Elerbee Engineering's corporate offices were the proper conservative blend of the functional and the aesthetic. The Elerbee logo, in the form of the Greek letter *sigma* enclosed within a three-foot triangle, loomed large in satin-finished stainless steel behind the reception area. The lobby's layout and furnishings were designed to provide an aura of warmth and distinction. Beyond, amid a series of long hallways, were secretarial stations and individual offices, large and small conference rooms with the latest in audiovisual niceties, a well-appointed library, a computer center, and various storage and file areas.

It was a well-appointed office, in a far corner off the beaten path, befitting an individual of status and taste. There was the thick carpeting, the dark mahogany furniture, the original art with the distinct semi-abstract theme, and a large, conspicuous, glass-topped wooden desk that seemed to shout out to any visitor that *here* resides a person of prominence, of primacy. The company's chief executive, Jeff Wylie, took a moment to sip the coffee that by now had cooled considerably. Seated to the front of Wylie's desk were Dave Paige, Larry Collier, and Jim Ogden, the three regional vice presidents.

It had been only two weeks since Langdon Elerbee's death, and it was clear to the top-executive team that the firm was still struggling to regain its normal operating tempo.

Wylie leaned back in his chair and calmly placed his folded hands in his lap. He was forty-six, tall and thin, blond, smooth-skinned, and immaculate in his navy suit with blue shirt and red-striped tie. His eyes were blue and clear, his jaw firm. His shoulders were sloped downward, more so than usual, as if shaped to allow for tight, headfirst passage. When he smiled, it was usually in a strained sort of way, as if the act of smiling was largely a waste of time for a man of such serious endeavors. Wylie displayed little evidence of humor and preferred instead to keep things businesslike when the corporate clock was ticking. And for Jeff Wylie, the corporate clock only rarely stopped ticking.

"So should I move him out of Fresno, then?" asked Larry Collier who, at age sixty, was the elder statesman among the three subordinates.

Wylie shrugged. "That's entirely your call. If you're willing to suffer through another six months of his bilge, then go ahead and leave him in place."

Collier paused, added a sigh of submission, and then finally nodded his understanding. The manager in Fresno was history.

Dave Paige sat alongside Collier and typed something into his laptop.

Wylie eyed the three men carefully. "I get the impression that some of you think I'm moving in the wrong direction by knocking some fluff off the operation," he said, his words having a strong, almost biting quality to them. "Anyone care to comment?"

There was a long silence before Collier finally cleared his throat and spoke up, saying, "Langdon's death and this damned business cycle that's out there, Jeff, it's still got everybody on edge. The timing's not especially good to be firing eight managers and ten staff people, in my opinion. I don't disagree that something needs to be done. I'm just saying that terminating eighteen people might not be the best move at this particular point."

Unlike Wylie, Collier had a weathered, wrinkled appearance, as if the loosely hanging skin of his face and neck had been formed with old leather. His reddish-brown hair had long ago moved elsewhere, except around the sides of his shiny crown. Responsible for the firm's Western Region, Collier had been in Elerbee's employ for over thirty years. He smoked heavily, suffered occasional coughing spasms, and often appeared nervous and overwrought. He had been a branch manager for many of his years, never failing to deliver both good work to his clients and nice profits to the corporate office. He was an excellent engineer—the quiet, steady Company Man whose willingness to go anywhere, at any time and without special condition, had finally resulted in his reward of high executive status.

"Why not?" pressed Wylie.

Collier thought for a moment. "I suppose it's because of the way my guys are trying to take everything in stride. They're trying to tough it out and not get too discouraged, to see things in a larger perspective. We're not that far from seeing this economy turn around, Jeff. It'll get better in a few more months. It's only a matter of time."

Wylie listened closely, saying nothing.

"Seems to me like it's one of those situations where you have to keep reminding yourself that everyone's nerve-endings are especially raw nowadays, and that the shock of Langdon's passing and the slow business climate will recover with a little time," Collier said. "It's part of the normal course of things, and it'll eventually right itself."

"I think the stuff about the 'nerve-endings' is a bit melodramatic, Larry," interjected Jim Ogden, age forty-four, an eighteen-year employee whose responsibilities covered the Eastern Region. An honors graduate of M.I.T., Ogden, like Dave Paige, was one of the young superstars who had quickly climbed to the upper rung of the corporate ladder. He had in fact been considered as the only other true contender for the Executive V.P. position which had subsequently been awarded to Paige. He was tall and thin, his dark eyes always probing, penetrating, his brown hair short and uncombed, his moustache always just a trifle out of trim.

"We've got to have performance, no matter what the conditions. And if we don't get it, then dammit we ought to sweep 'em aside and get somebody who'll earn their keep," Ogden asserted, eyeing Wylie for approval.

Paige leaned forward to get a better view of Ogden. "That's gallantly spoken, Jim, especially since none of the eight managers belong to you. Nevertheless, an inspiring, stunning piece of oratory—one I must confess almost brings me to a point of wetting my pants."

Ogden, on the other side of Collier from Paige, suddenly stiffened. He fought back the temptation to respond with a blast of his own, and instead said slowly, almost mockingly, "Then obviously you don't agree that we need results."

"Of course we need results," Paige answered. "I was simply objecting to your 'moralizing without actualizing' position. You should leave that to the members of the United States Congress."

"We can do without the sarcasm," Wylie said sharply, looking squarely at Paige.

Grinning, Paige glanced over at Ogden and winked, getting in return only another cold stare.

"Sorry about that," Paige said to no one in particular, and with little sincerity. Paige thought about commenting on the fact that at least five of Ogden's branches were performing at or below the levels of the eight operations in question. Something then drifted into his consciousness, roughly equivalent to "the better part of valor," and he quietly returned his attention to his laptop and his note taking, where he wrote:

    * My region's fees, profits, and project list up, up, up. Ogden's region down, down, down in same. Jeff's cogent analysis: Fire somebody (but not in Ogden's region).

    * Ogden has on new suit (charcoal). Tempted to comment on how distinguished he looks, but how much better he'd look with a shampoo that controls flaking.

    * This meeting's been going for two hours now; nothing's been decided; there is no more coffee; my stomach's growling--the things I have to put up with to be a big corporate cheese!

The meeting continued. Paige stifled a yawn. He was bored and tired, the latter in large part due to his having been up late the night before thinking about the strange twists and turns occurring in his life. He had thought of Langdon Elerbee, and how deeply saddened he was at the loss of a man he so deeply admired. And he had concluded in the wee morning hours that his former wife Valerie had been perfectly proper in divorcing the boorish jerk that he almost assuredly had become. He had spent some time in self-pity, and was moved out of his pathos only by the thought of the delightful weekend he had spent with daughter Sara a few weeks before. Eventually his melancholy had been displaced with more practical matters, such as his soon-to-be new position as Executive Vice President. He had wanted the job in the worst of ways, and he could think of absolutely nothing in his entire life, *nothing*, that he had wanted with equal or greater passion. Not even the woman he had married, he thought with brutal honesty. Not even Valerie.

The meeting continued.

    * This meeting's been going two hours and ten minutes, and nothing's been decided.

    * Decided: Nothing will be decided until someone decides something.

All previous decisions are herewith rescinded. Note: When something that's decided is rescinded, does it then default back to undecided? Or does it go off to some special place in the cosmos?

Two hours and twenty minutes!

"Where the hell are you, Dave?" Wylie asked sharply from across the desk.

Paige sat up and cleared his throat. "I was just working through a timeline," he said as he closed his laptop. "Sorry. What was the question?"

"You've contributed nothing thus far. What the hell's the matter with you?"

"Nothing's the matter," Paige answered, glancing down at his watch. "I was just distracted for a moment."

"Give me a thumbnail sketch of the state of your region," commanded Wylie.

Paige drew a deep breath and exhaled slowly. He had held his position as Vice President-Central Region for slightly less than a year, enough time to have determined that at least six of his contingent of twenty-one branch managers were marginal performers. He had to have people who could develop business, manage staffs of highly trained technical people, and produce profitable results in the wake. The choice was quickly becoming one of long-term development for the salvageable managers and immediate terminations for the other, more expendable group. Thus far, two of Paige's managers had been listed with the latter group.

"The region's in the process of going from fair-to-good, and when it gets there, it'll go from good-to-excellent in a far shorter time. The foundation's in place. Now it's a matter of making a few key staffing decisions and continuing to market the hell out of our services."

Wylie sat back, raising his eyebrows and lowering his head slightly. "Who's next on the review list, after Houston?"

"Kansas City, Albuquerque, St. Louis, Calgary—some of my bigger branches and some of my more nagging problems. As soon as they're on course, then the region reaches flank speed."

Wylie jotted a few notes and then tossed his notepad onto his desk. He shook his head, and then gave a disappointed look. "It's dragging us down."

"It's the best, most improved region you've got," Paige answered, trying hard not to sound defensive. "It's better than it was, and it'll be better tomorrow, and every day after that. We'll get there."

"When?"

"Soon."

"What will it take?"

Paige couldn't help but notice Wylie's unusually harsh tone and expression. "Good people, good decisions, good timing, good *everything*, Jeff. Do you want me to be more specific?"

Wylie frowned. "I want you to be more demanding in terms of getting the whole thing moving in the same direction at the same time."

Paige also frowned. "You might consider being a bit more realistic in light of where the region was when I got it, and where it is now. The progress is discernible, Jeff. I shouldn't have to sit here and point that out."

Wylie leaned forward slowly. Collier and Ogden shifted uncomfortably in their chairs and stared down at their laptops. Paige sat perfectly still, unsure but what only moments stood between his current lofty position and an airy plummet into the dark corridors of unemployment. He felt the need to swallow, to blink, but he did neither and kept his eyes riveted upon a small mole in the center of Wylie's forehead, between his eyes.

"The need to be realistic," Wylie spoke deliberately, "does not rest exclusively with me." He paused and allowed his words to enshroud Paige like a rising fog. "The bottom line is, things are changing. More demanding; more challenging; more competitive. We have to adjust. We have to set a faster pace, at a higher threshold, at a lower margin of error. And you've got to make all of that happen much more quickly."

Paige said nothing, although he did overhear Jim Ogden mutter something under his breath that Paige made out to be, "Goddamn spot on."

"I have a question," blurted Larry Collier in an attempt to abridge the now considerable tension pulsing through the room.

"Sure," Wylie said after a long breath in which he continued to stare at Paige. "Let's hear it."

"Has a decision been made on Dave's replacement once he goes to Executive V.P.?"

"As of this moment, no," Wylie answered, after which he returned his gold pen to the breast pocket of his starched white shirt.

Collier glanced over at Paige, saw the look on his friend's face, and became immediately concerned that Paige was on the verge of going ballistic. Ogden's twenty-nine branches in the Eastern Region were the oldest and thus the most established in the firm, but only moderately profitable as a group. Collier's eighteen branches in the Western Region were currently on a high-growth track, outdistancing all but Paige's group in its collective rate of growth in fees billed, although profits were still a major problem. And so Paige's Central Region branches, encompassing a geographical territory which was bounded to the east by the Mississippi River, to the west by the Continental Divide, and including the Canadian cities of Calgary, Regina, and Winnipeg, were entrenched at or near the top in almost every area of measured performance.

Wylie solicited any final questions. There was a brief silence, and Ogden and Collier closed their laptops and made ready to leave. Just as they stood, however, they turned to see Paige still seated, staring across at Wylie. Paige's expression was hardened and grim, as if he'd again seen the videotape of the hijacked 767 crashing into the South Tower in a huge fireball.

"I have one last question," Paige said, almost in a threatening tone.

Ogden and Collier took their seats again. The uneasiness returned to the room as if switched on like a light, this time in even greater thickness. Larry Collier was almost tempted to lean aside and whisper to Paige to leave it be, to back off for now and shut the holy hell up, to stifle himself and live to work another day. Larry Collier was fond of Dave Paige, greatly, as a friend and as a business associate. But he also knew there was a streak in Paige, potent enough to conceivably bring about his friend's undoing someday, no matter the immense talent and promise that otherwise defined Paige as an individual. And Collier didn't want that; not now, not ever. Elerbee Engineering needed Dave Paige, perhaps far more now than even Paige himself understood. Certainly Collier understood. But at that moment in Wylie's office, amid the anxiety that seemed to virtually choke him and constrict his throat, he couldn't bring himself to utter anything of the sort.

Wylie waited silently.

"My question is," Paige said deliberately, "now that things are changing, more demanding, more challenging, more competitive, and once I adjust, and set a faster pace at a higher threshold with a lower margin of error, and once I make all that happen much more quickly, and, by the way, still maintain the top position in overall regional performance," Paige said, pausing dramatically, then finally adding, "how the hell's *that* gonna make you feel?"

Wylie stared at Paige for what seemed an eternity. He eventually grinned slightly, sniffed, and answered, "Why don't we continue our conversation in private."

CHAPTER FIVE

It was a large brick house, nestled in an established, tree-lined, upper-middle-class neighborhood on Atlanta's northeast side. The Colliers, Larry and Dot, had lived in the home for the past twelve years after relocating from Los Angeles on yet another Elerbee-induced transfer. Their three children had by now grown up and left the nest, the youngest a junior in pre-med at Duke. It was a lovely neighborhood—quiet and picturesque with the tall, stately hardwoods and the well-maintained, reddish-brown, Williamsburg-style homes.

Saturday morning was always laid back and easy around the Collier household. Their routine began first with a breakfast of fruit and cereal, then coffee and newspaper in the relative cool of the screened patio. The air smelled of spring, of gardenia and pine and honeysuckle. The enclosed porch was crowded with hanging ferns, Fichus trees, and Philodendron. There was wicker furniture, white with thick, floral-design pads. A hand-woven basket beside a chair contained dozens of magazines ranging from home decorating to engineering-association material. Two ceiling fans stirred the air in a pulsating duet, creating a mesmerizing effect from the shadows and vibrations.

Dot Collier folded the front section of the newspaper and placed it beside her husband, seated nearby in a separate chair. Larry Collier was absorbed in the sports section, occasionally sipping from a beige ceramic mug with the blue letters *UCLA* painted across the side.

"By golly, I think they're going to do it again this year," Collier said with enthusiasm.

"Who's going to do what, dear?"

"The Braves. The club looks good again this year."

"You always say that. But then you always cheer for the Dodgers."

"Yeah, but this year the Braves will vindicate me with a World Series championship."

Dot sighed. "Swell."

"They will. You wait and see. Pitching, dear. They've got the pitching."

"You had an appointment with Dr. Rosenfeldt yesterday, right?" Dot asked, lighting the menthol cigarette she had removed from a leather case.

"Yeah, that's right."

"Well, what did he say?"

"He said I'm fine, but to stop smoking."

Dot laughed, and then began coughing loudly. She cleared her throat. "He tells you that every time. What about your blood pressure?"

"It's okay. I'm to stay on the medication."

"And your lab work?"

"It was mostly okay. Sugar's up a little, but not enough to worry about."

"Are you gonna stop smoking?"

Collier peered over the top of the newspaper. "Are you?"

Dot pointed at her husband. "I haven't had a mild coronary already. I don't have high blood pressure. I haven't had ulcers. I don't—"

"But you will, my dear."

Collier reached for a cigarette from his own pack and lit it with a disposable lighter. "Any more coffee?"

"I've got a fresh pot brewing," Dot answered. She left and returned a few moments later with coffee for both.

"When's David coming?" she asked.

"He said he'd be here around ten. Save him a cup."

"What's going to happen?" she asked, watching carefully.

"With whom?"

"With all of you—Jeff, David, everyone?"

"I think we're headed for problems with Jeff, Dave, and Jim."

"Well, tell me, dammit," she demanded.

Collier chuckled at his wife's insatiable curiosity. She sat erect, holding her cigarette up and away from her. Her white sweater was draped loosely about her shoulders, the arms crossed and tied in front. At age fifty-six, she was four years younger than her husband.

"Does Jeff have a preference?" Dot asked.

"Yes, for sure."

"Well then, who?"

"He favors Jim. They've been close for years, much the same way Dave was with Langdon."

"Why Jim?"

"They're compatible, I guess. Jim Ogden's a strange bird, though. He's one of the brightest people I've ever known, and also one of the most narrow-minded. He told us in a meeting yesterday that Affirmative Action was nothing more than a plot by the liberals to frustrate the historically high-achieving American system of free enterprise. And he blames a lot on Europe—France and Germany especially. Probably the Italians, too, but he doesn't mention them specifically. And if he sees an Arab or anyone even close to resembling a Middle East person—and God *forbid* if he spots one in an airport—he gets red in the face and starts mumbling a stream of profanities. He refers to them as 'terrorists,' no matter who they are or what they do. He happened to be in one of the New York branches one day—Syracuse, I think—when an Arabic guy came into the lobby to ask about a job. That's all, just there to see if he could find work. Well, Jim was coming back from lunch and he walks by and sees the guy, right? And he all but throws the poor devil out of the building, saying something about America being for the Americans. The branch manager somehow found out who the man was, and he attempted to smooth things over once Jim had left."

"Did the branch manager hire the man?"

"Are you kidding? And have Jim come down on him with both feet?"

"Did anything happen to Jim?"

"Jeff smoothed it over with Langdon, as I remember. It eventually blew over. But he's involved the company in five or six lawsuits over the years."

"Oh?"

"When Jim gets ready to terminate an employee, he does it without so much as a second thought. You can't do that nowadays, not without a file full of warnings and counselings and the like, and even then it's still shaky if it's brought before a court. But with Jim, if he's ready to fire a person, whether it's justified or not, he just does it. He's made some terrible decisions about the people he's hired, and he's made things even worse when he fired some of them without any specific cause."

"How does he keep getting away with that?"

"Beats me."

"What about David, then? How does Jeff feel about him?"

"I honestly think Jeff feels threatened by Dave. Dave's a smart kid, a lot of *savior-faire*. God knows he doesn't hesitate to speak his mind, and more often than not he's right on the mark. I think Jeff was always a little put out that Dave was closer to Langdon than he was himself. Jeff has seen Dave more as a potential rival than as a subordinate for the past year or so, maybe longer. It's had a negative impact on their relationship because Dave probably views it much the same way. Dave's never had a lot of respect for Jeff Wylie anyway—he calls him a 'snake,' and sometimes far worse. Dave once saw Jeff dressed in a white jumpsuit during a business reception and whispered to me that the basic conflict within Jeff Wylie is that part of him thinks he's Elvis Presley while another part thinks he's Jack Welch. Honest to God, I nearly gagged on my hors d'oeurves."

"So David's in trouble, huh? Is he a goner?"

"Maybe. Jeff can be petty and vindictive as hell. But Dave has this uncanny knack, I swear. Sometimes it's nothing short of amazing."

"How so?"

"Well, his region, for example. Jeff convinced Langdon to give the Central Region to Dave when we reorganized the company. Central was beyond repair, or so it was thought. A real dog of a region. Poor managers, poor morale, poor quality of services, poor *everything*. Everyone saw it as a managerial graveyard, including me. And somehow Jeff managed to hang it around Dave like a noose, and without the least bit of interference from Langdon. I'm sure Jeff saw it as the equivalent of Paige's Last Stand, that he'd go down with guns ablazin', but that he *would* go down. But I'll be damned if Dave didn't wade right in and begin to straighten it out almost immediately. The progress he's made to this point has been nothing short of amazing. And *that's* given Jeff a taste of the reflux, for sure."

"Does Jeff ever acknowledge David's success?"

"No. To the contrary, he hammers Dave about why the numbers aren't far better. It's so obvious that sometimes it's almost comical, although it's hardly comical to Dave."

Dot grimaced. "I'm sure it isn't."

"He's very unsettled by Dave. I suppose that's Jeff's way of reacting to it."

"Didn't Langdon almost fire Jeff a year or so ago?"

"Yeah."

"What was the reason? Didn't it have something to do with—"

"Jeff was screwing his secretary."

"Yeah, I remember now. It was the young brunette with the big boobs and even bigger hair."

"And Jeff thought he was being discrete, too."

"What happened to her?"

"She was transferred and eventually left the firm. It was almost as if it was all *her* fault."

Dot sighed. "I suppose he's learned his lesson."

Collier laughed. "Right. He quit screwing *his* secretary and started screwing Langdon's."

"You're kidding?"

"Nope. He's been seeing her for almost a year. It's gotten to be a joke. And this is the same guy who sends around the 'It's All About Integrity' pledges that everyone has to sign on a yearly basis. I'm pretty sure that

Langdon was right on the verge of cutting Jeff loose. He never told me so directly, but I knew he was having serious reservations about Jeff. Langdon mentioned to me not long ago about how he remembered when the company could barely meet its payroll in the early days, how we all sacrificed and fought through the hardships, but how we always kept the faith that what we were building would be worth our efforts. He told me that his vision for the company back then had largely been realized, but as long as he had an active role he damn sure wouldn't allow anyone with dubious character to damage the firm. I really believe his decision to sack Jeff was all but a done deal. Langdon was going to tolerate Jeff only long enough to get Dave ready for the C.E.O. job. I suppose now it's a fair question to ask whether he waited too long."

"No wonder David has such a problem with Jeff."

"Exactly."

"Does David still seek your advice?"

"Sure. Dave has a nice knack about knowing when and where he should go for counsel. And he has the good judgment to know how to use it once he's got it."

"He and Valerie were so cute. That's such a shame."

Collier laughed. "That's an area of his life he hasn't sought my counsel on."

Dot shook her head sadly. "Do you think they'll ever get back together?"

Collier gave a slight wrinkle of his nose, and then lit another cigarette. "I seriously doubt it. My impression is it's over between them."

A cool, steady breeze rustled among the pines and dogwoods. The wind chimes swayed in the breeze in a far corner of the patio. A pair of cardinals pecked away at the fresh seed stored in a feeder outside.

Dot noticed the look on her husband's face. "Are you all right, dear?"

Collier shrugged and said, "Sure, I'm fine."

But he wasn't, not entirely. At his age, Collier had developed an ability to deal with both the concept and the circumstance of death and dying. Intellectually and emotionally, he understood the process in a mature, philosophical way. Friends and associates his own age died more often now, and the exposure was more frequent and familiar than at any other time in his life. But Langdon Elerbee's death had grabbed him in a way unlike any other, excepting that of his own parents. He had never expected to work a day in his remaining professional life without the Old Man there, either running the company or growing pleasantly plump in his retirement, and Elerbee's passing had profoundly affected him. He felt cheated, as much for Elerbee's forfeiture of a comfortable retirement as for the own insecurity he now felt at being left alone in what he knew would be a dramatically, perhaps even disastrously, changing world.

It was almost as if part of him had died with Langdon Elerbee. And he just couldn't seem to shake it.

"Are you sure you're all right, dear?" Dot pressed.

"I'm sure," Collier said in his best attempt to sound reassuring. "Don't worry about me, dear. Everything's fine."

Paige arrived promptly at ten. The Colliers were waiting with warm greetings, coffee, and the fresh croissants Dot had finished baking only moments before. Dot stayed only long enough to enjoy a roll and make some small talk before excusing herself and leaving the guys to themselves.

Paige didn't waste any time once the two were alone. "What the hell's going to happen to our company, Larry?" he asked bluntly.

Collier smiled sagely. "I'm not entirely sure. My gut instinct tells me that things are going to be rocky for a little while."

"Your instincts are sound, my friend," Paige said in a somber tone. "Jeff all but told me the same thing yesterday afternoon."

"Oh?" said Collier, with eyebrows raised.

Paige nodded. "Yep. He told me that it's his intention to suspend my promotion to Executive V.P. until he can put together a comprehensive plan to take to the Board."

Collier quickly straightened. "Suspend? What the hell for? And for how long?"

Paige shrugged. "He didn't say for how long. I took it to mean that nothing would happen before the Board meets again in July. That gives him some breathing room to find a way to get rid of me and promote Jim Ogden."

"Damn," Collier said with disgust. "*Damn!*"

"Yeah, exactly," Paige said, chuckling. "I'm sure he kneels and thanks the Old Man's spirit every night for having given him such an opportunity."

"He'd have to have Grace Elerbee's agreement to get that past the Board. She's got Langdon's shares, and she'll keep that stock until she decides to sell, so she holds most of the cookies. Jeff can't force anything off the wall, not just yet, not unless he turns her against you. And hell, that's not going to happen."

Dot appeared and poured the last of the coffee into their cups. When she had returned to the main part of the house, Collier leaned over and reached inside the basket containing the magazines. He produced a silver flask of Bailey's.

"Can I interest you in a morning touch?"

"Sure, why not," Paige answered with a grin, holding out his coffee cup while Collier uncapped the bottle.

Collier poured a generous portion into each cup. He then sat back in his chair, crushed out his cigarette, and sipped twice. He took a deep breath. "I'm thinking that my best bet would be to get the hell out," he announced flatly.

Paige seemed surprised. "Retiring? Are you being serious?"

"I am."

"Why?"

"I don't like what I see coming, Dave. I don't enjoy it anymore—haven't for several years, tell you the truth. It's gotten too damned cold and impersonal."

Paige sipped his coffee and remained quiet.

"Elerbee Engineering's changing too much to suit me. It's just not the same as it was eight, ten years ago. It's much more short-sighted now. There's not as much loyalty, not as much 'family' in the way we deal with each other. It's hard to feel like I'm trusted anymore, which in turn makes me more suspicious. Maybe it's just a reflection of our society at large, but I don't like it."

Collier let out a long, loud sigh. "I don't like it either. I love this company more than anything else in my life—outside my own flesh and blood—and the thought of Jeff Wylie and Jim Ogden running roughshod over it, without Langdon around, makes me sick to my stomach. It literally makes me ill."

Paige nodded but said nothing.

"I mean, integrity in business relationships means a lot less than it used to. Everyone just uses everyone else for the short-term convenience of today, with little concern about building something that will last past tomorrow. And the loyalty thing bothers me. The employees don't seem to have any loyalty, this damned top management has no loyalty, except to itself. It's sad, especially when I can remember how rock solid the firm was at one time. We could trust one another, and count on one another to do the right thing for the organization. Nowadays it's every man for himself, like rodents in a trash pile."

Paige nodded again. He noticed the mist developing in Collier's eyes.

"It gets back to loyalty," Collier said emphatically. "Everybody's scared to death these days. Hundreds of thousands of white-collar types out of work. Millions more petrified that it'll be them today, or tomorrow, or for sure when they turn fifty and their prostate and marketability are growing at inverse rates. And somebody takes a red pen and strikes their name from the list. Just like that, without a second thought. And they're gone. *Bam*! Quick as a bolt of lightning."

"It's more a question of ethics," Paige replied. "And it all starts at the top."

Collier stopped and listened.

"I agree there's very little loyalty left," Paige continued, "but it's just a reflection of the bigger problem. The bigger problem deals with management's loss of its moral compass. Jeff Wylie thinks the female administrative help exists to service him in every way, and he gets away with it. Then he proposes to give himself a raise of ninety grand, bullies the Board into giving it to him, while at the same time we're still firing middle managers to trim our costs."

Paige paused, but it was clear his temperature was rising. "That sort of behavior, that sort of signal will creep into everything this firm does, and it'll erode the quality of our services, it'll poison our people, and it'll set us up for some major disappointments. Why, they could so devalue this company to the point where none of us would have any stock value left, or any pension benefits, or anything else. There are stories all over this country where some conniving idiot has taken control of an otherwise healthy company and driven it into oblivion. And the people who had been loyal, who had worked weekends and not taken their vacations and not seen their kids' Little League games and been unselfish in every way imaginable, those people were given pink slips instead of promotions. And a few were lucky enough to have some benefits left over after the dust settled, but a helluva lot of others were left with nothing but a letter about COBRA and a book on colored parachutes."

Collier's mood seemed to darken, but he remained silent.

"Do you know how much misery that kind of corporate catastrophe can involve?" Paige asked. "It's widespread, like ripples in water. All the hopes and dreams are gone in an instant, not to mention the welfare of family members and dependents. All the years of hard work, the diligence, the service to others—lost just as surely as if it were shit being burned in a barrel. Hundreds of thousands of man-years of honest effort flushed away by some seedy sons of bitches who give no consideration to the people who had the most to lose." Paige stopped and shook his head in disgust. "The executives who perpetrate those kinds of crimes upon humanity ought to be taken to the company break room and hanged by the testicles, I swear to God. Or, to be gender neutral, hanged in great pain by the most appropriate organ." He paused again, grinning. "It has to get better, Larry, and we'll make it better by taking the company back."

"Yeah, right," Collier said with a sigh, then a chuckle. "I feel the urge to sell my stock and cash out before something like that happens to Elerbee Engineering."

Paige mentally calculated that Collier's shares would be worth well over three million dollars, about twice the value of his own holdings.

"You know, you might want to do the same, Dave. You could find another job pronto. You'd be in big demand in our industry. And your investment wouldn't evaporate if Wylie and Ogden eventually run the Elerbee ship aground."

Paige remained expressionless. "Is that your advice to me, Larry?"

Collier shrugged and flicked an ash off his trousers. "If I were in your shoes, partner, I'd strongly consider leaving. Wylie's not going to give you the time of day now that Langdon's gone. He'll make things miserable for you. I'd think it over if I were you. Maybe test the waters, explore your options. You're young and mobile, and you'd be a helluva steal for any other firm in our industry."

Paige grinned slightly.

"I guess this modern world of business is no place for a sentimental old fool like me," Collier said with a forced chuckle.

"You're neither old nor a fool. Sentimental, maybe, but certainly not the other."

"Oh, but I am," said Collier, stopping to clear his throat. "I'm old and tired, like Langdon was. I've been thinking a lot about this over the past few days, and dammit I wouldn't be a bit surprised if all this stuff that's weighing me down, isn't the same sort of millstone that helped kill him."

"Think so?"

"Yeah, I do. Langdon appeared in most ways to be in good health, but hell, every man has his limits. And once they're exceeded, who knows what can happen."

Paige leaned forward, closer to Collier. "There's no need to retire, my friend," he said, his tone and expression suddenly hardening. "There's no need to wear any heavy millstones. And there's certainly no need to despair. Don't let these pretenders chase you out of the firm and away from the people and the work that have meant so much to you for so long."

Collier leaned in and listened carefully.

Paige spoke softly. "Do you want me to let you in on a little secret?"

Collier stared at Paige for a moment before finally nodding and saying, "Please."

"They'll never last, Larry. Jeff Wylie and Jim Ogden will not last at the top of this company because I'm not going to let them. I'm the only one who has even *half* a chance to knock them out. And when I say out, I mean nothing less than their removal from the firm. I don't have the shares, and I probably won't have the support of the Board when Wylie starts his bullying, but I'll beat them, even if I have to toss a grenade in each of their offices and hold the doors closed."

"You're outgunned, Dave. You may die nobly, but die you will, my young friend."

"I don't think so."

"Are you trying to tell me that without Langdon supporting you, that you won't get crushed under their combined weight?"

"I'm telling you that it's quite possible I may not get crushed at all."

"How? How the hell can you pull that off?"

"I can't fully answer that yet. But believe me, just as sure as I'm sitting here, I *will* stop those buffoons from trashing our company."

Collier sat back and laughed. "It's gotta be the booze, Dave. Something's sure as hell gotten to you."

Paige also laughed. "Nope, it's not the booze. It's the people involved, the circumstances, the way history works. It's the window of opportunity that always, *always* exists in moments like this. It's all of those things, Larry, and probably a good many more. But," he said, laughing again, "it's definitely not the booze."

"How then, dammit?" Collier said, straining to see a convincing sign. "Tell me how!"

Paige winked. "I can't answer that yet. But when I work everything out, I'll set it in motion, step back, and allow them to free-fall just as sure as if they'd jumped and forgotten their colored parachutes."

Collier's expression softened. "You're serious, aren't you?"

Paige smiled. "You bet I'm serious. I don't have all the particulars yet, but I'll develop the process and I'll bring it off. There's not the slightest doubt in my mind."

"Sort of sounds like you're issuing a *fatwa*."

Paige grinned. "I prefer to think of it more in Western terms, such as a frontal assault across an opposed enemy beachhead."

Collier smiled and shook his head. "I remember a quote from Churchill where he described someone as, 'The only bull I know who carries his own china shop around with him.' Why the hell do you come to mind when I think of that quotation?"

Paige laughed loudly. "I'll take that as a compliment."

"It was meant as such."

"And you should remember the Groucho Marx quote where he said, 'Who are you going to believe? Me or your own eyes?' Just keep watching, Larry. I don't want you to miss this."

The gleam suddenly appeared in Paige's eyes, and it was altogether convincing to Collier. He knew Paige well enough to believe that his young associate was capable of much, especially the unexpected. If Paige said it, *believed* it, then by God it was possible, perhaps even likely. And against all odds, too. Big odds, at that. And in the face of all logic, as well. Yet there it was, unmistakably etched across Paige's face, that look of confidence and strength and gumption that on other days in other places would have caused frightened young men to get up and follow him across that opposed enemy beachhead.

Collier laughed out loud, shattering the momentary silence on the patio. He reached toward the basket. "Let me offer you another morning touch."

CHAPTER SIX

"Good morning, Atlanta. It's Friday, it's six-thirty, and it's spec-*tac*-ular in our fair city. Sixty-six degrees and clear. The freeways are already slowing but hey, everything else is looking A-Okay. Here's a little something to help get things rolling, called *Celebration* . . ."

Paige arrived early at his downtown office. He had slept little the night before, so he immediately fueled himself with as much black coffee as he could comfortably ingest.

The in-box on his desk was overflowing. He already had sixty e-mails, more than half of his daily quotient of ninety, and it took him nearly an hour to read, delete, or file the messages. Except for his participation as a member of the Board of Directors which had met in Atlanta to expand Jeff Wylie's role, Paige had otherwise been out on the road for much of the four weeks since Langdon Elerbee's death. His travels had included St. Louis, Des Moines, Denver, Calgary, and Houston. Another branch manager had been replaced (Calgary), and one other was coming under Jeff Wylie's intense scrutiny (St. Louis). It had been another of those bleak, wrenching, search-and-destroy missions. Hopefully out of the havoc would rise some budding young superstars to carry the sick branches on to the greater glory of high profitability.

Or so the hope went.

Surprisingly, there were few phone messages. Maybe the other branch managers under his supervision preferred the dust to settle before drawing any attention to themselves. Maybe also, he mused, those same branch managers already knew all there was to know about the situations elsewhere, and thus needed no further elaboration. The word always got around quickly in Elerbee Engineering.

Sherry Painter, Paige's attractive assistant, arrived shortly before eight. She had permed her silky blond hair into an interesting, attractive disarray of curls and swirls, and she was anxious to see Paige's reaction. She stepped away from her desk after stowing her purse and returned a few moments later with fresh coffee for Paige and herself.

Paige milked the moment for all it was worth by staring straight-faced at Sherry before finally grinning and voicing his approval. She blushed and stood at the front of his desk, impatiently fingering the gold herringbone necklace that dangled outside her crimson sweater.

"Should I ask how the trip went?" she asked softly.

"Probably not," Paige answered with a quick grimace.

"Several branch managers called and asked who you were visiting next."

Paige laughed, and then asked if word of the terminations had spread throughout the region.

"Region? Dave, it's all over the company. Every time this happens, it's headline stuff."

And she was entirely correct. Sherry knew all too well the ways of Elerbee Engineering in such matters as firings, resignations (sometimes indistinguishable from firings), reprimands, scandals (actual or implied), and other assorted minutia which served to fill the gossip pipeline. She had anonymously labored in accounting for four of her six years with Elerbee, and she was familiar with the network of conduits which shared and spread the latest goings-on. But now, because of her proximity to the center of so much action, she herself had become a potential source. She was routinely called when rumors began buzzing; she was besieged when the rumors began transforming into facts. She handled it all with intelligence and skill, never compromising any sensitive information and never exacerbating any already difficult situation.

Two years earlier, Sherry had passed a harried Dave Paige in the hallway, only days after his previous assistant had resigned in favor of grad school. She had no way of knowing it at the time, but at that very moment Paige was on his way to arrange an interview with none other than Sherry herself after having received enthusiastic recommendations from several trusted colleagues. When he had noticed her in the hallway that morning, he had stopped and asked if she might be interested in leaving her present position and coming to work for him; she had replied yes. He had then asked if she was comfortable with Microsoft Word, Excel, and PowerPoint; she had again replied yes. He had asked if she would be willing to work longer and harder for the same money, perhaps even less; she had hesitated. He had grinned and said that since she was his first choice, that he'd be more than fair with the money if she'd agree to start first thing the following morning. When her boss, the accounting manager, objected to the prospect of losing his best employee so quickly, Paige apologized for ignoring the protocol but then went about arranging for Sherry's immediate transfer later that same afternoon. Since that time, she had become a key member, perhaps *the* key member, of Dave Paige's team.

Sherry started to leave, then stopped and glanced back. "I know there's lots to do with you being back and everything."

"Yeah, right."

"I know you're atrociously busy and everything."

"Right."

"Believe me, I know how pressed you are."

"What is it, Sherry?" Paige asked, looking up from the calendar on his laptop.

"Don't get me wrong, Dave. I'm perfectly willing to stay as long as it takes to get everything caught up. Even if it's midnight, *that's* how willing I am to stay and get the job done," she said, jabbing a finger into the air for emphasis.

"Sherry, what the hell gives?"

She hesitated a moment, then took a tentative step toward the desk. "Would it be okay if I left early today?" she asked in a pleading tone.

Paige shrugged. "Yeah, I suppose so. Why? What's up?"

"I need to do some shopping. Tracy's birthday is today and we're having a little party tonight."

Paige smiled, and then closed his laptop. "Gosh, how old is Tracy now? She's eight, isn't she?"

"Yes, eight. Can you believe it? My little baby's growing up in such a hurry."

Paige's respect and admiration for Sherry had always been high. She was an uncomplaining single parent who worked hard to provide the necessities for her child and herself. She was also an executive assistant of the highest quality. She had at one time worked as a doctor's receptionist to support the family while her husband completed law school. His thanks to her shortly after graduation had been to abruptly leave her and their infant daughter. Divorced for almost seven years, Sherry had been in little hurry to find another husband. Her physical attractiveness, however, was enough to turn more than a few heads when she ventured outside for a walk along Peachtree Street.

"Oh, I almost forgot," said Paige. He turned and reached behind his desk, into his credenza, and produced a card and a wrapped package. "Give Tracy a big hug for me," he said, offering the gift.

Sherry became emotional. She smiled warmly, waved, and then turned and left the office.

Paige reached into his bottom desk drawer and brought out a bound book. It was black, ledger-like, and inside were the words *Paige's Laws of*

Business. He opened the book and glanced over some of the many handwritten notations he had entered over the course of the past ten or so years. He reached for his pen and jotted the following:

*Don't get too panicky when things turn sour; it may just be temporary, but even if it's not, panic is impulsive and will add nothing positive.

*When you're hot, expect that most everyone will be your friend; and when you're not, expect the number to decline the very moment you fall off the chart. Don't take it personally.

*Even the best run companies have enormous imperfections; keep things in perspective.

Paige closed the book and leaned back, allowing his sub-conscious to internalize each of the messages.

Don Burroughs was facing about, toward his credenza, when Paige suddenly appeared.

"Let's talk," Paige said brusquely.

Burroughs was startled. When he glanced around, he saw Paige filling his doorway. Burroughs closed his briefcase, then stood to offer all the cordiality he could muster. "Come in, Dave, please," he said, extending his hand.

Paige ignored the outstretched hand and instead took a seat to Burroughs front. The personnel czar was impeccably dressed in dark suit with custom shirt and tie, cuff links, and bright red suspenders. He was big in the way a football lineman is big, with his salt-and-pepper hair swept back on the top and sides. His voice was deep and resonant, and his mannerisms suggested aristocratic nobility. Like any prince, he always looked good and smelled like a million bucks. Paige guessed that Burroughs was soft and physically lazy, though his own contact with the Vice President-Human Resources had been mostly limited to the workplace. Paige had always pictured Burroughs as the perfect sort for a televangelist, given his appearance and mannerisms, and thus believed that Burroughs had clearly missed his calling. Each time Paige envisioned Burroughs healing a sick old lady or a crippled old man, all with the magic of a touch, he had to suppress the urge to chuckle.

Paige took a report from a file folder and placed it on Burroughs' desk. "I've read the revised manpower-requirements analysis for the five-year plan. I take it you had something to do with this."

Burroughs straightened. "Well yes, I did."

"I've got a problem with it."

"Oh?" said Burroughs, blinking nervously.

"You didn't seem to pay any attention to the numbers I provided for the Central Region. My plan calls for one headcount number, and yours another. What the hell gives?"

Burroughs swallowed. He began to feel hot and flushed, the exact same way he always felt when he faced off with Dave Paige.

"I'd like to know why my numbers weren't used," Paige said, pressing harder. "Did you decide they were worthless? That I didn't know what the hell I was doing?"

"I went over this with several others in your absence, Dave."

Paige's eyes narrowed. "Tell me why you felt the need to go over with someone else the numbers that I had already approved. Who the hell's running the Central Region, anyway?"

Beads of perspiration suddenly began glistening on Burroughs' forehead, like vapor droplets on an icy bottle. "There were some assumptions that—"

"What assumptions? And made by whom?"

"I discussed this with Jim and Jeff, and—"

"Who, dammit? Tell me who authorized you to change the manpower requirements for *my* region in *my* portion of the five-year plan?"

Burroughs coughed, and then began scribbling on a sheet of paper on his desk. "The changes were merely part of the normal give-and-take that these long-range things usually involve. In the end, all the changes were approved by Jeff."

"I know how the planning process works," said Paige. "Do you think I just came aboard last week? That I'm freshly arrived here from Antarctica?"

"Of course not," Burroughs answered, still looking down.

Paige abruptly rose. Burroughs remained seated and avoided any further eye contact.

"My advice to you," Paige said slowly, "would be to never again change anything you get from me without first contacting me and giving me the courtesy of knowing that what I've submitted is being altered, and the reasons why. You don't arbitrarily change things that deal with my region. You don't make decisions for me. You don't represent me in my absence. You don't involve yourself in any way in the ongoing operations of my branches without first going through me for approval."

Burroughs still didn't look up. It was in such moments as these that he'd always assumed he'd have his fatal heart attack when the time came for his personal moment of truth. His chest pounded the reminder to him.

"I don't like what's happened here," Paige continued, "and I don't intend to have this conversation again. I hope I've made myself clear, because if it happens again," Paige said, pausing and then adding softly, "then you'll have only yourself to blame when you come to work one morning and suddenly find yourself up to your nipples in the Mother of All Wars."

Paige started to leave but then suddenly stopped. "Oh, one other thing. Never again address anything to me that contains the phrase, 'It has come to my attention.' Just so we're clear, what does or does not come to your attention matters to me slightly less than jack shit."

When Burroughs finally did look up some time later, Paige was gone.

Many of the Elerbee Engineering people referred to it as the Conference Center. It was within easy walking distance of the office, just a block removed from Peachtree Street. It was officially named Richardson's, and its co-owner, a middle-aged, gray-bearded bear of a man and a former Atlanta Falcons football player, was always there with his high-fives and loud laughter. Art Richardson was six years retired from the game, his everyday reminder being a constant limp from his oft-injured right knee which had blown out one time too many, the last on the frozen tundra of Green Bay. He and a few business buddies had discussed a venture over poker one night, and before long they had thrown caution to the wind and flung themselves full bore into the ownership of a downtown bar and grille.

The windows were stained glass, the interior a comingling of polished brass and hardwood. There was a long bar behind which two bartenders busily practiced their craft. Four waitresses served the customers in the booths and at the tables. There were rows of framed black-and-white photos of old rock stars—the pioneers—on the surrounding walls. In fact, there were dozens of photos, certainly enough to stir conversation, especially among the younger patrons. No small wonder, then, that the music inside was decidedly that of the Sixties and Seventies. And the clientele was predominantly thirtyish, mid-to-late, with the rest being somewhat younger, somewhat older.

The smell of the place was primarily that of broiling beef; secondarily, of beer, varnish, and perfume.

There were at least a dozen regulars from Elerbee Engineering who congregated nearly every weekday evening at a section of tables—*their* tables—at the far end of the room, opposite the entrance. They came in all flavors: Engineers, accountants, data processors, secretaries, and occasionally a top executive. They were mostly decorous, though they laughed often and boisterously, and sometimes argued over business-world matters. They didn't stay late as a usual practice, but they were hardly tentative customers while they were there. There was a code of conduct among them which by no means encouraged drunkenness, but if it did happen, and it sometimes did, the inebriated would be driven home courtesy of the more sober.

Paige took a seat at a corner table with his longtime pal, Ted Haygood. Even though adjacent tables were filled with Elerbee people, Paige and his guest were able to enjoy a private conversation with few interruptions.

The lively song *Sooner or Later* provided the background music.

"So what can I get y'all?" called Chrissie, the young, well-endowed waitress in the skin-tight jeans who worked the corner section.

"Two draft beers," Paige called over the noise, almost in a shout. "And a basket of something crunchy."

Chrissie smiled, displaying her perfect teeth and ruby red lips. "Sure, Dave. Two beers and a box of rock salt." She giggled and turned away toward the bar.

"God almighty, I'd rip her limb from limb," Haygood remarked lustily.

Paige chuckled. "You'd likely end up in a coma, pal, if you ever caught up with her in the dark."

Chrissie soon returned with drinks and pretzels. "Um, Dave, the guys at the other tables said that, um, if you'd buy 'em a round of drinks, then they'd like respect you forever."

Paige glanced at the sly, grinning faces around him. Some raised their glasses in salute.

"Tell them respect is something that can't be bought," he said loudly, pausing, then grinning and adding, "but bring 'em a round and charge it to me any damn way."

The group cheered and applauded.

Bus Stop filled the speakers.

Years before, Ted Haygood and Dave Paige had been fraternity brothers at college in Indiana. They had remained close ever since, especially when their careers had reunited them in Atlanta. The tall, red-haired, marathon-thin Haygood, a native Chicagoan, was an accountant and partner in the international CPA firm he had joined straight out of college. He also served as Paige's financial adviser, modeling investment plans and tax options on several personal-computer programs that he and Paige had jointly developed.

The Paiges and Haygoods had been close for years, and when Valerie Paige had moved back to Pittsburgh immediately following the divorce, Shannon Haygood had been distraught at losing her best friend. The Haygoods had seen it coming, but it had nevertheless been a difficult blow to absorb after all the years of close friendship.

"Tough day today, huh?" Haygood asked the suddenly distant Paige.

"Nah, just thinking."

"Yeah? About what? About being in the sack with that delightful little fox Chrissie?"

"No, but now that you mention it, it's not such a bad thought."

"Be an even better act."

"I don't doubt that."

"So what's up?"

"Ah, just some stuff going on at the office."

"If your place is as bad as mine, nothing's ever serene and steady. My managing partner thinks that the absence of a bonafide crisis is excuse enough to create one. Nothing's laid back and predictable anymore. Anywhere."

"Right," Paige said quickly. "And it's getting worse at a near exponential rate, I'm afraid."

"What about the Executive V.P. slot? You've still got a lock on it, right?"

Paige shrugged. "I don't think so, not after what's happened. Ogden's got his head so far up Jeff Wylie's ass that it's sometimes mistaken for a growth on Wylie's colon. I've got a bad feeling about the whole thing."

"You mean Wylie's gonna try to screw you out of the promotion?"

"I think so, yeah."

Haygood frowned, the wrinkles showing. "What sort of unethical bastard are you working for, Dave?"

Paige gave a strained smile. "I'm not sure, but your description's right on both counts."

"Why don't you look around, man?"

Paige shook his head resolutely. "Not just yet. Wylie and Ogden each have the capacity to step on their own private parts. And when they do, and if I can hang on until then, I can be back in the picture."

"So the central question would seem to be: Can you hang on until then?"

"Well," said Paige, looking down at his mug, "I believe I can, yes. But in all honesty, I'm afraid it's an open question."

A fresh round of drinks arrived a bit later, courtesy of the group from data processing.

"Computer geeks are good for something after all," Haygood said under his breath after he and Paige had smiled and waved their thanks to the others seated nearby, but then added in a low voice, "but very damned little, if you ask me. You must have a different strain in your firm than we've got in ours. I've always thought that if they ever stopped tinkering with their computers, they'd probably be into something like serial murder."

Paige chuckled.

"No, seriously," pressed Haygood. "Engineers are pretty weird—pardon me, Dave, but they really are—and accountants can be damned strange, too. And lawyers? Jesus H. Christ, they're hopeless. And the doctors, well, they *are* Jesus H. Christ. And if you don't believe it, just ask the pompous bastards. But computer geeks, they're just plain scary!"

Paige laughed loudly. "You have a way of capturing the very essence of the professions, Ted."

They talked on, admiring Chrissie and declining the offer of another drink from another table of Elerbee patrons.

Haygood finally leaned in Paige's direction and asked in a soft voice, "Are you coming around yet? After the thing with Valerie, I mean?"

Paige looked away and took a deep breath, then nodded. "I'm fine, Ted. Thanks."

"Is she still at her sister's place in Pittsburgh?"

"No, she has her own place now."

"Any plans to," Haygood said, pausing, "get back in circulation?"

"I've thought about it," Paige said, laughing self-consciously. "I think about it every time I roll over in that empty bed."

"Any candidates?"

"Not currently, no."

"Isn't there someone at Elerbee you could, you know, see regularly?"

Paige frowned. "That wouldn't work. It's the thing about the 'company ink,' man. That can get way too complicated, and it rarely if ever enhances one's career. Besides, that's just not my style."

"Shannon wants to match you up."

"Tell Shannon thanks," Paige said, grinning and sipping his beer, "but not just yet."

"Then just get out there and go for it, my man."

Paige frowned again. "With whom? And don't you read the newspapers about the dangers of that nowadays? It scares the hell out of me."

"They're plenty of clean, great-looking women in Atlanta."

"Yeah, right. Divorced with two young kids. Besides, I'm too old to get back into that meat-market thing. I wouldn't even know where to start."

"Bullshit. You're not too old. You're mature, urbane, successful, and most women would kill for a guy like you."

Paige laughed.

Haygood shook his head in mild disgust. "A bottle of wine and a night of passionate lovemaking would make a new man out of you, my friend."

"If that's a suggestion, then I most heartily agree. But," Paige said, frowning and turning away, "if it's an invitation, then I most ardently refuse."

There was only a quick moment of silence before they each erupted in laughter.

Chrissie showed up with change from the two twenties Paige had given her for the tab. "Will there be anything else, Dave?" she asked with a suggestive grin.

"Not tonight, Chrissie," Paige said, shaking his head in disappointment.

She brushed him with her hip when she leaned forward to remove the empty mugs. "Okay, then, if that's the way you want it."

She turned and walked away. Her stupendously round backside in the incredibly tight jeans became a point of interest for nearly all the men and perhaps even a few of the women in the crowded place. Paige swept a handful of his hair to the side, and, turning to Haygood, took in a deep breath and shrugged.

CHAPTER SEVEN

"You need to know about this guy," Sherry Painter said in a loud whisper as she peered into Dave Paige's office.

"Which guy?" Paige whispered in return, on hold with the telephone to his ear. "And why are we whispering?"

"This consultant guy," Sherry answered in a normal tone.

The party on the other end of the line suddenly began speaking again. "Five minutes," Paige mouthed, holding up five fingers for emphasis.

Sherry soon returned to Paige's office and took a seat in one of the two chairs in front of his desk. She had a spiral notebook in her hand and a look of displeasure on her face.

"This is the big-shot consultant from the accounting firm who's best buddies with Jeff Wylie," Sherry said in a hushed tone. "All of the people on the systems-project team say he's an arrogant bully and a complete jerk. Apparently he ran all over Jim Ogden in the meeting the last time he was here two months ago. Other than that, I hear he's an absolute delight. Anyway, I knew you were sitting in with the team this morning, and I wanted to let you know this character will also be in the room."

"I just got off the phone with Ted Haygood, who works at the same firm," said Paige.

"Yeah? What did Ted have to say about him?"

"That he's a partner, based out of Chicago; that he's an asshole with an ego the size of the Sears Tower; and that Ted and his colleagues hate to look up and see him in the Atlanta office."

Sherry nodded. "Right. Just an altogether terrific guy."

"Should I sling an AK-47 across my back?" Paige asked, grinning.

Sherry shrugged and got up to leave. "Just consider yourself forewarned."

Jeff Wylie had only recently assigned Paige the overall responsibility for the systems-project after Jim Ogden had successfully lobbied for his own removal, citing his need to spend more time with his branches. Paige had protested the sudden change, arguing his own need to be with his branches and clients, but to no avail. A new financial and administrative software package had been purchased by Elerbee Engineering, and the outside accounting firm, Jarred & Holtzclaw, was assisting Elerbee's undermanned systems specialists in the testing and conversion. It was slow, tedious, detailed work, and the pressure to get the project done quickly and seamlessly was great. The project was running behind schedule, and Paige had summoned the key members of the team, both the internal and consultant members, to bring him up to speed on the progress and the pending issues.

The meeting participants were seated around the table when Paige entered the conference room. Coffee, juice, and bottled water were available, and someone had kindly donated two boxes of donuts. The six Elerbee members, four males and two females, like Paige dressed in business attire, all smiled and nodded as Paige came into the room. Paige grinned when he noticed each of the Elerbee employees with partially consumed donuts in hand, some even with the evidence of sugary powder on their mouths and shirts. An attractive woman smartly dressed in a navy-blue business suit, whom Paige knew as Diane Tresvant, the consultant project manager, was seated near the head of the table. At the head of the table was a tall, jowly, heavyset man with bright blue eyes and dark thinning hair, who wore an expensive suit, starched white shirt, suspenders, and bright silk tie with matching pocket square, all with a sort of imperial, authoritative, self-assured demeanor.

"I'm going to assume that you're Dave Paige," the man said in a booming voice as he rose from his chair and offered his outstretched hand.

"You've assumed correctly," Paige said, noticing his firm handshake and imposing physical presence.

"I'm Patrick Tierney from Jarred & Holtzclaw. Very pleased to make your acquaintance, Dave."

"Likewise," said Paige as he also greeted Diane and slid into the chair beside her.

Paige opened his laptop to the agenda he had created and circulated to the team members. He had several areas of concern—adherence to schedule, budget issues, staffing limitations, software bugs and fixes—and he wanted to hear from the team what additional resources they felt they needed. Earlier, Wylie had made it clear that the project carried the highest priority, that its delivery on time and within budget was critical, and that Paige would be held accountable for the results, even though Paige's entry had been months after the project's beginning. Paige wanted answers, needed answers, and came to the meeting prepared to ask all the right questions.

Tierney sat up in his chair and cleared his throat. "Dave, with your indulgence, I'd like to begin the meeting with a few comments."

Paige hesitated a moment, grinning slightly to mask his irritation, before finally closing his laptop and saying, "Please proceed."

Tierney proceeded to lecture the team members, sternly, with his index finger tapping the table for emphasis, about the slip in the schedule for the project's completion.

"Let me just start by saying that we've still got a long way to go to close this project out successfully," Tierney began. "Our progress has been marginal, at best, and that's simply not good enough. You're all professionals and you all know what needs to be done. Diane tells me the effort is good, but at this point I can't yet translate that effort into the results we should be seeing, the results we're expecting. You've indicated that you have everything you need to get on schedule and stay on schedule. I don't find it worthwhile to keep having this discussion, especially when we all know the priority that this project carries. Jeff Wylie expects this to be delivered on time, and I'm frankly tired of having to tell him that we can't seem to catch up. I would expect this team to work as long and as hard as it takes to keep to the schedule, even if it means working weekends. We have to be responsible and accountable, people, and we have to do what it takes to do our jobs."

Paige sat and listened, saying nothing. He noticed the Elerbee employees alternately glancing over at him, and he could see and feel their obvious discomfort. Diane Tresvant kept her eyes fixed upon the notepad on her lap.

Tierney continued. "Ladies and gentlemen, I want to see results. That's what this is all about. That's why we have our jobs, to deliver results. That's the *only* reason we have our jobs. This isn't the Department of Motor Vehicles; this is a for-profit business entity in the *private* sector. Therefore, we have to perform; we have to deliver; we have to do what we're being *paid* to do. I don't want to have to come here and have this discussion again. We've already done that plenty enough, in all honesty. Now it's time to get off our duffs and deliver. Each one of you has a decision to make today. Each one of you needs to decide today that you're on board, and that you're willing to put in the necessary time and effort to get this project back on track."

Paige remained silent. The Elerbee employees began to take on the appearance of school kids being scolded by an irate principal, with their slumping shoulders, their avoidance of eye contact with Tierney, their facial expressions reflecting the weighty mix of fear, guilt, and anger that churned within.

Tierney leaned back in his chair. "So, here's what I'd like to do. I'd like for you to decide as a team what it's going to take to complete this project on time, with specifics and a timeline, and then be willing to commit to it today."

Tierney glanced at his watch. "I'll give you an hour. I'm going to leave the room, and when I come back, we'll see where you are."

Tierney pushed back in his chair and stood. "One hour."

Tierney took one step before Paige said sharply, *"Keep your seat!"*

All heads in the room turned toward Paige, at once, like a gathering of Meerkats.

"I beg your pardon," said the stunned Tierney.

"Take your seat. As long as Elerbee Engineering continues to pay your consulting fee, you'll take your direction from me, effective immediately."

Paige stood and pointed to Tierney's empty chair, in which the latter reluctantly sat after pausing and staring disbelievingly at Paige.

Paige nodded and then looked out at the others. "With all due respect, Patrick, here's what's going to happen next: First, I'd like the two project leaders, Steve and Diane, to review the agenda items with the team and determine if I've left anything off, and if so, to add those topics for discussion; second, if there is anyone else needed for this meeting, either in person or by phone, then so advise me and I'll get them here; and third, clear your calendars for the rest of the day and order pizza for lunch, since we're going to be here awhile."

Paige noticed the slight smiles on the faces of the Elerbee employees. Diane Tresvant glanced up at Paige, her expression mirroring the awkwardness she was feeling.

"Okay, project leaders, it's all yours. I'll be back in thirty minutes," Paige said. He then leaned toward Tierney. "Could we speak in private?"

Tierney followed Paige the short distance to Paige's office, the consultant's face and body language reflecting his great displeasure. Sherry Painter looked up only briefly from her computer screen until it suddenly registered who was passing near her desk. She couldn't help staring as the two men walked by and entered Paige's office, closing the door behind them.

"Can I offer you some coffee?" Paige asked once they were seated.

"No, but you can offer me an explanation about why you thought it necessary to make a fool out of me in front of the group," Tierney said in a sharp tone.

Paige took a deep breath and glared at Tierney for a moment. "You are an ass of the highest order—a gold-medal, best-in-class, world-champion ass, at that—and as for me, I hardly needed to make a fool out of you. You did an absolutely splendid job of that yourself."

"I resent that."

"Then suck it up. There's more on the way."

Tierney shook his head as he glanced around the office interior. "This project's in the crapper. You have no idea what you've gotten yourself into. You've got a dog on your hands, and you're sure as hell being watched closely by Jeff Wylie. Do you honestly want to manage this thing without my help?"

Paige began laughing.

"Oh, you find that humorous, do you?" said Tierney, his voice constricted, his face reddening, his composure escaping nearer to a point of no return.

"I do, yes," said Paige, his expression suddenly hardening as he leaned forward toward Tierney. "But here's what I *don't* find humorous: I don't like the fact that we pay you a substantial consulting fee to occasionally pop into our offices and proceed to harangue and berate our people; I don't like your off-the-charts pomposity and arrogance, again when we're paying the bill as your client; and I don't intend to compete with you for the leadership and overall direction of this project. That, sir, just ain't gonna happen."

Paige waited a moment for Tierney to absorb his words.

Tierney got up to leave.

"Stop!" Paige said firmly, also standing.

"This conversation's over," Tierney replied.

"I said stop. This conversation's *not* over."

"I was hired by the C.E.O. of this firm. You're not the C.E.O.. As a matter of fact, you're essentially nothing, nill, nada. I don't know where you get off thinking you're someone of importance around here, but I've got news for you: You're not! And just for the record, I don't have to take this crap from you, pal," Tierney said, still standing.

"I am not your pal. And here's what you *do* have to take from me: Just for the record, you are henceforth relieved of any further participation on this project. You can grab your briefcase and head for the exit. I don't care to see you in this building again, ever. You should not bill another hour—another *minute*—of your time to this project or this firm. There will be no need for you to interface with any of my Elerbee team members. Not now, not ever. Diane Tresvant can represent your firm and continue in her role, but as for you, you're done, sir. Your services are no longer needed."

"You know that won't fly with Jeff Wylie."

"Jeff Wylie's not running the project; I am. And I have decided today that your time is up."

Tierney laughed, then turned and walked out of Paige's office.

Sherry Painter waited several minutes before she tapped on Paige's office door and looked inside.

"What happened?" she asked Paige, who was still standing and staring out his office window.

"Everything's cool, Sherry," he replied nonchalantly, still looking away.

Sherry stepped inside the office and closed the door behind her. "There's a major buzz going around the office about what happened in the conference room. One of the project guys came out to go to the bathroom, raised his arms in the air and said, 'Paige a winner by TKO.' What the heck happened in there?"

"Everything's cool," Paige repeated.

"Well, then what happened in here?"

Paige turned and faced Sherry, his hands in his pockets and his demeanor calm and unrevealing. "We just worked everything out, that's all. We needed to reach an understanding and we did. It was short and to the point, nothing more than that."

"Did he lose his temper and get mad?"

"No."

"Did you lose your temper?"

"No. I knew exactly where it was at all times."

Sherry smiled and took the cue, deciding against pressing the matter. "Are you okay?"

"I'm fine," Paige said, nodding.

Sherry nodded in return before leaving the office. Paige glanced at his watch and sat back against his credenza, his arms folded across his chest. He was due back in the conference room in ten minutes, and he was expecting Jeff Wylie's imminent appearance at his door and the start of yet another in their ongoing series of nasty confrontations.

But Wylie didn't come.

Paige went back into the conference room and oversaw a productive, two-hour, high-energy meeting. The team was enthusiastic about bringing the project back on schedule, and longer workdays were agreed upon as the primary method. Afterward, Paige pulled Diane Tresvant aside in the hallway.

"I know I put you in a terribly awkward position, Diane," he said in a lowered voice, "and I sincerely apologize for that. But I also want to tell you that I have great confidence in you, and I want you to continue to assist us on this project. I've heard nothing but good things about you, and I value your project-management skills. What happened with Patrick was between him and me, and should have no bearing on you or your duties with this team."

Diane smiled and thanked Paige.

And, oddly, Paige never heard from Jeff Wylie about the Tierney incident.

Paige sat in his office after the long day, his tie loosened and his fatigue showing in his eyes. It was near midnight, and he was reminded of how hungry he was when his stomach once again called out its discontentment. Hours earlier, the soda and cheese crackers just hadn't been enough. It was in such moments as these, when he had cleared not just his desk but also his brain, when his very last reserves of energy had been extinguished, when both his calendar and his state of mind were ready to roll the day over into history, that Paige became reflective.

He opened his Paige's Laws of Business.

Just like on the playground, the physical bullies in business will step aside in confusion if you come at them fearlessly and ferociously, which they don't normally expect. The intellectual bullies are nothing without their feelings of power and dominance, so their sense of preeminence has to be the specific target. When they lose their power source, their inability to persuade is magnified, and their influence is nullified. Those who attempt to be both physical and intellectual bullies will inevitably self-destruct, as is their core tendency anyway.

Never, never, never gloat in victory. Leave that to the drunks and the punks. It's a destructive, rather than constructive, behavior.

However, always celebrate a victory. Each victory is typically hard-earned, and often has a short shelf life. It should be savored and appreciated for all its worth. And watch what happens when you give away the credit to others.

CHAPTER EIGHT

The May month-end results were published at the beginning of June. The message: Elerbee Engineering was holding its own. Revenue was up 1% over the comparable period of a year ago; net profits were up 5%, to the delight of Jeff Wylie. The firm was mostly healthy and on target, no small feat in an economy that was still soft and fragile.

Wylie gathered his full staff for an early-morning session in the headquarters' conference room. There, under the oil portrait of its founder, the top management of Elerbee Engineering held its quarterly review. Collier, Ogden, and Paige were present, along with the finance, quality, engineering, and marketing chiefs. Don Burroughs from human resources was also there, as regal as ever. Each of the regional managers brought with them a series of PowerPoint presentations on their laptops with which to chart, graph, and bullet-point their respective results, with Wylie guiding the session through its customary format.

Ogden was first up. Fees had risen in all but five of his twenty-nine branches; profits were up modestly, but in higher proportion than the increase in fees; there was a fair mix of project types, and decent prospects for a continuation of same. And there were other highlights: The Eastern Region laid claim to the company's most profitable of all branches, in Atlanta; and the company's single largest project, a group of research buildings in the Raleigh-Durham area. The Eastern Region had recruited and hired eighteen new engineers through the first five months of 2002, ten of whom had graduated with masters degrees at the top of their respective classes. The other eight were only slightly less impressive. The region's weakest branch, in Cincinnati, had shown an increase in fees billed in May, the first such increase over the previous month in almost a year.

"A very encouraging sign," Wylie commented.

And there was more: Ogden had directed a task force which had developed a training manual that covered in detail virtually every phase of branch operations, from proposal preparation to final billing. Copies of the bound manual were distributed to all present.

"Simply an outstanding effort," Wylie commented.

There was even more. Elerbee Engineering had been awarded a commendation by a leading community relief organization for its efforts in providing volunteer services and in raising considerable sums of money from Elerbee employees. The corporate effort had been spearheaded by none other than Jim Ogden, who had of course delegated all the work but who now absorbed all the accolades.

Still more. Ogden, it seems, had been appointed as a high-ranking officer in a prestigious national engineering society, succeeding Dave Paige and providing considerable public-relations potential for the firm.

"Our heartiest congratulations," Wylie commented.

When Ogden finally took his seat and surrendered the floor to Paige, he had the unmistakable look of triumph on his face; similar, Paige thought, to the way Hitler must have looked when he had entered Vienna during the *Anschluss*.

Ogden nodded at Wylie, with Wylie nodding slightly in return before turning his attention to Paige.

Paige followed with a report on the Central Region. Fees were up only a meager 2% over last year, though profits had risen 12% over the same period. The recent managerial changes, Paige insisted, would no doubt bring favorable results, though perhaps not immediately. The project list was strong, stronger now than at any time in the previous six months. And there were new projects on the horizon, for which new engineers would be needed—a noticeable departure from the hand-to-mouth basis on which the region's twenty-one branches had subsisted for almost a year. The area encompassing much of the region was still economically depressed, Paige pointed out. But, he added quickly, Elerbee Engineering was getting its share.

The trends were mostly favorable. There was depth—in projects and in people—which had previously not existed. New business was being sought more systematically, more aggressively, than had been the case before. There were more leads on larger projects, more leads on smaller projects, more *leads*, and more contacts following up the leads, than ever before. The morale of the employees in the central branches was good, and getting better. There was measurable progress; there was more consistency. A far more demanding pace was being set at the top, for sure, but the region was mostly following in step.

There were no miracle strokes, no singular milestone achievements, but Paige's group was clearly at the top of the heap. Ogden's group was closing the gap, however, and Paige was suddenly no longer out of reach.

"Thanks, Dave. We'll be watching with interest," Wylie said.

Larry Collier's review of the Western Region was short and succinct. Growth in fees was weak, weakest of the three. In fact, the region was well behind the pace of the previous year. And the costs associated with the region's operations had risen in far greater proportion, painting the region's profit picture in hues of pink and red. As a consequence, a general belt-tightening in each of the eighteen branches was underway, Collier explained. Things would henceforth be more closely controlled.

Don Burroughs' review of the manpower levels of the firm, both current and projected, was done without great fanfare. However, Burroughs did manage to point out in his short presentation that Jim Ogden's region was almost singularly responsible for the employment of the company's otherwise modest numbers of minority engineers and managers. "A more determined effort," was the prescription given by Burroughs to the two regions belonging to Paige and Collier.

Paige went ballistic. His region had introduced the firm's first African American and first female branch managers earlier in the year, and he hadn't failed to notice that Ogden had been fed a steady stream of minority candidates by Burroughs, far more than had been directed to either Paige or Collier. After Paige's blunt suggestion that Burroughs "get off his dead ass" and provide some leadership in the targeting of specific minority candidates, Jeff Wylie was compelled to intervene and restore the general order. Burroughs' forehead immediately broke out in little beads of perspiration, which Paige glanced over and noticed and only barely contained his laughter.

The topics were eventually fulfilled when the staff members had completed their business presentations. Paige sensed that the eye contact between Wylie and Ogden—one his boss, the other his contemporary and bitter rival—mirrored the unspoken but understood tectonic shift now well underway in the fundamental nature of things in the Elerbee Engineering.

Thus Paige's worst fears were being validated. He envisioned himself as gradually slipping away into the abyss of a career vacuum—an executive who was once an insider but who now finds himself clearly on the outside; an alien; an overachiever who, for reasons outside his own control, suddenly finds himself no worse a loser than if his achievements and contributions had been diminutive. The Old Man was dead, and Paige was dying. Or so he felt. And it was starting to eat away at him in a dreadful way, as if all the small bites he had thus far managed to endure were now suddenly culminating in a critical, irrevocable loss of blood and flesh.

Wylie gave a brief summary and then drew the meeting to a close. Promptly, Burroughs was the first out the door, spilling and ignoring the cold coffee on the leg of his trousers.

Once back in his office, Paige closed the door and directed that Sherry hold his calls. He needed some time to think. Two days earlier and prior to daybreak, he had left for Chicago to attend a two-day management seminar sponsored by a national engineering society. The meeting's first day had been barely worthwhile, and Paige had seriously considered boarding the company jet and flying back to Atlanta. Instead, he had foregone the Elerbee aircraft and purchased with his own funds a round-trip ticket from O'Hare to Philadelphia, only because he knew how anal Wylie had become about the operating costs of the jet, as well as Paige's alleged monopolistic tendencies over its use. He just didn't want the additional hassle at this point. So he had set out on his own to pay his daughter another pleasant, if unexpected, visit.

The time with Sara had been well spent and satisfying, even though the events at work were always in his head, never far from the surface, as difficult to shake as a summer cold. Sara had noticed his distraction, had even commented on it, and he had immediately fallen into an even deeper funk.

This is not good, he kept thinking.

Screw Wylie, he thought once he had settled back into his chair and made himself comfortable behind his closed office door. He was finally about to reach one of those peaceful, easy feelings when there came an unexpected, loud knock on his door.

"Yeah?" he called out sharply.

Jim Ogden opened the door and peered inside. "Got a minute?" he asked, and without waiting for an answer immediately stepped inside and closed the door behind him.

Paige said nothing.

"I need to make you aware of something," Ogden said in a hushed voice.

Paige gave a resigned shrug. "Then the floor is now yours."

Ogden remained standing and scratched at an old stain in the middle of his dark blue tie. "Becker and Associates. You know them, right?"

"Yeah, sure. The engineering-consulting arm of Becker International. What about them?"

"I understand they're looking for someone to head up their soils-engineering operation. They do sixty, seventy million a year, mostly in the northeast. The parent, Becker International, will go about a billion five, give or take a few hundred mil. I competed with Becker and Associates when I was running the Baltimore Branch, yet Becker International was one of my bigger clients. Kind of screwy, I suppose. Anyway, Becker and Associates has always been small potatoes, even though they've done some damn good work over the years. Now all of a sudden they're interested in growing the company, and the word I get is they want to talk to someone from here."

"Oh? Who?"

"I don't know. I'd guess it'd be someone here in Atlanta. Have you heard anything?"

"No, nothing."

Ogden gave a shrug and glanced past Paige, out the window on the opposite end of the office. "I've got a contact up there who told me they're looking for the best man they can find. The job sounds as if it'd involve running the whole freakin' show, building the business and coordinating all the soils projects. And man, they handle a hell of a lot of projects."

"Any interest on your part?" Paige asked pointedly.

Ogden grinned and stroked his moustache with his index finger, his dark eyes suddenly fixed upon Paige. "Not really. I might talk to them out of courtesy if they call, but I really have no burning interest."

There was a clumsy moment of silence.

"Philadelphia's an okay town. But Becker's about as solid as they come. It'd be a hell of an opportunity, the kind that doesn't come around but once in a blue moon," Ogden said convincingly.

"Okay, I'll buy that. Go on."

"It'd be a super chance to go in there and make a big splash."

Their eyes met for an instant before Ogden looked away.

"Oh, by the way," said Ogden. "Were you aware that your new assistant's been designated?"

"No," Paige answered, cocking his head slightly. "And I wasn't aware that my assistant was *going* to be designated. Who the hell made the choice for me?"

"Jeff, with Vince Kincaid's blessing, since the guy's coming from finance."

Paige said nothing, intending to ask Wylie later on for an explanation of the unusual protocol.

"You'll like him, though," Ogden said, grinning and lowering his voice to barely above a whisper. "He's the only black dude in the bunch, and you're getting him."

Ogden chuckled.

"Is that all?" Paige asked impatiently.

Ogden turned slightly and reached for the door knob. "Yep, that's it, but like I said earlier, I do have a contact at Becker. He's not *that* high-ranking, but he could see to it that the word got out. All I'd have to do is put a bug in his ear."

"Then by all means, Jim, call him up and tell him to put your name in play."

Ogden laughed. "I was thinking more in terms of your name."

"It could be your moment in the sun," Paige said with a heavy dose of sarcasm in his tone. "You should seize it and squeeze it."

Ogden squinted slightly, then nodded slowly. "Make no mistake, my man. That's precisely what I intend to do."

Richardson's was heavily crowded. The regulars were augmented by a contingent of food brokers in town for a convention. Paige sat at a table with Ted Haygood, his CPA friend who had called earlier and suggested they bypass the heavy evening traffic and meet instead for a cocktail. Chrissie, the waitress, moved about her section delivering drinks and drawing stares. The owner stopped by the table and encouraged Paige and Haygood to sample the hors d'oeuvres— hot, spicy chicken wings. "A little taste of napalm," the owner said with a wink.

In the background came *Alone Again (Naturally)*.

The first round of beers came compliments of Ted Haygood. "I just wish you'd get out more, man," he had said before raising his glass.

Paige shrugged. "Yeah, well, maybe I will. Cheers."

"Yeah?"

"Yeah. Now shut up and drink."

At a nearby table, a bulky lady in her early fifties with a hairy mole on her chin and a space between her bottom teeth was attempting to sing along to the words of *Cherish* despite a voice that resembled a foghorn. Haygood, who faced the lady, was having difficulty keeping a straight face.

"Must be Mellow Night, or something," Haygood observed.

"Why don't you ask her to dance? Maybe that'd shut her up."

"Think she'd look any better at close range?"

Paige stole a quick glance. "Nope."

They said nothing for several moments, each amazed at how poorly the nearby lady carried a tune.

Paige sighed. "Ted, I think I'm weakening."

"Well then, let's move to another table, dammit."

"No, not that. I'm talking about life in general."

Haygood appeared surprised. "Where the hell did *that* come from?"

"I think I may be losing it," Paige answered, shaking his head from side to side. "This stuff at work is finally getting to me, I think."

"Ah," said Haygood, waving off Paige's pessimism. "You're just tired, man. You need a break."

"I need more than a break. I need a mega-vitamin. I need a trip to Australia. I need a new boss. I need the job I'd been awarded. And I'll need a friggin' miracle to pull this thing off now. Wylie's getting his boy Ogden all lined up to become Number Two. I'll be lucky to stay employed until the Board meeting next month in New Orleans."

The muscles in Paige's face tightened. He drew a long, deep breath. "Damn, what a difference a death makes."

"You're giving up and throwing in the towel? Am I really hearing this? From you, of all people?"

"What the hell else can I do? I'm a political outcast. One of my own branch managers told me yesterday that he'd talked with one of Jim Ogden's guys who told him that Ogden has already drawn up an organization chart that he plans to propose after he's become Executive V.P.. And guess where I am in that organization?"

Haygood remained silent.

"I'm not," Paige said, looking away for a moment.

Chrissie brought the round ordered by Paige. Her perfume was enticing.

"You look so sad, Dave," she said after placing the mugs on the table. "Is something wrong?"

Paige looked at her and smiled. "Everything's perfect, Chrissie."

"That's good," she replied, reaching for the empty mugs. "That's *very* good."

Paige followed her with his eyes as she turned and walked away. "Dear God, I do need a break."

Haygood laughed, then sipped the fresh beer. "By the way, Diane tells me that she's meeting with you again in a few days."

"Correct," said Paige, still trying to follow Chrissie on the far side of the room. "We're scheduled to meet soon."

"I think Diane's got a thing for you, Dave."

Paige looked up from his beer. "What makes you think that?"

"Just the way she talks about you, mostly. It's not something she'd be so foolish to make obvious, but it's there, in my humble opinion. She's initiated several conversations about Elerbee Engineering in general and about Dave Paige specifically, almost as if she wanted to send you a message through me. Besides, before she started working with you guys on the systems project, she hadn't said so much as 'boo' to me in almost three years. And now I'm one of her favorite people in Atlanta. She couldn't wait to tell me about your having kicked Patrick Tierney's ass off the project and out of the building. She said she wanted to stand up and cheer when you blew Tierney away in the team meeting, but she knew it would've ended her employment with the firm. She really likes your style, man. Whether you realize it or not, you've got a not-so-secret admirer in Diane."

"Interesting," Paige said thoughtfully.

Haygood grinned slightly. "I thought you'd think so."

"Any idea what she's like outside the office?"

"Divorced, no kids. She's focused, serious, and she can be tough as nails when she needs to be. She's smart as a whip, and she'll likely make partner soon, and for all the right reasons. And," said Haygood, grinning mischievously, "she's a distance runner and in the event you haven't noticed, she's in fabulous physical condition, a real hardbody. And if all of that's not enough, she's also interested."

"C'mon, Ted," Paige said, slightly irritated. "She's never given me any such indication."

"Then maybe you should ask her out, is all I'm saying. She's a lot like you, man. I swear to God, a lot."

"What's that supposed to mean?"

"That she's one hell of a driven person, is what it means."

"Diane and I have a business relationship. She's a consultant to me and my firm. That's the entire extent of our relationship. We're not lovers; we're certainly not broadcasting our loneliness to each other. We have a *business* relationship. And a pretty good one, I might add. I know that may seem unlikely, maybe even implausible to you, but that's all there is. Period. Okay?"

Haygood threw up his hands. "Okay, fine. You call it like you see it, bro. But I just thought you'd like to know she's interested in you."

"Thanks," Paige said with a nod. "I'll keep that in mind."

"You do that."

"I will."

Chrissie passed nearby.

"I absolutely, positively will."

CHAPTER NINE

Jim Ogden awakened at nine, far later than usual. He knew as a consequence that he'd be hopelessly out of sync for the rest of the day. It always happened that way after a night like the last one. Beside him, still asleep, lay Nina.

Goddamned scotch and red wine, he thought.

They had started out the previous evening during Happy Hour, and then proceeded to drink until the wee hours of the morning before he had finally taken her to bed and ravished her young body. Now his head felt stuffy and thick, and the aspirin had not yet delivered the needed cure. He coughed, and then reached for a tissue on the nightstand.

"Good morning," she said in a soft, dreamy voice.

"Morning. Are you feeling okay?"

"I'm feeling fine. What is today? Is it Friday?"

"Yep, all day."

"Are you going to the office?"

"Of course," Ogden said as he wiped the tissue across his nose, and then wadded and tossed it in the direction of the bathroom.

"Coming back tonight?"

"No."

"Why not?"

Ogden climbed out of the bed and reached for the grey slacks that were draped over a nearby chair. "Are we going to have to get into all that again?"

Nina sat up, covering herself with the satin sheet. She ran her hand through her freshly cut short hair, and then shook it into place. "Why not?"

Ogden took a seat on the edge of the bed and began pulling on his socks. "Look, as soon as things straighten out a bit, then we can start being together more. I promise," he said as he turned to touch her face with his hand.

"When?"

"In a month or so, baby, just like I've been saying all along."

"And you've also been saying you're going to leave your wife so we can stop living this lie."

"Yep, that's the plan."

"So what'd you tell her this time?"

"The usual—that I'm leaving town on a business trip."

"What if she tries to contact you?"

"She won't."

"I don't like this, Jim. I'm not comfortable with it. I've never been comfortable with it. I've told you before that I want a normal life."

"You're adjusting nicely."

"And you're telling me that you *do* like it, that you don't mind this false arrangement?"

Ogden said nothing and instead began searching for a clean shirt in the walk-in closet.

"I'm not a leper, Jim."

Ogden peered out from the closet. "Why do you say such ridiculous stuff as that?"

"I don't like being used."

"You've been used all your life, Nina," Ogden said, suddenly touchy. "Everybody you've ever been around has used you. I've treated you a hell of a lot better than the others, but yeah, I'm using you, too. Just like you're using me. Now stop coming at me with that 'used' nonsense."

Later, Ogden was already into his second cup of coffee when Nina came down the stairs. She took a seat on the sofa, her smooth legs crossed underneath her. She wore a black tank-top with faded, cutoff jeans. Her legs were long and firm, and her entire body was toned from the many hours spent at the spa. She wore no makeup except for yesterday's eye shadow.

"I want you to leave, Jim."

Ogden's eyes remained fixed on a newspaper. "Coffee?"

"Did you hear me? Did you hear what I said? I said I want you to leave and not come back."

"I heard you."

"I don't want you coming back here ever again."

There was a long, awkward silence. Ogden folded away the newspaper and tossed it aside. He leaned forward on the table, propping on his elbows. "Why?" he asked as he watched her from afar.

"I'm not comfortable with our relationship, that's why," she said, glancing briefly toward the ceiling and then looking away.

Ogden poured a fresh cup of coffee and took it to her. He sat in a chair nearby, turning to face her. Her expression was firm and unyielding, and her eyes avoided his altogether. He admired her features—her cheekbones and rounded lips; the nipples protruding from beneath the tank-top; the smooth, bare skin of her shoulders. She was attractive, even in modest attire. Tall at five-foot nine, and elegantly thin, she was merely twenty-four, twenty years his junior. And despite her youth, she was already well on her way toward establishing herself professionally as an accomplished photographer. She worked out of her older brother's studio, sometimes using his lab, sometimes his special equipment, but the talent behind the camera was unmistakably hers. She was steadily building a reputation as a talented freelancer.

They had met the previous October, a month after the end of her ill-fated affair with a former art professor. She had consequently dropped out of college, taken an apartment, and begun developing her photography from a part-time avocation into a burgeoning, full-time practice. The occasion of their first meeting occurred when she had photographed the wedding of Ogden's Elerbee Engineering secretary, Beth. He had desperately wanted to stay away—he hated weddings, for he knew all too well that they often cooled, indeed sometimes froze—but he and his wife Mary had come anyway, for Beth. And so he had smiled and congratulated and complimented, and he had even danced with the lovely Beth at the lovely reception. But it was the foxy photographer he had spotted at the onset who had captured his attention. She was quietly professional, with a reserved smile and an ability to manage a wedding crowd without becoming obtrusive. And she was young, far younger than he. They had talked, and then later that night had met for a drink, away from the wedding activity. Within two weeks, Ogden had become a frequent overnight guest in her apartment.

"Let's talk about it, okay?" he said comfortingly.

"There's nothing to talk about. You can leave and do away with the risk of someone 'discovering' us together."

Ogden leaned back in the chair. "Nina honey, look, why don't—"

"It's not gonna work, Jim. You won't talk me out of it this time. I won't listen to you anymore. So don't bother, dammit."

She turned away defiantly.

"Okay," he said with sorrow. "I had something important I was going to tell you, but I can see now there's no need."

"You have no plans for us."

"You're wrong, Nina. I have very definite plans for us."

"You can't expect me to believe that. Not now. Not after all this time."

Ogden got up and walked to the table where he took one last sip of the cool brown liquid in his coffee mug. He then turned to face her. "There's something important happening in mid-July, in New Orleans. It's the organization thing I've told you about. And my chances of being promoted to a major position in the firm are very good. Actually, my chances are better than 'very good' because it's doubtful that Dave Paige will even make it to July at the rate he's going. But even if he does, it'll still be me, I'm certain."

Nina appeared indifferent.

"Nina, I'll be the one chosen. And once that happens, once I'm promoted, there won't be as much scrutiny over me, especially on all the stuff concerning my private life. I'll get a big raise—big enough to afford another house. And once I'm settled in, that's when the two of us could finally be together, the way we've both wanted. God knows I've been waiting a long time for this, baby, and now it's right on the verge of happening."

Ogden started toward the stairway. He stopped at the base of the stairs and turned toward her. "That's what so sad about all of this. New Orleans is only a month away. It's not as if it'd have to be this way forever. One more month and it would've been far different." He slumped, his hands in his pockets. "I'm really disappointed. I've been working my ass off so all this could happen, and everything's right on schedule. It's been a long time coming, but things are working out just like I thought they would. And now you hit me with this."

Nina kept looking away, her head lowered.

"Damn," he said with a resigned shrug, "I guess I'll just get my things."

Nina turned and looked in his direction. Her eyes were moist and reddened. "You've never bothered to tell me you love me," she said in a breaking voice. "Not once, Jim."

"Yeah, I know," he said remorsefully. "And I'm sorry, baby, I really am. I know I'm not one to talk a lot about my feelings, but the truth is, I love you a great deal, Nina. Just because I fail to say it doesn't mean I don't feel it. I feel it every day, every minute. It's the only thing that keeps me going sometimes. And I've never felt it as strongly as I do at this very moment. Nina, I love you, and I need you, and I want you. And I can't bear the thought of not having you."

Ogden turned and climbed the stairs to the bedroom. Upstairs, he glanced at his watch—it was nearly ten. The traffic would be lighter now, and he'd have an easier drive to the office. When he went to the closet to get his shirt and tie, he sensed another presence in the room.

"Will you make love to me before you go?"

He turned and saw her standing alongside the bed, her face wet with tears.

"Before I go for the last time?"

"Not necessarily," she said, watching carefully for his show of approval.

He left his shirt hanging in the closet. As he approached her, he could see her struggling to maintain her self-control. He embraced her tenderly, calming her, cradling her head against his shoulder. After a moment, she sat down on the bed and proceeded to undress by pulling her top over her head.

Ogden undressed quickly and slid into bed beside her. She was soft and warm, her body velvety smooth and unblemished. He kissed her, and then ran his hand along her thigh.

Afterwards, still breathing heavily, he kissed the tip of her nose. "No more talk of breaking off our relationship," he said as he nuzzled her smooth cheek. "You belong with me." They rolled onto their sides and faced one another. Ogden ran his hand along her shoulder and arm.

"Do you really think we could move into a house later on in the summer?"

"I do, yes."

"Will it depend on the promotion?"

"Yeah, but like I told you, my chances are very, very good."

"What about the thing with Dave Paige? You said he may not make it, right?"

"That's right."

"Why?"

"He can't stand the heat he's getting from Jeff. Plus, his old lady divorced him and now he's all alone and miserable. If anything else presents itself, he'll jump at the chance to bail out of Elerbee Engineering. He's all but dead and gone."

Ogden leaned and kissed Nina on the neck. "It's all starting to come together, baby."

"For us," she added.

"That's right. For us."

"What about the other guy?"

"What other guy?"

"The other one besides you and Dave Paige."

"His name's Larry Collier. I'm not sure he's got the stamina to hang on much longer in any capacity. His health's terrible. Hell, he may not live until New Orleans," Ogden said with a chuckle.

"That's sad."

"Yeah."

Nina suddenly sat up and reached toward the nightstand, near her side of the bed. She opened the top drawer and unfastened a gold cigarette case. She removed a pre-rolled joint and lit it with book matches.

"Care to join me?" she asked after a deep inhalation.

"No, not now. I'm leaving in ten minutes."

She inhaled again. "When will you be back?" she asked, her voice scratchy from the hot smoke.

Ogden smiled. "Tomorrow afternoon, early."

"I know what you're smiling about."

"Oh?"

"I'm not breaking it off, Jim, because you said you loved me—you said it!—and because of the other things we talked about, like maybe getting into a house of our own. You said all that, Jim."

Ogden turned away from the smoke. "That's right, I did. And I meant it."

"But there's one thing you didn't get into."

"Damn," Ogden mumbled under his breath. He quickly rolled out of the bed.

"C'mon, Jim. You didn't mention anything about our getting married."

"Anything's possible," he replied as he leaned over to step into his slacks.

Nina extinguished her smoke by carefully crushing its end into a glass ashtray. A portion of it remained—less than half—which she placed back into the cigarette case. She slumped back onto the bed. She was exposed from the waist up, and made no effort to cover herself with the sheet. She ran her hand slowly through her hair.

"What about what I just said?"

"We'll talk later."

Ogden leaned and kissed her on the lips, feeling her warm mouth from the hot smoke. She made an attempt to pull him closer but he quickly stepped back.

"No, baby. I'm already late."

He pulled the sheet up and covered her bare front, then kissed the top of her head.

She sighed. "Please hand me my appointment book before you leave. It's on the dresser."

Ogden tossed her leather-bound book onto the bed, beside her. Her eyelids appeared heavy as she looked up and smiled. She looked down at her book and flipped the pages until she came to the month of July.

"I'm going to keep things open so I can travel to New Orleans with you," she declared.

Ogden winced slightly. "Yeah, fine."

"That's okay, isn't it?"

"It's okay, yeah."

"I won't be in the way or anything, right?"

"No. It'll be fine."

"I can't wait to visit New Orleans again. And I want to be there with you when you get your new job. We can share the big moment together."

"That's fine, baby," Ogden said as he started toward the door.

"Have a nice day," he heard her say as he descended the stairs to the living room. He picked up his car keys from the breakfast table, took a final sip from an earlier glass of orange juice, and grabbed his briefcase before heading toward the door.

A smile crept over his face as he closed the door behind him.

CHAPTER TEN

"Good morning, Atlanta. It's Monday, it's six-thirty, and it's raining all over the metro area. Right now, the temperature's at a breezy fifty-nine degrees, and there's more rain in the forecast. The street's are slippery and the traffic's dreadful, so allow for a little extra time this morning—like a calendar week! But hey, Atlanta, cheer up. Everything's gonna be okay. Here's something to get you started off this morning, called, you guessed it, *Rainy Days and Mondays* . . ."

Paige's morning began with a flurry.

First he met with the company's credit manager, a stern, humorless man who gave the impression of believing in absolutely nothing that wasn't supported by registered documents. Together they reviewed the status of the past-dues in the Central Region. Paige was surprised when the man concluded the meeting with several complimentary remarks about the overall soundness of the region's receivables, as well as noting what he described as a "new attitude" emanating from the branch managers in the Central Region.

I like this guy, Paige thought.

There was also a brief meeting with the corporate marketing team to discuss the progress of several large proposals in the Central Region. Things seemed to be moving smoothly on all fronts—good projects in hand, good projects in store, good feelings about both.

I like these guys, he thought.

Next, he reviewed an econometric forecast, sitting in with the vice presidents of marketing and finance, as well as with Jim Ogden and Larry Collier. The report was a compendium of market trends and growth assumptions compiled from an imposing statistical database. A member of the accounting staff had developed the format—a Georgia M.B.A. who was scheduled to become Paige's full-time assistant. The young African-American was named Hal Mortensen, and Paige immediately liked him after listening to him turn drab, raw statistical data into insightful, reasoned analyses. This guy can play, Paige thought to himself as he watched and listened.

Between meetings, Paige returned to his office and reached for his book, *Paige's Laws of Business*. He took a moment to crystallize his thoughts before reaching for his pen and writing:

*The more someone has to justify his own position, the more that same someone will look at a problem not in terms of its ultimate solution, but more in terms of quickly fixing the blame elsewhere.

*Some of the most ruthless people in business can also be some of the biggest cowards. Beware of the ass-kissers, for they're as quick to slash as they are to smack, and both acts are performed chiefly from the rear.

Next on Paige's schedule involved a bi-weekly overview meeting with the systems-project group. A heated argument ensued not five minutes into the session between the data-processing representative and the operations representative over the scheduled implementation date.

"August first ain't gonna work," said Judah Hammond, the operations assistant. "The software company's in California, and our own data-processing folks don't come down on them hard enough to make sure they turn the tapes around as quickly as possible. Nope, no way will August first work."

"The software company's doing just fine," countered Don Wilkinson, the data-processing assistant. "If you users would make sure you do the testing in accordance with the schedule, then any delays in turning the tapes around would be a lot less disruptive."

"We are doing the testing."

"Not as timely as you should."

"That's just not true."

"It damn well is."

From the head of the conference table, Paige raised his hand and quieted the two combatants. He glanced quickly at Diane Tresvant, the outside consultant from Jarred & Holtzclaw CPAs, who had wisely chosen to defer to Paige and stay out of what was essentially an internal territorial squabble.

"Let me clarify one point before we go any further, gentlemen, and that is, the August first conversion is not negotiable. Not now, not ever. It's a fixed point, and I insist you think of it that way."

The two men facing one another from across the table sat back in their chairs and listened.

"I will expect you two to meet and iron out any difficulties we may have with testing and programming, as many times as conditions warrant. And I don't expect there to be any more finger-pointing over the basic issues that we in this room have control over. Am I coming through loud and clear?"

The two nodded.

"Because if I'm not, if for any reason you're not hearing me loudly and clearly, and we get to August first and we're not ready to convert, then it is *I* who will be doing the finger-pointing, and not you. So if there's anything else we need to get out on the table, anything that will keep us from meeting our time line, then let's hear it now."

"We'll work it out, Dave," said Wilkinson, who nodded toward Hammond. "And we'll get back on track posthaste."

"Any problems with that?" Paige asked as he turned and looked at Hammond.

Hammond shook his head. "No. Don's right. We'll work it out."

Before adjourning the meeting, Paige asked Diane Tresvant to remain in the room for a brief discussion following the meeting's end. Diane sat across the wooden conference table from Paige, her open laptop beside her on the table and a yellow notepad in front of her. She wore an attractive grey jacket and skirt, with white blouse, and her short brown hair was neatly parted in the middle.

Paige leaned back in the cushioned chair after the room had cleared of the others. "Straight answer to a straight question, Diane."

She nodded. "Okay, shoot."

"Can we meet the August first conversion date?"

"Yes," Diane said without hesitation. "The software company's taking the programming bugs we're finding and making the fixes quickly, which is good. We're almost through the testing matrix, and assuming that we don't have any major crashes elsewhere—and we shouldn't—then we're good to go for August first. I like our chances, Dave, I really do. Especially now that you've got everybody re-focused."

Paige sipped from a bottle of water, remaining silent.

"And besides," she continued, "your team has gotten a lot more accustomed to working with my guys. They're functioning a lot more efficiently now, not like at first. So we're getting better traction there, too."

"Diane, this is the single most important thing you've ever done in your life up to this point," Paige said bluntly. "It has to go precisely according to plan."

Diane blinked, then recovered quickly. "We'll make it, Dave. I have every confidence."

"If we don't," Paige continued, staring hard into her eyes, "then you and I will most likely find ourselves working the night shift at Mickey D's."

Diane smiled slightly. "If I didn't understand before, I certainly do now."

Paige returned his pen to his pocket. "Got any questions of me?"

"No," Diane said, shaking her head. "I think we've covered everything to my satisfaction."

Diane closed her laptop and then slid her chair back to stand.

"Just one moment more," Paige said, still seated across the table.

Diane relaxed in her seat.

"One other thing, but on a bit of a different note," Paige said, changing not only the subject but his own tone and carriage. He relaxed, becoming less stiff and formal. He smiled and appeared slightly self-conscious. "I'll need you to hear me out on this."

Diane shrugged and smiled in return. "I'm listening."

Paige took a deep breath and chuckled slightly. An uncomfortable silence ensued for several seconds until Paige shifted in his chair once, then twice. He cleared his throat and chuckled again.

"Is something wrong, Dave?"

"No," Paige answered quickly in a higher than normal tone. "Nothing's wrong. Everything's fine, really."

Diane's expression reflected her sudden confusion.

"Listen, Diane, I have access to a place in the Rockies, about an hour from Denver. There's plenty to do and the scenery is absolutely spectacular. If you're partial to incredible natural beauty," Paige said, pausing to read her reaction, "you'd love everything about it. But even if you're not," he said, pausing again and chuckling slightly, "I still think you'd enjoy it."

Diane leaned slightly forward, with an expression that seemed to say, Yeah? And?

"I'd like very much if you'd join me there for the weekend," Paige said. "I realize this is a bit sudden, and I doubt that you expected anything like this when you walked into the room this morning. But I'd be honored to have you join me. It really is such a refreshing place. And if your schedule is as hectic as I think it is, then that would make it all the better for you to take a little time off to enjoy what is undoubtedly one of the more naturally beautiful spots on the face of the earth. So what do you say, Ms. Tresvant, CPA? Would you join me as my guest to see the majestic Colorado Rockies?"

Diane blushed for a moment, unsure. "I, uh, Dave, I'm not—"

"I understand the client-relationship thing may be a problem for you," Paige said quickly. "But don't get too bogged down with that. It's not like we're going to divulge any super-sensitive national-security information, or anything. And the whole thing will be handled with the appropriate discretion, you can be sure."

Still blushing, Diane smiled and cleared her throat. She reached for a nearby bottle of water. "Well, I can say with absolute *certainty* that I wasn't expecting this when I showed up here this morning."

"I really like the way you handle yourself, Diane. I like the results you get. I think we have a lot in common. And if that's not enough," Paige said, pausing and staring straight into her eyes, "I also happen to find you extremely attractive."

She said nothing.

"I honestly think you'd thoroughly enjoy yourself. The mountains are a lovely place, and I'd certainly do my best to be a first-rate host. By the time Monday rolled around, you'd be a new person, guaranteed."

She cleared her throat again, but still said nothing.

"So? Will you join me this weekend?"

"I'm seeing someone."

Paige shrugged. "I had a wife once."

Diane frowned.

Paige grinned. "We're divorced. And it doesn't matter to me that you're involved with someone else. I'd still like to show you the mountain place."

"It wouldn't be professional, Dave. It just wouldn't be right," she said in objection. "Besides, I've already made plans for the weekend. And on top of all that, I just told you I'm seeing someone."

"I don't care who you're seeing," Paige said with a shrug. "I don't care that you have plans for the weekend. I don't care that you work for a company that works for my company. I don't care about any of that. I'd like to take you to the mountains, and I'd like for you to do whatever it takes to do that, this weekend. We can leave for Denver on Friday night and come back on Sunday afternoon. It'll be you and me, Diane, and I very much like the thought of that."

Paige didn't take his eyes off her, almost as if he were attempting to absorb her. She crossed and uncrossed her legs once, then finally reached again for the water bottle.

"God, you don't have a subtle bone in your body," she said after moistening her dry mouth.

Paige grinned.

"Really, Dave, I—"

"Diane," he said abruptly, "I'm aware that I've once again put you in a terribly awkward position. If you truly don't want to go, then as far as I'm concerned this never happened, and it will certainly have no affect whatsoever on our business relationship. I want you to believe that, because I mean it sincerely. And if you feel that way, if you'd rather not go, then please, say so. And just understand that my intentions were entirely noble, that I really did want to spend time with you outside the office, getting to know you better. And I do apologize for my," he said, stopping and grinning boyishly, "lack of subtlety."

Diane smiled slightly, and then took another sip of water.

"If it makes you feel any better," Paige said, still grinning, "I've been a nervous wreck all morning thinking about how I'd approach you. I must've gone over a dozen different scripts in my head—even rehearsed one or two out loud on the drive in—and I finally decided that I'd just come right out and ask you, you know, adult to adult."

Diane almost choked on her water as she suddenly began laughing. "Adult to adult, huh?" she said, still giggling.

"Exactly."

She sat up and recovered her composure. "I don't suppose it occurred to you to start off this 'budding relationship' with say, dinner and a movie? Here in Atlanta, I mean?"

"It did, yeah."

There was a brief silence.

"So?" Diane pressed.

"So what?"

"So why did you decide that the very first time you'd ask to see me would be to offer to take me to Colorado?"

Paige blinked twice, then nodded. "I see your point. We really haven't had time enough to explain to each other that we don't have herpes or AIDS or criminal records, that we eat certain foods and have certain values and like certain things and don't like certain other things—stuff like that, right?"

Diane nodded, smiling slightly. "Stuff like that, yeah."

"Well," Paige said, shrugging, "then let's go grab some dinner tonight and get all that cleared up. What do you say?"

Diane laughed out loud.

Paige leaned forward in his chair. "Listen, Diane, the last time I asked a lady for a date, Ronald Reagan was in the White House. If I'm a little rocky, then keep in mind that I'm two decades out of practice. But my intentions are wholly honorable, and I can't emphasize enough that I'm sincerely interested in you."

She stared hard at Paige.

"And remember, Ms. Tresvant, this is the single most important thing you will have done up to this point in your life."

She grinned. "Where have I heard that before?"

Paige shifted in his chair. "Let me ask you a question."

She cocked her head slightly to the side.

"Are you afraid of flying?"

"Of course not," she said, looking at him strangely. "I fly all the time."

"Then one more question," Paige said quickly. "Do you like the mountains?"

She smiled. "Yes, Dave, I like the mountains."

"Okay, then," Paige said after a deep breath. "Please allow me one final question."

She chuckled, then shook her head slightly and gave a resigned shrug. "What's one more going to matter now?"

Paige smiled. "Do you prefer red wine, or white?"

"I told you already that I'm seeing someone."

"You did, yes. I remember that part."

"And that this is all a bit sudden."

"Yep. I remember that, too."

"This could also become a lot more complicated than either of us can foresee."

Paige nodded, smiling. "I understand that. But it's a risk that I'm quite willing to take. I have very good and trustworthy instincts, and right now my instincts are telling me—screaming at me!—that I'm doing the right thing with the right person at the right time."

They sat staring at one another a moment longer before Paige finally nodded his head, smiled slightly, and said, "Whatever risk exists, you're worth it. I wouldn't have asked you otherwise. I want to be with you, to get to know you, to learn everything about you. I want to know your favorite color, whether you like dogs or cats, what books you read, what desserts you fancy, which sports you follow. And when I get to know all of those superficial things about you, then I'll want to know you on a deeper, more personal level. And I'm still waiting to hear which wine you prefer."

He cocked his head slightly and grinned. "Step out there and take a chance on me, Diane, just like I'm ready to do with you. Come with me to Colorado."

She hesitated at first, her expression hard and uncompromising. She sat perfectly still, as if the electrical demands inside her head were leaving little of her energy to disperse elsewhere. Her breathing was steady and controlled, her eyes locked upon Paige. It took a while—maybe half a minute—before her facial features softened and the slightest of smiles appeared on her lips, just for an instant. She cleared her throat softly, and then nodded politely. "White wine will do nicely, I think."

Paige's concentration had waned severely by mid-afternoon. He had thought of little else but Diane Tresvant since their morning encounter. Even Sherry, ever the perceptive assistant, had noticed the change in her boss—something about his being *too* formal with Ms. Tresvant when he had seen her to the lobby at the meeting's conclusion. Sherry knew her boss but she also knew to keep those sorts of things at arm's length, and she consequently said nothing.

Hal Mortensen, Paige's young assistant, began moving his few things into a small empty office on executive row. Like Collier and Ogden, who for some time had already been assigned full-time assistants, Paige welcomed the additional help. Besides, the young man appeared to be intelligent and resourceful, and he had handled himself well in his presentation of the forecasting report.

Paige waited until Mortensen had completed his move into his new office before walking in just as Mortensen was arranging an assortment of desktop paraphernalia, including a large photo of a very lovely young lady.

"Hello there."

Mortensen quickly got to his feet. "Hello, Mr. Paige," he said enthusiastically, hand outstretched.

"Call me Dave. And let's get started," Paige said, finding a legal pad in a cardboard box and handing it over to Mortensen.

Mortensen hesitated a split second before accepting the pad from Paige.

Paige sat on a corner of the desk, arms folded. "Our current practice with regard to the financing of our equipment needs, and I'm specifically referring to our trucks and drilling equipment, is to purchase outright, rather than lease. This is, of course, a company-wide practice. But I'm not certain that it's necessarily the best practice, given the potential alternative uses of capital."

Mortensen stopped to quickly adjust his glasses, and then continued to write.

"Given the fact that most managers are paid largely on the basis of a pre-tax return-on-investment, and also given the rather substantial costs associated with this equipment when bought new, *and* given the costs of capital, I'd like you to quantify for me just which of these methods is our best approach—lease or purchase."

Mortensen nodded. "Okay," he said confidently.

"When you've completed that, I'd then like you to examine our published fee schedule, with particular emphasis on the different levels in our hourly engineering rates, and project what a flat five-dollar per-hour increase on an across-the-board basis would generate in additional fees for the remainder of this year, assuming we maintain the targeted levels. Then I'd like you to poll my branch managers and get their opinions on how the proposed increase might impact them from a competitive standpoint."

"Got it," said Mortensen, still writing.

"And finally, but I'd like this to be first on your hit list, give me your written comments on the administrative strengths and weaknesses of each of the branches in the Central Region, based only upon your direct experience with them. If you've had no contact with certain branches, then note such. And where you detail weaknesses in a particular branch, give me your recommendations on what would be needed to remedy the situation. Then tell me which single branch, within or outside my region, is considered by you to be the absolute best—the gold standard. And tell me why. Okay?"

"Okay," Mortensen said, grinning. "This ought to keep me going for a while."

"There's plenty more after that," said Paige, standing. "Sherry can assist you as needed, and I'll be happy to help when I'm in the office."

"Great, Dave," said Mortensen, still grinning. "I'm really looking forward to working with you. I've heard so much about you."

Paige laughed softly. "Don't believe a word of it." He turned and started to leave, then noticed again the girl in the picture. "By the way, how old are you, Hal?"

"Twenty-six, sir," Mortensen answered firmly, as if such a ripe old age would duly impress Paige.

Paige nodded. "Remember this: You have just crossed paths with Opportunity. If you hadn't noticed it, I'm here to confirm it for you. And I'm delighted to have you on my staff. So, if you bust your ass for me, hotshot; if you bite off all you can chew and then come back and bite again and again; if you come in here and make this a better region with better systems and better information and better procedures; if you give the Central Region all you've got, every day, every way, then I'll do all I can to make you a superstar before your thirtieth birthday."

Mortensen was momentarily embarrassed when he realized his mouth had suddenly opened.

"Do you think you can handle that?"

Mortensen seemed ready to explode with inspiration. "Absolutely, Dave. I can handle it."

"Good. Always keep that in front of you, because that's what I'll be expecting from you. By the way, who's the pretty young lady in the picture?"

"That's my fiancée, Monica," Mortensen answered proudly.

Paige paused in the doorway, turned, and then winked. Mortensen waited until Paige had disappeared from the office before he pumped his fist at his side and, with teeth clenched, growled, "Yes. *Yes!*"

Paige had just completed a phone conversation with a large client when Sherry stuck her head inside the office door. A mischievous grin was etched across her face. She pointed in the direction of Mortensen's office, and then said in a voice only barely above a whisper, "He's so psyched he's about to burst. I haven't seen that much youthful energy in this part of the building in ages. What did you say to him?"

"That if he does well, he'll get a bonus of a million bucks, just like all the rest of my staff," Paige answered, also in whispered fashion.

"Is that a fact?" Sherry asked, eyebrows raised. "A million bucks, huh?"

"You betcha."

"Well, I'm certainly glad to hear that. A million dollars is gonna cure a lot of my ailments. I'd like to express my sincerest thanks to you, Mr. Paige."

"Don't mention it, Ms. Painter."

She gave him a curious look and then left.

Paige was also feeling good. He didn't care about Wylie and his pet Ogden, at least for the moment. He didn't care that the deck was stacked decidedly against his being named Executive Vice President after already having been selected. He didn't even care that Valerie was off in Pittsburgh, likely gone forever, possibly even seeing and sharing a bed with other men. The entire matter of the breakup didn't seem as catastrophic now as it only recently had. He was climbing back; he was still a player—against all odds yet still alive and advancing. And when he thought of Diane Tresvant, when he was stirred by the images flickering on and off like a movie reel inside his head, he felt attractive and virile once again. He welcomed the return of those feelings, almost as if they were long, lost friends. Things were better, definitely; better than in quite some time.

Then there was the phone call from St. Louis.

Porter Caldwell, an associate of Paige's from their early Elerbee days together in Atlanta, as well as the current manager of the St. Louis Branch, called in the late afternoon with disconcerting news. Caldwell proceeded to inform Paige that an Elerbee Engineering technician from the St. Louis office had been discovered by an influential member of a client company to have been, by all appearances, drunk and unable to perform his duties. On the client's job site, no less. And during working hours.

"Holy shit!" Paige shouted.

The client, a large Midwestern developer, was also justifiably irate. As a consequence, the client had immediately suspended all of Elerbee's data-gathering on the soils investigation for the project—a proposed office-building complex to the northwest of downtown St. Louis. Elerbee Engineering, one of the proudest of the proud, had been unceremoniously booted off a job site.

"My ass is in a pickle," said the hapless Caldwell.

Bosco Properties, the client, was demanding an explanation of the incident. Why, they had asked Caldwell, should they ever again consider a company whose representatives were drunk on the job in the early afternoon?

"Will they meet with us, Porter?"

"I can ask. When?"

"Tomorrow, the earlier the better. Dammit, get us in front of those guys, no matter what."

"Okay, I'll try. I'll call back as soon as I've got something."

"One way or the other."

"Right, one way or the other."

Paige leaned back in his chair and began to formulate a crisis-management plan. His inclination was to advise Wylie immediately, in the event the Bosco people were themselves attempting to reach the firm's top executive. But Paige wanted more information, more hard facts, and he therefore decided to roll the dice and await Caldwell's return call before alerting Wylie to the problem.

Paige began jotting his questions onto a notepad: Who was the technician? Who was the project engineer? Who was the client's representative on the job site? What was the size of the total project? What was the percentage of completion of the field work? Of the lab work? Of the engineering work? Are we currently doing other work with Bosco? If so, what? If not, is something else proposed? If so, what?

Paige silently prayed that Bosco Properties would hold off on contacting Wylie, at least for the present. He wanted time to get the facts—*all* the facts—and to go to Wylie with a recommended course of action. Good grief, he thought. This isn't going to be pleasant.

The phone rang. It was Caldwell.

"They'll meet with us in the morning, in their offices downtown."

Paige nodded. "I'll leave tonight. Who'll be there?"

"A virtual Who's Who of Bosco Properties."

Swell, Paige thought to himself in disgust.

"Okay, Porter. I need some answers."

The technician had been a foreman with one of the drilling crews who had been performing a series of soil test borings on the project site. The borings would later be analyzed in the laboratory and used as a basis for the engineering findings and recommendations concerning the foundations of the various structures. The other two members of the crew had operated the drilling rig while the foreman had been comatose in the cab of a support vehicle. It was during such a moment that the client had happened upon their location. An empty liquor bottle had been on the seat of the truck, beside the foreman; another empty bottle was in the floorboard. The foreman had been sprawled inside, eyes closed and mouth agape, amid the bottles and the loud music of the radio. The assistants had been instructed by the client to complete the boring and then promptly leave the site. Notification of the situation had been rendered to Elerbee's project engineer several minutes later by telephone.

Paige asked for and received answers to the questions he had intended for Caldwell. Bosco Properties, while not the largest of the branch's clients, was certainly among the better. Two other separate proposals were pending—one a warehouse project and the other a shopping strip. Neither was currently underway, however.

"Find out how many borings may have been done without the foreman's supervision," Paige ordered. "And look at the driller's logs from the previous borings to see if there might be any discrepancies or inconsistencies."

"Okay."

"Talk to those drillers, dammit. Find out the straight scoop."

"Right."

"I'll be out there sometime tonight," Paige said, remembering that the company jet was down for maintenance, "depending on when I can get a flight." The conversation with Caldwell ended. Paige then called Jeff Wylie and asked for an immediate meeting. He gathered his notes and walked down the hall to the large office in the corner.

"There's a problem in St. Louis."

Wylie listened as Paige brought him up to speed on the situation. Wylie was clearly dismayed, but held his comments until Paige had summarized the problem and outlined the plan to meet with the Bosco Properties people in St. Louis the next day.

Wylie's focus was directed more toward Paige's minimizing the potential damage to the firm's reputation. He seemed less concerned with ensuring that the data, and the resultant engineering report, not be compromised by the incident.

"Get us back on that job," Wylie said matter-of-factly, "and while you're at it, bring Porter Caldwell back on his shield."

Paige blinked and shifted in his chair.

"This isn't the first time something like this has happened in St. Louis on Porter's watch," Wylie continued. "If you'll check, you'll probably find that it's not even the first time something like this has happened with this particular foreman. Porter's been counseled before, but he does nothing but whine and complain that good foremen, good technicians, good *whatever*, are hard to find. There's enough risk in what we do without leaving the data gathering to a drunk, for crissakes. But apparently Porter hasn't gotten that message. Or worse yet, he chose to ignore it."

Wylie's eyes were cold and piercing. "I'm certain that we don't need a man like Porter Caldwell running a big branch like St. Louis," he said, his voice rising. "Matter of fact, I'm fairly sure that we don't need a man like Porter Caldwell running *anything* in Elcrbce Engineering. And if we can't get ourselves back on that job site and finish that project on time and within budget, and restore that client, then I'm not sure that we should confine the housecleaning to St. Louis alone."

Paige drew a deep breath and shifted again. He swallowed and then cleared his throat. "Let me see if I've got this straight: I meet with the Bosco Properties people in the morning in St. Louis. Based on the results of the meeting, if Bosco Properties stays, Porter goes. However, if Bosco Properties goes, Porter goes and I go. Is that about it in a nutshell, Jeff?"

Wylie stared hard at Paige. A cold, eerie silence, thick enough to break off in icy chunks, pushed each man deeper into his seat.

"You have a responsibility," Wylie said slowly, "and you'd better start shouldering it."

"Just exactly what are you saying?" Paige said calmly.

"I'm saying that you've finally gotten burned—gotten *us* burned—for having tolerated an incompetent sap like Porter Caldwell for as long as you have."

"For as long as *I* have? *You're* the one who hired Porter and you're the one who promoted him to branch manager and sent him to St. Louis. If you're going to flog me with something, Jeff, try to do it with better historical precision. Besides, I don't buy your description of Porter being an incompetent sap. That's simply not the case, based on my close observation of that whole situation in St. Louis."

"Your skills at close observation," Wylie said in a voice filled with sarcasm, "have failed you this time, I'm afraid."

Paige felt the dizziness from the blood rushing to his head. He struggled to retain his self-control.

"I'm not at all pleased with your performance, Paige. I'm not pleased with the contempt you hold for many of your colleagues, and I'm not pleased with the arrogance you enjoy displaying in your dealings with them, or even with some of our trusted consultants. You're not a team player; you prefer to go your own separate way. I also sense that you hold me in rather low esteem, as well. The bottom line is, you just don't seem to be a very happy camper."

Wylie sniffed and flicked at a speck of lint on his shirtsleeve. "Is anything I'm saying reaching you? Or do you consider it just another ration of drivel from someone you hold in low regard anyway?"

Paige was lucid enough to realize that an honest answer was not in his own best interests. He said nothing for the moment.

"Well? Are you going to respond?"

"Tell me what you want me to do, Jeff. If you want me to go to St. Louis tonight, then say so. If you want me to resign—now, right this minute—then let me know that, too. But whichever you choose," Paige stopped and stared coldly at Wylie, "don't screw with me. That won't work for either of us."

Wylie stared back, just as hard. "Let's get one thing straight: If you can't play on my team, under my rules, then I'll expect you to make a decision. The bottom line is, you're on thin ice. You would be well advised to tread lightly."

Paige took that to mean he was still employed. He nodded slowly. "Then I'll go to St. Louis tonight."

Wylie took a deep breath and looked away, saying only, "Go fix the goddamn thing."

The June weather in St. Louis was hot and sticky up into the late evening. Caldwell and Paige sat across from one another at the small, circular table in the corner of Paige's downtown hotel room. Outside the full-length window they could see the illuminated Busch Stadium only a few blocks away where the Cardinals were playing to a packed house.

Paige's questioning of Caldwell had been relentless from the moment they had met at the baggage-claim area of Lambert International. After two hours—two long, hard, bear-down hours—Paige was finally beginning to feel comfortable with all the circumstances surrounding the incident.

"Why the hell didn't you tell me this kind of thing had happened before, Porter?"

Caldwell leaned forward, his chin supported by his hand. His brown hair was mussed and his dark eyes were bloodshot. "I thought you knew," he said softly.

Paige stared across the table at his long-time friend. He remembered the squatty Caldwell, so awkward in the old days on the Elerbee basketball team, and a one-man wrecking crew in flag football. He remembered having carried Caldwell up the stairs to his apartment—fireman's style—after one or two of the games when afterwards they had visited a few joints where adult beverages had been served. He also remembered something about Caldwell having returned the favor. Paige genuinely liked Caldwell, always had, and the thought of firing his old chum was unpleasant enough that he refused to even think about it, at least until after the meeting with Bosco Properties.

"Okay," Paige said as he leaned back with his hands propped behind his head. "Anything else I need to know?"

Caldwell pondered a moment. "That should cover it. You ought to have the full picture by now."

"Good."

Caldwell ran his fingers through his thick brown hair. "Wanna go for a quick beer?"

"I don't think so," Paige answered with a yawn. "I'm gonna look over my notes and then call it a night."

"Suit yourself, man. Oh, by the way, Annie sends her love."

Paige thought of Caldwell's lovely wife, of their two daughters, and the prospect of their namesake being suddenly unemployed. "Give my best to Annie and the girls," he said, looking away.

Caldwell stood and began tossing some papers into his brown attaché case. "I'll be back at seven to meet you for breakfast."

Paige nodded. "Fine."

Caldwell reached for his coat and slung it over his shoulder. His collar was open, his tie loose. "See you in the morning, chief."

"Yeah, in the morning."

Caldwell started toward the door. He stopped suddenly and turned toward Paige. "Everything's cool, huh Dave?"

Paige stared out the window at the bright stadium lights, his back toward Caldwell. No, Porter, everything's not cool, he thought. Jeff Wylie's major issue wasn't as much with Porter Caldwell as it was with Dave Paige. Porter Caldwell just happened to be in the way, unfortunately. Caldwell's long friendship with Paige, which had hitherto been viewed by

Caldwell as positive and career-enhancing, now brought him close enough to the powder keg between Wylie and Paige that he stood a good chance of being caught in the bursting radius. It bothered Paige that someone as fundamentally decent and competent as Caldwell could be sentenced to corporate execution for all the wrong reasons. It bothered him, yes, but it didn't surprise him. Not anymore. Not with Wylie.

"Good night, Porter," Paige said finally.

Several more moments passed before Paige eventually heard the opening and closing of the door.

It was a corner office, large with thick pile carpeting and full windows on two sides. Located atop thirty stories, the office overlooked downtown St. Louis and out across the brown waters of the Mississippi River, into Illinois. They sat on a small sofa, Paige and Caldwell, and looked across a square coffee table at Joe Tetranova, a Bosco vice president who seemed to be the only Bosco executive in the room who wasn't scowling. Also facing them in a chair was Frank DePass, the Bosco project manager who had discovered Elerbee's intoxicated foreman during his site visit. Alongside him was Mike Bartholomew, president of Bosco Properties. Another man whose name Paige had promptly forgotten—the controller, he thought—sat in a metal-framed chair between and to the rear of Bartholomew and DePass. Bartholomew's large wooden desk and leather chair were at the opposite end of the room, facing them. Unoccupied, yet conspicuous.

Tetranova leaned forward slightly. "Thank you, gentlemen, for arranging to come out here to help us solve our mutual problem."

Paige nodded. "We also thank you gentlemen for taking the time to meet with us. I can assure you that Elerbee Engineering is interested in resolving this issue, and to your complete satisfaction."

Tetranova asked DePass to review the circumstances leading up to and including DePass' discovery of the Elerbee employee in the cab of the support vehicle. As he listened, Paige became confident that his own understanding of the incident squared with DePass' account.

"It's also come to my attention that this isn't the first time something like this has happened with this guy. Is that correct?" asked DePass, staring directly at Paige.

Paige momentarily hesitated to see if Caldwell might respond. He did not.

"That's correct, Mr. DePass," said Paige. "But I don't want to leave the impression that Elerbee Engineering condones behavior of the type under discussion here."

"Well, it's obvious that your man has a problem," DePass said coldly. "And it's obvious he causing you people some problems. What I don't like is that he's causing *me* some problems."

"I'm not happy about that either, Mr. DePass," Paige said. "And I make no excuses for the improper behavior of our employee. There are no excuses. I think what's important, though, is for us to tell you what we've done, and are doing, to make certain that our final report to you is of the highest technical quality, as you have every right to expect. The important point here, the point I want to make is—"

"Mr. Paige," interrupted Bartholomew, "we shall be the ones to make the points here. Jacob, what's the story on the budget?"

The bald, portly man seated between DePass and Bartholomew produced a worksheet in small print. "The interim billings from Elerbee total sixty-four thousand dollars, as of this date. This represents the field-investigation phase and some lab fees. No engineering fees; just borings and lab. Okay?"

Paige drew a quick mental picture of the budget, which included charges for drilling, lab work, and the engineering fee for managing the project and preparing the report. He nodded and at the same time noticed out of the corner of his eye Caldwell's nervous fidgeting.

"The proposal indicated that the field phase would cost sixty-eight thousand five-hundred. So you've billed us for ninety-three percent of the field phase. Okay? But based on the number of borings you've billed us for against the number cited in your proposal, you've only completed seventy percent of the field investigation. I'm wondering, okay, what the story is, 'cause I've never received any requests from you people for any increases in the budget. Will there be cutbacks in the lab or reporting phases to make up for the overage, or what?"

Paige cleared his throat. "I can assure you that there will be no budget overruns, nor will there be any shortcuts in the different phases of the project. Mr. Caldwell and I will see to that, you can be sure."

"There will be no shortcomings," Caldwell repeated.

"No additional shortcomings, is what you really mean," said Bartholomew, peering over his reading glasses.

Caldwell nodded self-consciously. "That's correct, sir."

Bartholomew removed his glasses and crossed his arms over his chest. "Let's see now," he said, glancing to his left at the worksheet. "This is mostly small potatoes, on the whole. I mean, it's not that big a percentage of the total delivered price. But it is a cost, gentlemen. And it sure as hell seems sloppy."

Paige and Caldwell, both grim-faced, acknowledged their assent with their silence.

"You've got a guy on our site who's drunk on his ass, and he's supposed to be providing your engineers with information on the soil conditions. And he's drunk, for cryin' out loud. *Drunk*! And if that's not enough, you're showing signs of going well over your own proposed budget. We asked you what this job would cost us; you told us and we gave you a contract for the amount you specified. And now it seems that it may not be enough to finish the whole program. What the hell are we supposed to think of all this? Are we supposed to have confidence in you people that you know what you're doing? Still? After all this?"

There was a moment of silence before Paige spoke up, saying, "May I respond to that?"

"By all means," Bartholomew answered with a trace of sarcasm.

"Somebody sure as hell needs to," interjected DePass.

Paige took a deep breath. "If I were in your position, gentlemen, given all that's happened over the recent past, I'd have to make a business decision that would most likely involve going on without Elerbee Engineering."

The Bosco people were expressionless, though it was clear they were listening intently. Porter Caldwell's expression changed as if he'd just seen a poisonous snake at his feet.

"And if that happens," Paige continued, "if you do decide to break with us, then I'll understand. Believe me, gentlemen, I do appreciate the fact that you have a business to run, that you have stockholders and clients and employees who expect you to operate your business efficiently and profitably. And I make no excuses for Elerbee Engineering's shortcomings in the role we accepted to assist you on your project. We haven't performed up to the standards that either of us demands. So," Paige said, pausing for a sideways glance at the pale Caldwell, "if you choose another soils consultant, then as far as I'm concerned we'll have no one to blame but ourselves. Please let me emphasize to you that I don't want that as a course of action, that I want us to remain as your soils consultant. But if it's not to be, if we can't work through this thing, then, as I say, I'll understand."

Bartholomew sniffed and looked away for a moment, otherwise breaking what had become a weighty silence.

"Permit me one other comment," added Paige. "The driller foreman in question has been discharged, after twenty-two years of service with our firm. There had been previous problems with this individual—to the point that a year ago we had him entered into an in-patient rehabilitation program here in St. Louis. One of our managers showed enough concern about the individual that he had personally attended a few Alcoholics Anonymous sessions with him, just as a way of demonstrating our concern and our support. That same manager also made it clear that he was always available to talk, at the office or at home, if this individual ever felt the need to do so. And he did. And they talked. Often. Sometimes at two o'clock on a Sunday morning. And I'm proud of that manager for making the effort, for trying to reach out to another human being and doing the right thing. And I'm sorry, deeply sorry, that those efforts didn't work out—for *any* of us, as it turns out. And even though we finally ended up having to make a hard decision about this individual, I'm still proud of Porter for trying."

Paige turned and looked again at Caldwell, nodding.

"As for the matter of the budget overruns, I will personally assure you that, if allowed to continue, Elerbee Engineering will perform in accordance with our proposal—nothing less than the programs we promised to deliver and certainly nothing exceeding our overall fee estimate. We have reassigned the particular project engineer to other duties, and if we are allowed to continue on the Bosco project, we will assign it to one of our senior engineers and absorb the difference in their billing rates. We will do the work as planned and you will be charged what we proposed and what you budgeted, and nothing more."

Paige paused a moment, sensing that his audience was with him. Except DePass, who had what amounted to a sneer on his face.

"We're ethical people, gentlemen, as you are. We won't hide from you if things go poorly, and we won't shortchange you because of any difficulties of our own making. We won't make excuses and we won't leave you high and dry. We'll do it right, even if we have to do part or all of it gratis. What you get from us will have complete engineering integrity, I assure you. It will be our best effort—the sort of effort you expected from us when you favored us with the project to begin with. And there will be no further surprises."

Bartholomew glanced over at DePass. "Any comments, Frank?"

"It all sounds well and good," said DePass, unconvinced.

"And?"

"I guess I'd be willing to try them again, but not without some reservations."

Paige nodded to DePass.

"Joe, anything from you?" Bartholomew asked of Tetranova.

Tetranova straightened. "I feel good about the things Dave's said. I don't think the problems are so big that we can't sit down and talk about 'em and work 'em out. I see this meeting as having been a step in that direction."

Good guy/bad guy, Paige thought. Here it comes.

Bartholomew stared alternately at Paige and Caldwell. "My initial inclination was to go out and find another consultant, and to fire you people outright."

Bartholomew's words hung in the air, especially the much dreaded *fire*, which seemed to echo off the walls as if shouted from a deep canyon.

"I'm not sure that I still shouldn't do that," he continued. "But in the spirit of giving second chances, which is apparently what you attempted with your old-timer—though I'd guess that his second chances came in bundles, over that many years—then we'll permit Elerbee Engineering to move back onto the site and continue with the project, given the 'clarifying' conditions as outlined by you, Mr. Paige."

Caldwell breathed a quiet sigh of relief.

"I would suggest that the work proceed as planned—on time, within budget, and nothing less than the best, most sober people you have."

Paige resented Bartholomew's parting dig, but under the circumstances said nothing in response.

The meeting concluded when Bartholomew stood. They all shook on it, and things ended on a friendly note.

On the drive to the office, Paige blasted Caldwell about the budget issues.

"Didn't you know?" Paige asked in aggravation and disbelief.

"Honestly, I didn't realize it was as bad as it is," Caldwell answered in obvious embarrassment.

Paige shook his head and said nothing further about it.

Caldwell later drove Paige to the airport after the two of them had had a serious clearing of the air with several project engineers at the branch office. They headed northwest on the Mark Twain Expressway, toward Lambert International, in the comfort of Caldwell's new Toyota. Neither man spoke, and only the sound of an easy-listening FM station filtered out the noises of the road.

Paige busily jotted notes onto the outside of his airline-ticket envelope. Caldwell reached down and turned off the radio.

"Be straight with me, Dave."

Paige continued writing. "Yeah, okay. Go ahead."

"How close was I to getting canned?"

Paige glanced over at his friend. "That's not important now, Porter. You just keep the branch on the course we've established."

Caldwell turned into the airport's entrance and maneuvered the car into an open space against the curb. Paige reached behind the seat and grabbed his briefcase from the back, which he then opened and tossed inside some notes and a portable calculator. They got out and walked to the rear of the car where Paige collected his single bag, which he handed over to a nearby attendant.

"I want to hear from you on this project," Paige said firmly.

"You will, for sure. Thanks for coming out and giving me a hand."

The strain of the past few days was clearly evident on Caldwell's face. His shoulders seemed to sag, as if weighted with bags of flour. He stood next to Paige, one hand shielding his eyes, the other resting on his hip.

"Tell me honestly, Dave. Is Jeff Wylie pissed?"

Paige hesitated a moment before saying, "Let me handle Wylie, okay?"

"But is he pissed? I need to know that."

"Yeah," Paige nodded, "he's pissed. But I think it'll blow over. Don't worry about it, Porter. Concentrate on St. Louis and stay close to Bosco Properties. I'll work things out with Wylie."

Caldwell sighed, and then nodded. "Have a safe trip home, boss," he said, offering his hand. "And thanks again for your help."

They stood together a moment longer before Paige turned and walked toward the terminal building.

"I couldn't have done it without you," Caldwell said to himself as Paige disappeared behind the glass doors.

CHAPTER ELEVEN

Paige took a seat on a stool in the hotel bar and ordered a beer. It was the end of what had become a two-day marathon of reviewing, planning, and strategizing the branch's operations with his management team in Albuquerque, New Mexico. Satisfied with the results, Paige had politely declined another long dinner session with the group and instead planned to order room service and get some needed rest before his early flight back to Atlanta the following morning. Besides, he had accumulated nearly two-hundred e-mail messages over the past two days and would need most of the evening to satisfy the intrusive beast that e-mail had inexorably morphed into. A half-dozen voice mails were also lying in wait.

Paige loosened his tie and enjoyed the icy cold beer in the frosted glass. The bar was noisy but not overly crowded, with Happy Hour business patrons in groups of two and four and eight at the tables around the perimeter.

"Wanna see a menu, cap'n?" the bartender asked, a pleasant, late-fortyish, soft-spoken man with a shiny-bald crown. He wore slacks and a white dress shirt with a thin black tie, and over years of plying his trade he had acquired the skill of seeing everything in short, unobtrusive glances while busy with the multiple tasks at hand.

"No, I'm good for now," Paige answered as he began listening to the voice messages on his cell phone.

He sat with the phone to his ear as he scrolled through messages from Hal Mortensen, Sherry Painter, and two branch managers before he heard the welcomed voice of Diane Tresvant. Paige's expression suddenly changed when Diane explained in a somber tone that she'd been having second thoughts about their upcoming Colorado trip, that she'd reluctantly come to the conclusion that it would be in their respective best interests for her to break the date and remain in Atlanta, and that she sincerely hoped he would understand. She offered her regrets, pausing for a long moment and then giggling like a schoolgirl before finally declaring that she was only joking, and was in fact anxiously looking forward to their time in the Rockies together.

"I can hardly wait," she said in a soft, sensuous voice before ending the message.

Paige smiled and put his cell phone away, then glanced at his watch. He would call Diane later and wake her from her sleep, and chastise her for causing his heart to miss a beat.

He was about to settle his tab when the bartender placed a fresh beer in front of him.

"Compliments of the lady at the other end of the bar," the man said with a nod and a slight smile. "Cheers, cap'n."

An attractive blonde, tanned, trim, and well-dressed in business attire, with shoulder-length hair neatly parted near the middle, looked up from her handheld PDA and smiled at Paige.

Paige smiled in return and nodded his thanks. He finished off his first beer while studying the lovely lady at the opposite end of the bar. She wore no wedding ring, and except for a silver necklace, no other jewelry. She was a professional of some type, he decided. She's comfortable with gadgets, he surmised as he watched her easily navigate her PDA. Could she be in I.T., maybe? No, not likely. A lawyer, maybe? Possibly. She's dressed to kill and presents a terrific first impression. Sales, perhaps? Yeah, probably sales. Real estate? Or office equipment? Or software? Or pharmaceuticals? His mind raced through the various possibilities, all while watching her sipping from the glass of white wine and occasionally searching for an almond from the mix the bartender had placed before her.

That's it, he decided. She's a pharmaceutical rep.

Paige grabbed his beer and moved toward the lady.

"Thanks for the drink. Mind if I join you?"

"Not at all," she said, smiling. "And you're very welcome."

"I'm Dave Paige," he said, slipping onto the stool beside her and then extending his hand.

"Hello, Dave. My name's Paula Markham."

They shook hands. Paula brushed her hair behind her ear, then looked at Paige and smiled.

"So what did you decide I do for a living?" she asked with a sly grin. "You didn't settle upon 'hooker,' did you?"

Paige hesitated a moment, wondering if his sudden embarrassment was showing. "Of course not. Pharmaceutical rep seemed far more plausible."

Paula laughed. "Not quite, but I can live with that, I suppose."

Paige motioned to the bartender and pointed to Paula's nearly empty wine glass. "So, now that you've told me what you aren't, Paula, will you tell me what you are?"

She put her PDA away in her purse and turned her attention toward Paige. "Well, for starters, I own a training company, based out of Los Angeles."

"Ah. Tell me more."

"I have nine employees total, about forty clients, and I'm at a point, thankfully, where I'm going to need to add people to keep up with the growth. I work with clients in such areas as team building, conflict resolution, executive profiling, and management selection and succession, among others."

Paige nodded his understanding. "And who do you work with?"

"My clients are corporations of all sizes, universities, city, state, and federal governments, and I've also done some work for the U.S. military. I also teach a course in behavioral science at an L.A. community college."

"Is that all you do?" Paige said with a laugh.

"I manage to stay busy."

"So you're a shrink?"

"I am, indeed. What about you? How do you spend your days?"

"I'm a V.P. in an engineering company, and I have P&L responsibility for twenty-one branches in the central U.S. and Canada. The firm's headquartered in Atlanta, which is where I live. And I have to say that my schedule's pretty tame compared to yours," Paige said with a chuckle.

The bartender refreshed Paula's wine glass.

They made small talk for perhaps fifteen minutes, about the smog in L.A. and the humidity in Atlanta, and the traffic in both. Paula laughed easily, had a magnificent smile, and seemed sincere and without pretense.

"Ah, they're leaving," Paula said, pointing off to the side. "Would you like to claim their table and continue our chat with a little more privacy?"

"Sure," Paige replied as he picked up their drinks and followed Paula.

They talked openly for the next hour about the details of their careers, and then about the fringes of their personal lives. Paula became animated when she expressed her love of her work, her passion for being able to have a discernibly positive impact upon people and their organizations. She spoke of how she found being a business owner not only demanding and unrelenting, but also invigorating and fulfilling. She revealed that shortly after earning her doctoral degree, her husband of just four years, a Navy fighter pilot, had been killed in a mid-air crash some nine years ago; that she was childless from the marriage, and had since not remarried; and that she dated only intermittently, and then only with a select group of male acquaintances.

"If I'm destined to be an old maid," Paula said, following with a throaty laugh, "then I'd damn well prefer to be a wealthy one."

Paige spoke of his professional dilemma in what appeared now to be his rescinded promotion to E.V.P., and the intense, ongoing gamesmanship consuming the firm's top executives since the death of the founder. He loved the company and wanted very badly to remain, he asserted, but each passing day seemed to shift the firm's center of gravity a little further away from him—bit by bit, craftily, unremittingly, and soon, he feared, irreversibly, akin to the hapless frog in the gradually warming water.

Paige eventually spoke of his divorce from Valerie less than a year earlier, and how he was still adjusting to its harsh, gut-wrenching realities. Paula noticed the change in his demeanor, the disappointment evident in his voice and eyes, the way he cleared his throat and sat in silence for an uncomfortable moment. He became lively again only when the subject turned to Sara and her life and accomplishments.

"She's wonderful," Paige said, smiling after a recital of Sara's many favorable qualities. "She's my girl."

"I can tell," Paula replied, nodding.

Paula asked lots of questions, about Paige's philosophies on business and life and love, about corporate ethics and fairness, about the sorts of people Paige liked and those he disliked, and the reasons why. She listened carefully, his answers usually leading to other questions.

"I've never before had a lady buy me a drink in a bar, and I've never before had a session with a shrink," Paige finally said, laughing. "I'm breaking new ground tonight."

"And all with the same person," Paula added.

Paige managed his sobriety, but Paula was becoming noticeably more appealing the more they talked. Her physical beauty was obvious, but she was also quick, insightful, and generally well-informed. There was an underlying strength and resiliency in her that Paige quickly detected, no doubt the result of her building a business and meeting her payrolls; or perhaps more likely, the precipitating factor in giving her the gumption to step out on her own in the first place.

They had another round of drinks, and then decided to have something to eat—soup and sandwiches—while remaining in the bar.

"So, is there anyone special, Dave?" Paula asked between sips of steaming French onion soup. "As in romantically special?"

"Not yet," he answered with a shake of his head.

"Is that a 'not yet' as in nope, nothing, zero; or, as in a work-in-progress with a value other than zero?"

"I'll know in a couple of weeks," Paige answered, laughing self-consciously.

Paige inferred from Paula's arched eyebrows that she was curious to hear more, but he said nothing further.

They finished their dinner, and after the table was cleared Paige motioned to the bartender for one more round of drinks.

"This is it for me," Paula said when the wine was delivered. "I've got six million e-mails to sort through."

Paige looked at Paula and grinned.

"What? Why are you grinning?"

"Tell me something."

"Okay. What?"

"You're a trained psychologist. You know the way organizations function and the way people behave in the real world. You know the sorts of struggles and intrigues that routinely take place among the top-management tier. You know that vacuums are created when a key owner or executive suddenly leaves or dies. You know and are familiar with *all* that stuff. Given that, take what I've told you about the situation at my firm, and what you've managed to learn about me thus far tonight, and tell me how you'd advise me if I was your client."

"The first thing I'd do is explain that you'll get an hour's consultation and a written report for five-hundred bucks, with fifteen minutes of follow-up at your discretion."

Paula's expression was firm and businesslike.

Paige nodded. "I see. But here's my counter: I don't need an hour, and I don't want a written report or a follow-up. Would wine and food cover your fee, in this case?"

Paula smiled and nodded. "Yes, food and drink will be a perfectly acceptable substitute tonight, Mr. Paige, along with the value of your exceptional company."

Paige took a deep breath and exhaled slowly. "So, what the hell should I do, Dr. Paula Markham?"

Paula sat back in her seat and sipped her wine, a deliberative but otherwise noncommittal expression deeply set into her face, her unblinking pale-blue eyes fixed intently upon Paige, piercing into and reaching the very back of his skull, like a pair of powder-blue lasers. A minute passed, slowly, then another, as Paige swallowed and wondered however briefly just what it was he had asked for, and what it was he was about to get. Finally, she sipped again before pushing her wine glass off to the side and leaning forward with her elbows on the table, her clasped hands supporting her chin.

"Okay, Dave. Like it or not, here's my take: You're an insatiable overachiever, the consummate Type A. You're restless and tireless and clearly ambitious. You're fair and even-handed, and you've built a reputation as a person of integrity. You place value on great results, but you also appreciate great effort, especially the 'above and beyond' kind, and you sure as hell don't abide sloppiness or laziness. Everything you've ever gotten in your life—everything— has been a result of your own hard work. You walk into a room and the energy level invariably increases, never decreases. It's in the way you carry yourself, the manner in which you speak, the eye contact you make, and the distinct impression you give off as a careful, attentive listener, which is *far* less common in executives like yourself than you might think. You don't strike me as being afraid of confrontation—to the contrary, I get a certain vibe that you may actually enjoy it, *need* it, at times, perhaps even often. You don't like who you don't like, and you see no reason why they shouldn't have the benefit of knowing it.

"You're also conflicted about your failed marriage, since failure is neither a concept nor a result you have much familiarity with. You're conflicted about being at a point in your career where the seeds of antagonism you've planted and allowed to grow in other corporate carnivores may now suddenly flower and reach out for you like a Venus Flytrap, and you don't quite know what to do about it, which frustrates you greatly. You're conflicted about remaining with a firm you love, which has been stable and nurturing and comfortable, but now which is none of that, and in fact perhaps even the polar opposite. You feel a sense of loss, not just about your chairman and mentor, but about the mental image you've had of the firm for all these years, almost as if it, too, is about to be laid to rest."

Paula turned her head slightly, trying to gauge Paige's reaction. "Is this making any sense?"

Paige nodded slowly, seemingly transfixed. It was as if he were sitting on a beach at the water's edge, only vaguely aware of his surroundings, the rhythmic crashing of the waves, the cool sudsy water washing over his skin, the sand giving way beneath him as the water recedes and giving off the momentary sensation of falling into a hole. "Please continue," he said softly.

"So what to do?" Paula asked with a shrug, then a chuckle. "If I had the perfect answer, the perfect solution to your situation, then I wouldn't be trading it just for dinner and drinks."

Paige grinned. "I wasn't necessarily expecting perfection."

"Good, because my world is just like yours, and it's a far cry from perfect. But I do think I have something I can give you to chew on and digest that will hopefully provide a morsel or two of value. And I'll always be willing to act as a sounding board after tonight, if you could see any usefulness there. So, okay, here's the best advice I can give you, Dave, having known you as I have for two hours or so, and never having set foot in your company: You must make a brutally hard, brutally honest, objective, unemotional assessment of your circumstances, and then, but *only* then, devise your plan to either stay with or leave the firm. That sounds simplistic, I know, but the sort of assessment I'm asking you to make is not easy, believe me. Being honest with ourselves is never easy, and sometimes downright depressing. If you're not on the verge of nausea, literally, then you're not doing it right. Pain is gain, and you've got to do the work. There is simply no other way.

"Neither decision is without risk, obviously, so you should also consider which course would bring you the most satisfaction, as best you can determine, but only after you've had that tough-minded, clear-eyed appraisal. I think you'll find that your objectivity in this decision will likely be the most challenging portion of the entire exercise. But it's also the most important. You have to face your vulnerabilities and imperfections, your areas of weakness that you'll never fix either because you don't want to, or because you can't, and assess what limitations that may bring, and what consequences might follow. And then measure that against your strengths, which would include what I perceive to be your substantial willpower, which in the end can be a differentiator.

"So, here we are. You've done the work and you're ready to make a decision. But if, in the end, your head tells you to do one thing and your heart another, and again your assessment has been done with all the proper due diligence, then by all means follow your instincts. You didn't get to where you are without well-honed instincts, so don't be afraid to follow your gut. And please, remember this: You can make a mistake and eventually recover your footing. It's not war, Dave. You won't die or cause anyone else to die if you screw up and get this wrong. It might not be pleasant, granted, but you'll live to fight another day. Stay true to yourself, true to your values. You're a good man, best I can tell, and good people are *always* in demand. Please keep that in mind. A little perspective is never a bad thing."

Paula again turned her head slightly. "Whew! Did that help?"

He stared at her for a long moment, still silent and trancelike, as if allowing the last of her words to become fully absorbed, properly labeled, and transported to the appropriate storage bin in his brain. "More than you know," he finally said, appreciatively. "You have an uncommon amount of common sense and a remarkable insightfulness and wisdom about you,

Paula. I thank you for your counsel and your candor. Is there anything I can do for you to return the favor?"

"You can hire me," Paula said with a laugh. "I'd love to work for you."

"I can't make any promises, but after all the dust settles, wherever I end up, I'd like to talk to you about several areas of opportunity that I've already begun to think about. I really like what I've heard from you tonight, and I think you could help."

Paula reached inside her purse and produced a business card. She wrote on the back of the card and passed it to Paige. "My personal e-mail address is on the back. You can contact me there, or through the office. And my cell number is on the card."

Paige reached into his wallet and provided a card of his own.

Once the bill was settled by Paige, he glanced over and noticed Paula quietly staring at him as she ran her fingers along the bottom of her necklace.

"Thank you for buying me that beer," Paige said with a grin and a wink. "I got to meet a very beautiful, intelligent, interesting woman that I might have missed otherwise. You've been terrific company, Paula. I've enjoyed every minute we've spent together."

She smiled and shrugged. "It just struck me that you appeared to be someone I should meet. It was a nice return on the investment of a beer. You're also terrific company, Dave."

Paula paused, then added, "And to be honest, I'd like to share more of it."

Paige took a long, slow breath. "I'd like that."

They stared at one another a moment longer before Paula cleared her throat and reached for her purse.

"Well, I need to deal with those six million e-mails," she said as she rose.

Paula extended her hand to Paige. "Maybe we'll meet again somewhere down the road."

Paige also stood. "Good night, Paula."

He stood for a moment longer and watched her leave, noticing when she glanced back over her shoulder as she reached the doorway, savoring the sight of her striking beauty once more, wondering if he was allowing such a treasure to slip from his grasp forever.

It was another airplane, another Diet Coke and peanuts, the beginning of the end of another trip. He got lucky with an upgrade this time as he sat looking out his first-class window seat, his fellow business traveler sound asleep beside him. He glanced out at the hills and canyons below, unsure whether he was still in New Mexico. He glanced at his watch and then guessed that beneath him was the Texas Panhandle.

The guy next to him was beginning to snore. A flight attendant announced that the movie was being delayed because of a problem with the projection equipment. A heavyset man across the aisle was drinking whiskey in the early morning and laughing loudly at something his companion was saying, causing the guy next to Paige to snort and stir from his sleep, and then begin a noisy licking of his lips. A woman seated directly behind Paige was coughing as steadily as if she had contracted tuberculosis and had every intention of sharing it with all of those within range of her flying droplets.

Paige smiled. Nice up here in first class, he thought. He found his pen and opened his *Paige's Laws of Business*.

Willpower can be the key differentiator, in the end. Never underestimate its importance.

We all have freedom of choice; none of us, however, has freedom from consequences.

My belief is that the razor's edge in performance is gained in an all-out parlaying of one's greatest strengths rather than generally improving upon one's weaknesses. What benefits a team more— improving the average players or having the superstars play like superstars?

CHAPTER TWELVE

Dave Paige and his companion Diane Tresvant arrived at Denver International Airport on a cool, overcast Friday night. They rented a car and, after a steak dinner at a downtown restaurant, decided on the spur of the moment to remain in Denver for a full night's rest before an early morning Saturday start. It was late, and they'd both had long days at work.

They got an early start the next morning, though a full night's rest had turned out to be elusive.

The weather was cool and cloudy on Saturday morning, and since Paige was familiar with the area he decided to show Diane a sampling of the Colorado countryside with detours to the brewery town of Golden, a casino in the old mining town of Black Hawk, and a gold mine in Idaho Springs. When they finally turned onto I-70, a sudden rainstorm greeted them near the Eisenhower Tunnel which, after five miles or so, dissipated as suddenly as it had appeared. The mountains were lovely, and as they passed the resort town of Dillon, Paige turned off the road at a rest stop to admire the beauty of Lake Dillon and the surrounding high country, where they could also look back to the east and see the approaching storm they had previously encountered as it rolled in over the tops of the mountains.

They reached Copper Mountain by mid-afternoon. Paige's local manager in Elerbee's Denver office had made the necessary arrangements, and a one-bedroom condo which had been reserved in Paige's name was ready and waiting. The condo had a woodsy look and smell to it, its interior rustic, with exposed beams, a fireplace in the center, the kitchen and living room on opposite sides of the fireplace. There were sliding glass doors which led to a wooden deck and provided an unobscured view of the mountain and the quiet ski runs.

When Paige had unloaded their things from the trunk of the rented Jeep Cherokee, they ventured outside for a visit to the nearby village—street shops and restaurants compressed onto a quaint, convenient tract. They lunched on club sandwiches before Paige took Diane into a ski shop where they bought sweatshirts, jogging suits, and other souvenirs. They had seriously considered going for a long walk, but instead opted for the solitude of the resort.

They ended up in the bedroom with glasses of white wine and their new clothes unceremoniously tossed into a corner. Diane's was the first lipstick Paige had tasted in months, and it only served to make him want more. She was warm, her skin erotically soft. Her legs were smooth, her hips firm and rounded. She breathed deeply when he kissed her, more deeply when his hand began moving over her legs. She kissed him hard in return, her moist lips and tongue as active and accomplished in their use as were his. Her sounds were maddeningly arousing to him, as were her movements, her scents, her touches. She was his, as ready and sensuous and responsive as the night before. Their passion was unrestrained, and for each it was intensely exhilarating and fulfilling. Afterwards, Diane gave a contented sigh. "Nice trip so far," she said with a husky little laugh.

Paige rolled onto his side and faced her. Beads of perspiration glistened high on her forehead, and her hair was damp at the temples. He reached over with his thumb and dabbed at a streak of smudged eye shadow. Diane, meanwhile, weaved her fingers through the matted hairs on his chest, straightening and combing them back to life.

"So what's next for the famous Dave Paige?" she said with a faint giggle.

"Dinner, I think."

"No, no," said Diane, giggling again. "I meant, what's next for you at Elerbee Engineering."

Paige smiled. "Gosh, who knows?"

"I've heard all about the big Executive Vice President thing that you were already supposed to have."

"Yeah?"

"Sure. I've also heard that you've run afoul of Jeff Wylie a ton of times.

Are you still eligible for the position?"

"Technically, yeah. Practically, I'm not so sure."

"Who'll make the selection? The Board?"

"Well, Langdon Elerbee initially made the selection and the Board approved it. I'm not altogether sure what will happen now."

"Then Wylie will have the final say?"

"Wylie will make the appointment, right. The Board will go along with whatever he wants."

"But you're on the Board, right?"

"Yeah, but I'm just one vote. Enough of the rest of them are sufficiently intimidated by Wylie that he can essentially do whatever the hell he wants."

"What's your plan if you don't get it? Will you stay with the firm?"

Paige smiled. "I've got another month to work that out. The Board meets in mid-July in New Orleans."

"Where's the ownership concentrated? Does Wylie hold a majority of shares?"

"No," Paige said with a shake of his head. "Grace Elerbee still holds a majority. I'm sure she'll eventually sell her shares back to the firm, but at this point she's the largest individual shareholder."

"Are there any restrictions on who she could sell her shares to? Could she sell to anyone?"

"Do you always ask questions two at a time, Diane?"

She laughed and reached beneath the covers. "I can't imagine why I'm thinking in terms of pairs today."

"I like the way you think," said Paige, leaning and kissing her on the tip of her nose, "almost as much as I like the way you—"

"Yeah? The way I what?" she asked, kissing and pressing against him.

"You're a woman of many skills, Diane, not the least of which is your ability to arouse in me a desire to ravish you."

Their kisses became more fervid.

"Then ravish, shall we?"

And they did, well up into the late evening.

They went for a walk after dinner, then stopped at the lodge located at the foot of the runs where they enjoyed a rest and a refreshing drink. The ski areas were visible from the glassed-in building, and there was a large deck outside for those who wished to have their lungs filled with the thin mountain air. The outside temperature was chilly, and most opted for the ambience within, with the fresh flowers and the quiet music and the large, hardwood bar where the remedies for sore muscles and bruised bodies were routinely dispensed.

Paige and Diane took a corner table.

Diane slid back her glass of white wine and reached down to the ankle she had twisted slightly when she had stepped into a slight depression.

"Still hurt?" Paige asked as he sipped his beer.

"A little, yeah."

"Is it swelled?"

She shook her head. "It's no problem, really."

But her hand remained upon her ankle. After some coaxing, Paige had her place her leg upon his thigh, underneath the table, where he was able to roll down her sock and determine that the ankle did indeed have some minor swelling.

"Need to get some ice on it," he declared after his diagnosis was complete. "The sooner the better."

Diane grinned. "Might be a little restrictive."

Paige also grinned. "Yeah, but not prohibitive. Besides, the total welfare of both your mind and your body is my responsibility this weekend."

"That's nice," she said, staring at him for a long moment. She finally sighed and looked away. "And I really did want to go dancing tonight."

"I'm betting we'll think of something else," Paige said with a chuckle.

"Did I ever tell you what the people in my office call you?" she asked.

Paige gave a curious look. "No. What?"

"After the systems meeting with Patrick Tierney when you threw him out of your building—"

"I didn't throw him out of my building."

"For all practical purposes, you most certainly did. Anyway—and I'm sure this originated with your friend Ted Haygood—when word spread around the firm that you and Patrick had had the confrontation and the big, bad Patrick Tierney had left with his tail between his legs, you instantly became 'The Legendary Dave Paige,'" explained the giggling Diane, drawing quotation marks in the air with her fingers. "One guy even said he'd pay big money for a movie of it so he could show it at the office Christmas party."

"That's ridiculous. And how did the word get out? You and Patrick were the only ones there from your firm."

"That's not important."

"Because you came back told everyone, right?"

"Um, I may have mentioned it; I can't remember for sure. But still, it's hilarious. You're now such a hero at my firm that you could come to work and they'd make you a partner immediately. I swear, our managing partner wants to buy you a steak dinner, *that's* how much he appreciated your taking down that obnoxious jerk."

"You may have mentioned it?"

"Maybe," said Diane, her eyes twinkling. "Like I said, now you're a hero to everyone in our office. And that would include me."

Paige reached across and took her hand in his. She was lovely in the light, and for the first time in a long while he was stirred from within. There was something about her that had been deeply piercing him, accelerating his heart rate and flashing a neurologic cocktail of images, impulses, and possibilities across his brain. The more he watched her, listened to her, made love to her, the more convinced he became that these fresh new feelings that were seizing and overtaking him were like old friends reappearing from out of the past.

Welcome back, he thought.

They talked on a bit longer, about their interests, about relationships, about life and life's meaning, and how one's work fits into the overall mosaic.

"So, Mr. Dave Paige, how would you describe your business philosophy?" she asked, leaning forward with her chin propped upon her clasped hands.

Paige smiled when he remembered the same conversation with Paula Markham. He thought for a moment before answering, "Well, I suppose it's pretty simple, really. I believe in God, in hard work, in human decency, in the American system of free enterprise—and therefore I pray every day that my hard-working managers will do the right thing and make the right decisions and produce the highest profits."

Diane leaned back in laughter. "I should've seen that coming."

Paige reached across and took her hands in his. "C'mon, we need to get you back and see to that ankle."

Her eyes gleamed in the ambient light.

He held her hands a moment longer, then leaned across and gently kissed her before moving alongside her to support her as she rose from her chair.

It was mid-morning Sunday before a groggy Diane awakened to the smell of bacon and coffee. She arrived in the kitchen wearing jeans and a black sweatshirt with *Colorado* emblazoned across the front in gold letters, a gift from Paige. She limped only slightly, and for the most part her twisted ankle supported her weight with little difficulty.

"Good morning," Paige called from his spot in front of the stove.

"Hi," she answered as she took a seat on a stool at the kitchen's breakfast bar.

Paige poured coffee into the ceramic cup he had already positioned atop the counter. He then leaned across the counter and kissed her, long and slow. Her mouth was warm, and she smelled of soap and light perfume.

"So the ankle's better?"

"Yep. Your treatment has just about made me whole again. I'm a new person."

Paige stopped and glanced at her. "I'm certainly glad to hear that," he said, noticing her eyes squarely upon him. Several seconds elapsed before Paige grinned and handed her a box of assorted donuts.

He returned his attention to the stove and its surroundings where he had quickly flung together an accumulation of egg shells, plastic wrappers, cups, knives, bowls, and seasonings.

"The house special is eggs with cheese, onions, and green peppers, with bacon on the side. Can you handle it?" he asked.

"An omelet?"

"Oh no," he replied with a shake of his head. "It's officially called eggs with cheese, onions, and green peppers."

"With bacon on the side. Yeah," she answered, giggling, "I can handle it."

It happened again during breakfast—they each stopped at the same moment and stared at one another. Paige was tempted to ask Diane what she was thinking, why she was staring. But he said nothing, merely filling his eyes with her lovely face and eventually returning to his surprisingly good meal. They took a walk afterwards, and then checked out and left Copper Mountain. They drove back toward Denver in clear, cool weather, and made a stop in the high country near Mt. Evans at Echo Lake. They were alone, and except for the animal tracks along the perimeter of the lake, no other evidence of civilization intruded upon them. The view was breathtaking, with the ponderosa pine and white aspen, the reds and browns of the exposed rock, the surrounding mountains covered at the top in white, and the cool, steady breeze.

"Now I can understand why people would want to live out here permanently and soak up this amazing scenery," Diane observed as she clung to Paige's arm. "I just want you to know that I've not only enjoyed all of this," she said with a sweeping gesture, "but I've also thoroughly enjoyed being with you."

Paige grinned. "I knew you'd enjoy Colorado, but I wasn't altogether sure about the other part. I'm glad to hear that. Thanks."

He kissed her softly, and then held her close. "And I can't think of anybody I'd rather be here with than you."

"Yeah, right," she said with a disbelieving chuckle. "I'm sure you can have your pick."

He held her at arms length. "You might not believe this, but I haven't been 'picking' since my divorce. Until now, until you."

"You're not serious."

"I am, yes."

"Wow," Diane said in amazement. "I wouldn't have guessed that."

They walked only a few feet more when Diane stopped again. "What was she like?" she asked, measuring Paige's reaction.

"Who?"

"Your ex-wife."

Paige grinned and appeared momentarily self-conscious. He pondered his answer for a moment, and then said softly, "Headstrong as hell." He chuckled, and his expression changed. "She's wonderful in some ways; impossible in others. She has lots of interests, and I've come to believe that it's all because her attention span is so short. And I don't mean that in a derogatory way. Valerie's a remarkably bright girl. She absorbs things quickly, and she has an endless curiosity."

"So what happened between you and Valerie?"

Paige grinned, then reached out to take her arm as they turned and started walking slowly back toward the Jeep. "What happened between me and Valerie," he said, grinning again, "isn't very easy to summarize, I'm afraid."

"You don't have to answer if you'd rather not. I understand."

"Oh, I don't mind. It's just that I'm not sure of all the reasons. But it roughly follows this line: Valerie wanted a career. Then she wanted children. Then she wanted a career again. Then we started a family. Then she started a career. Then she became bored—with her job, with me, with her life with me, with everything. She liked Atlanta, but she really missed her family back in Pittsburgh. She didn't like being alone, yet she didn't try to make a lot of new friends. She had plenty of money, a hot new car, a comfortable lifestyle—the upper-middle-class suburban dream. But she wasn't happy, and in the end I guess that was enough to make her feel like she needed to walk away from it, from me."

Diane said nothing as they walked along in step.

"Maybe she'll find what she's looking for. I hope so, because it's been pretty elusive so far." Paige turned toward her as they walked. "What about you? How serious are you with the guy you've been dating?"

She shrugged. "So-so, I guess."

"What does that mean?"

She glanced away quickly. "I don't think it's anything super serious. We see each other fairly often, but we're both free to see others if we choose."

"So what does your not-so-super-serious guy do for a living?"

"He's a consultant."

"Okay," Paige said, immediately trying to conjure up an image of what the guy must look like. "What kind of consulting?"

"Mergers and acquisitions," she answered with a nod, as if the rest should be obvious.

"I see," he finally said, stopping and looking into her eyes. "Now can I ask you a personal question?"

Diane smiled. "Dave, my marriage didn't survive because I was more successful in my career than my husband, or so he thought. And he couldn't deal with it—the fact that I made more and traveled more and had a nice, neat professional career. He made it such an issue that I finally couldn't deal with it either. I felt guilty, and for all the wrong reasons. And so he ended up leaving and going back to Ohio where he bought a building-supply company and took up with a Korean girl."

"But you've survived," Paige said admiringly.

"Oh sure. So far, anyway. Tell me about Sara."

Paige's expression immediately changed, and he grinned like a proud papa before launching into a five-minute description of the one person that Diane could see was the delight of his life.

"I'd love to meet her," she remarked when Paige had finished.

"I want you to meet her. You'd like her."

"I'm certain I would," she said, looking deeply into his happy eyes.

Diane's dark hair blew in the breeze. Her appealing fragrance seemed to swirl in the air around Paige, enveloping him in a tantalizing aura of allure. The combined sight and sound and smell of her were tantamount to an intoxicant, and as long as he remained close to her he could have what amounted to an inconspicuous high. When he could resist no longer, when the urge to feel and taste and absorb her became overpowering, he reached for her, kissing her and feeling her warmth, his own passion surging through him like an avalanche of thick snow roaring down a mountain.

When he pulled away and mentioned something about their having a plane to catch, Diane sighed softly and reached to kiss him ever more deeply.

"Ever made love in a Jeep Cherokee?" he asked, still intermittently kissing her lips, face, and neck. He felt her lips form into a smile.

"Of course not," she answered as she stole a quick glance at their surroundings. "But that shouldn't necessarily disqualify me."

"It doesn't," Paige said as they quickly began walking toward the vehicle.

It was late when Paige arrived back at his condo, and there was a curious message on his answering machine: It was from Robert Becker, president of Becker International, who had left a number and requested a call in return. When Paige dialed the number, it was answered by Becker who was relaxing in the spa of his upper Chesapeake Bay cabin. Would Paige mind meeting with him, Becker asked, in a couple of weeks when Becker would be in Atlanta? About what? Paige inquired. About several things—*opportunities*, as Becker described it. Well okay, Paige replied. Sure.

Excellent, Becker said. He would call later to set up a time and place. He thanked Paige and wished him well, and said he'd see him soon. Then he mentioned it again—*opportunities*—and said in closing that he thought Paige would find what he had to say extraordinarily interesting.

Fine, Paige said. He'd be there. Looked forward to it.

After hanging up, Paige stood in the kitchen of his quiet condo for some time, still reminded of Diane by the faint remnant of her perfume on his clothing, still pondering the reasons behind Becker's contacting him. He remembered the conversation with Jim Ogden about Becker International's search for someone to head up the subsidiary Becker and Associates. That must be it, Paige concluded.

Or might it involve something else? After all, Becker had used the plural.

Opportunities; Becker International; Becker and Associates; sittin' in a spa on the bay; timing; politics; Board of Directors; Central Region; Jeff Wylie; Jim Ogden; Grace Elerbee; Executive Vice President.

Good grief! he thought. It all seemed to be running together like a Billy Joel song.

Opportunities.

Yeah, right. Opportunities.

CHAPTER THIRTEEN

"Good morning, Atlanta. It's seven o'clock, and we're in for a warm Monday. It's already seventy degrees, and the highs are expected to reach into the upper-eighties today. Hey, watch out for the accident on I-75 near the Chattahoochee. There's a three-car pileup, and traffic's backing up all the way to Canada! Here's something to get the week off and rolling, called *Take Me to the River* . . ."

Paige glanced ahead at the traffic and saw little else beyond the endless stream of red brake lights snaking its way over the horizon. He wasn't moving; he had no alternate choices; he was condemned to a wait of unknown duration, one of those maddeningly random snags that every commuter abhors.

"Damn!"

It was nearly eight when he finally reached his office. On his way past Sherry's desk, she looked up, unsmiling, and said, "We need to talk. Call me when you're ready."

"Five minutes," Paige answered, hoping in that time to compose himself from the strain of the freeway entanglement.

At the appointed time, Sherry brought in coffee for both. She closed the door and took a seat facing Paige's desk.

"There's a bunch of rumors going around," she said before Paige had taken the first sip from the ceramic cup.

Paige leaned back in his chair. "Rumors? What sort of rumors?"

"Such as, there are three managers leaving."

Paige winced. "Who?"

"Larry Collier's one. Porter Caldwell's two."

Paige seemed humored. "Yeah, right. Who's the third?"

Sherry's expression was suddenly gloomy. "Dave, please don't pressure me about my source, but this person hasn't been wrong yet. And that's what has me so concerned," she said in such a lugubrious tone that the words seemed to drip off her tongue and form in a pool on the floor.

Paige's expression also changed, and he could sense that Sherry was closing in on a full-fledged cry. "Who's the third?" he repeated with a trace of impatience.

Sherry swallowed hard and paused a moment before blinking and uttering in a barely audible tone, "David Paige."

Paige gave a shocked look, then recovered and offered a slight grin. "Sherry, your previously reliable source has just swung and missed. I already know about Collier and I know nothing about Caldwell, but I definitely know about Paige—and he isn't leaving."

Sherry gave a contemplative, penetrating look into his eyes. She could find nothing to indicate that he was hiding anything from her, which wasn't his style; or that he might even be planning something of the kind further down the road, as a way of keeping his options open, which was his style. In every way she could quickly measure, he appeared to be the same as always—a condition that appeased her for the moment. She gave a relieved sigh and swallowed hard.

"Any more rumors this morning?" Paige asked causally.

"No. Well, yes, kinda."

Her discomfort grew. She shifted, cleared her throat, and looked away, off to the side. Her lips were pursed into a tight line across her face.

"Well, what?"

She took another deep breath, and then exhaled loudly. "One of my good friends in accounting told me there's a rumor going around that you and I are sleeping together." She gave a dejected shake of her head and then blushed a bright red, almost the color of her knit blouse. She paused a moment to let her embarrassment ebb, then turned and looked at Paige. "There are people in this company who think that I got my job—that I'm *keeping* my job—based on what I do in the sack rather than what I do in the office. And I don't like it, Dave. I resent it. I resent it a lot!" she said with an almost childlike pout.

Paige nodded sympathetically. "I can see that."

"Some of these morons believe everything they hear, too. *Everything*!" she exclaimed, anxiously tapping her pen against the notepad she held.

Paige sat up and leaned forward. "You're in a very visible position, and you're also very attractive. How do you think that washes with someone who's in a low-profile job and has a problem with their own self-esteem? Those rumors are inevitable, I'm afraid. And I know how mean and false those things can be. And yeah, there are probably people who'll believe it as a way of somehow getting even with a person they view with envy. Just don't waste your time or energy worrying about it, because you'll never be able to control that sort of jealousy."

"I suppose you're right," Sherry said, seemingly more composed. She became quiet, though her aggravation was still unmistakable. She stood up and stepped toward the door.

"By the way," Paige called, grinning slightly. "What did you tell your friend in accounting, the one who told you about the rumor?"

"I thanked her for telling me, and I told her to forget it because it wasn't true," she said matter-of-factly, adding, "unfortunately," and then walking out of the office.

Jeff Wylie waited until mid-morning to gather his staff in the large conference room. The rumors concerning Collier and Caldwell turned out to be true: Collier was retiring immediately after the New Orleans board meeting and convention in July; Porter Caldwell was leaving his post in St. Louis to pursue a teaching career. Nobody seemed particularly surprised about Collier—he had notified Paige soon after making his decision—and given his questionable health, his retirement seemed to make perfect sense. Caldwell was another matter, however, at least to Paige. Wylie seemed pleased, almost congratulatory when he looked at Paige and mentioned something about the probability that the greater good of the firm is being served in Caldwell's resignation.

Bring Porter Caldwell back on his shield.

Caldwell, Paige remembered, had seemed fine on the previous Friday after the Bosco Properties fence had been mended. Paige had been satisfied that he had saved both Bosco and Caldwell, and that the whole thing would blow over as soon as, and as *long* as, things returned to normal. A few quiet months, Paige remembered thinking, and the whole thing with Caldwell would be reprieved.

After the meeting, Paige sat alone behind the closed door of his quiet office. He had asked Sherry to hold all his calls. He swiveled around in his chair and gazed out his window at the city beyond him. When he tried to reach Porter Caldwell by telephone, he was told that Caldwell had not yet arrived at his office. When he tried Caldwell's home number, there was no answer. Paige leaned back and propped his feet atop his credenza. He didn't like the way the day was starting.

He was tired. He hadn't slept much the previous evening after returning home late from a trip to his Southwest branches. He had been hungry, but he hadn't bothered to eat. Instead, he had quaffed down several beers and then gone to bed alone. The net result was that he was not only tired but hungry and thirsty and a little bit headachy, and in such a condition, he needed very badly to be left alone.

It was June, and the clock was incessantly ticking toward the July meeting and Jeff Wylie's presumed unveiling of his new organizational structure. There wasn't much time, Paige knew. Time enough for a colossal gaffe, sure; that was always a lurking possibility. But hardly enough time to initiate anything major and have those results credited before July. As a general rule, change moved very slowly through the conservative Elerbee Engineering. There was a fixed corporate pace—an equilibrium—and any short-term attempts to heighten that tempo would often yield only marginal results, if indeed any results at all. Branch operations were generally more decentralized than not, thus inhibiting any immediate, large-scale responsiveness to change. And while change was by no means foreign to Elerbee, it tended to move at something quite less than the speed of sound.

And now something would have to be done about St. Louis.

But the sobering reality was simply that good results on Paige's part were no longer a factor in the organizational equation anyway.

Dammit, Porter! he thought again.

There was a sudden knock on his office door. Jeff Wylie glanced inside and called out to Paige.

"Might I bother you for a moment?"

Paige wheeled around in his chair and stood. "Sure, no bother."

Wylie stepped inside and pushed the door shut. He wore a look of unabashed admiration on his face—a condition in their relationship so infrequent of late that it quickly became as embarrassing to Wylie as it was flustering to Paige.

Wylie cleared his throat. "I just wanted to stop in and tell you what a nice job you did in St. Louis. I know I didn't bring it up in the meeting, but I didn't want to let the day go by without mentioning to you how impressed I was."

"Thanks, Jeff," Paige said, adding, "but which part of the St. Louis thing are you referring to?"

Wylie gave a strange look. "All of it: Smoothing things over with the client; getting us on site again; cleaning up the house and getting it back in order, including getting rid of Porter."

For a fraction of a second Paige considered letting it pass. However something inside him refused—that same something in his character that he had known about for years; that same something that was at once so virtuous and diabolic that it became altogether impossible for him to tell whether it was self-righteousness or self-destruction. The only thing he knew for certain was that it was there, always had been, and probably always would be.

"The part about Porter wasn't intended," Paige asserted. "As a matter of fact, that part wasn't in my plan at all."

Wylie's expression changed.

"To be perfectly honest, I'm disappointed at what Porter's doing. I told you before I went to St. Louis that I thought Porter was effective, and nothing that's happened since then has changed my mind. I had every intention of keeping him on the job."

Wylie smiled condescendingly and paused before reaching for the door. "I see. Well, I won't waste any more of your time. It seems as if I may have made an incorrect assumption."

No shit, Paige thought but didn't say.

"Maybe someday you'll see how it's all supposed to work," said Wylie, turning and leaving, closing the door behind him. Paige stood a moment longer before finally plopping back into his chair. He felt overcome with anxiety and frustration, as much by his own doing as by the circumstances in which he found himself. He held Wylie and Ogden in utter contempt not only as individuals but as business managers, yet in a strange way he admired the fact that each was reaching out and seizing his moment in the sun. Paige felt with each passing day he was losing control of his life, a condition for which he was seemingly unequipped to handle. His destiny now seemed to be in the hands of people he loathed, and he helped himself little by continually antagonizing them, deliberate or otherwise. But mostly deliberate, he knew only too well.

There had to be a better way, he thought. Surely it wasn't mere destiny that had caused both his marriage and his business career to so suddenly and thoroughly vaporize. There had to be a reason. And there had to be a fix. There *had* to be. And it would have to be found quickly, for July was soon approaching. He reached into his shirt pocket and retrieved a folded slip of paper.

Bob Becker, Becker International.

Dinner at Pano's and Paul's.

Tonight, 8:00 pm.

Paige relaxed at Richardson's shortly after work at the invitation of the retiring Larry Collier. They took a seat at a corner table and ordered mugs of cold beer.

Collier smiled and winked at Paige. "I'm gonna leave the rat race to you and the others, ole buddy."

"I wish you were staying," said Paige, touching his glass to Collier's. "I'm going to miss you, my good friend."

"Thanks. It's a load off my mind to have finally made the decision," said Collier, a look of peace and contentment about him. "I'm feeling better already, I swear. Incidentally, have you had a chance to think about a replacement for Porter?"

"Yeah. It's gonna be Mike Petrovic."

Collier gave a curious stare. Mike Petrovic was the current manager of the Pittsburgh Branch, Paige's old stomping ground but now a part of the Eastern Region and thus under the operational control of Jim Ogden. Petrovic had been originally hired by Paige, and had eventually been named as Paige's successor in Pittsburgh where he had since gone on to become one of the premier branch managers in the firm.

Collier signaled his agreement with a nod. "I'm impressed. How did you manage to pull that one off?"

Paige stared at Collier for a moment, unblinking, before answering in a flat, unemotional voice, "I just did it, Larry. I picked up the damned phone and I called Mike and I did it. Period."

Collier gave an even stranger look. "Would you mind explaining that?"

"I just did it, that's all. I called Mike and offered him the job this afternoon. He and his wife grew up in St. Louis, and he was excited about getting an opportunity to go back. So I told him to get his things in order and have his young ass out there in two weeks."

Paige was unsmiling, and it became apparent to Collier that what he had just heard was factual.

"Jesus Christ, Dave! He's not even your man. You did this without consulting Ogden or Wylie or anybody else? You can't *do* that!"

Paige calmly sipped his beer. "I've already sent my young guy Mortensen out to St. Louis. He's going to pull things together administratively so Mike can hit the ground running when he gets there."

"Mother Mary!" said the incredulous Collier, shaking his head. "Do you really think they'll let you get away with this? C'mon, Dave, who do you think you're fooling?"

Paige nodded nonchalantly. "It'll fly. You watch."

"Who the hell's gonna replace *him*, now?"

"That's Ogden's problem. I'm sure he'll deal with it when he finds out," Paige said with an innocent laugh.

Collier took a deep breath and slumped down in his chair. "I swear to God, this takes the cake. Now they'll deep-six your ass for sure, my young friend." Collier shook his head again, still in disbelief. "Have you got another job lined up?"

"No," Paige answered, chuckling. "They won't do anything, Larry. They'll blow off a bunch of steam, but nothing will happen. Mike's going to be in here day after tomorrow from Pittsburgh, and I'll tell Wylie and Ogden about it after Mike and I have had a chance to work out a few final details."

Collier sat up. "You're off-the-chart crazy, Dave!" he said loud enough to draw several stares. "And you're not being fair with Mike."

"I told Mike everything. I also told him to trust me. He's been around me long enough to know how I work."

"Jay-sus," Collier said, exasperated. "I don't want to be around when Wylie and Ogden find out about this. I think you may have signed your own corporate death warrant, cowboy."

"As I said before, they won't do anything," Paige said sharply, leaning toward Collier. "As long as Grace Elerbee holds all that stock, they won't touch me. They know the relationship I had with Langdon, and they damn well know that Grace hasn't forgotten it, either. The moment she sells her stock back to the company, I'm toast. I understand that as well as anyone. But as long as she holds, and as long as she continues to sit on the Board, and as long as everyone knows she's still taking an active part in the running of the company, then Wylie will have to tolerate me. I know it; you know it; Wylie knows it; hell, the American people know it. And you can bet that I'm going to play my full hand while I still have a few cards left."

Collier listened with interest. There was an intensity, a sense of urgency in Paige's words and demeanor that seemed to sweep across the table and grab Collier, energizing him as if he were wired into the same power source.

"Larry, I'm going to find a way to take this company away from those two. And to do that," Paige said, pausing, "I'll need your support and your influence with the other members of the Board."

Collier stared into Paige's determined eyes. It was almost as if he could see reflected an ugly, damaging, executive-row power struggle—the potential of which caused him immediate concern over Elerbee Engineering's ability to survive another high-echelon cataclysm. But when he considered Elerbee Engineering being totally dominated by Wylie and Ogden—especially Ogden—the scenario involving the power struggle seemed far more palatable.

"I've told you before that I'm going to do it, Larry. And dammit, I will. I'll find a way to take this company away from those two and discard them like animal droppings and then get on with building what you and I know this firm's capable of becoming."

"You won't get much help. There's no loyalty anymore. What little help I can give you won't be nearly enough. They'll overwhelm you, my friend."

"No!" Paige said sharply. "They *won't* overwhelm me. And there's still plenty of loyalty in the workforce. Companies are different today than in the past, I agree. But I *don't* agree that loyalty's a thing of the past. No enduring, successful human relationship can take place without it, and it'll be there when I need it most, Larry. It'll *be* there, believe me."

Collier stared again, finally shrugging and reaching over to touch his mug to Paige's. "I'll be damned, but I'm starting to believe you."

"Then help me, Larry. Stick with me and let me be able to count on you when the time comes."

"You'll have my help," Collier spoke calmly, "to the fullest extent I can provide it."

Paige nodded solemnly, his jaw firmly set. "Outstanding," Paige said, raising his glass in a salute to Collier. "I knew I'd be able to count on you."

Bob Becker was waiting in the lobby of the restaurant by the time Paige arrived at eight. Though they had not previously met, Paige somehow knew that, among the half-dozen businessmen crowded into the small lobby, the balding, mid-fortyish man in the conservative grey suit was Bob Becker. And in return, it seemed to Paige that Becker immediately recognized him as well. They greeted one another cordially, each hurrying to get in one of those discreet, head-to-toe, first-impression glances that often sets the tone of the early going. They were properly seated at a table in a far corner and were soon thereafter served a round of drinks. The restaurant was crowded, though Paige's survey of the nearby tables turned up no familiar faces.

The stocky Becker offered up a "Cheers" before sipping from his drink. His complexion was ruddy, as if he spent large amounts of time outdoors. He had a seemingly easy manner, though lurking just beneath the surface was an intensity that Paige quickly detected. It was more in the eyes than in the voice—the same look that had for years been referred to by the employees of Becker International as the Philly Stare.

"I adore your city," Becker said with a sweeping gesture. "It's lovely with all the trees and hills."

"Atlanta used to be one of the world's best kept secrets," Paige said with a grin. "But no longer, I'm afraid."

"Ah yes, the traffic," said Becker, smiling. "I seem to remember that you spent some time in Pittsburgh. By the way, are you familiar with Becker and Associates?"

"Only that it's the soils-and-materials arm of Becker International."

"Then let me tell you a little bit about the company and our plans for it."

The conversation proceeded through the course of the meal, and was mostly light and superficial. Paige listened with interest to Becker's ambitious plans for Becker and Associates. He responded with circumspection to Becker's gentle probing of the Elerbee Engineering situation in the aftermath of the death of its founder. Becker later produced a single sheet of paper—an organization chart of the entire network of the Becker International companies, including Becker Design, Becker Construction, and Becker and Associates.

They had coffee afterwards, after the table had been cleared.

"Do you ever get to New York?" Becker asked between sips of hot, steaming coffee.

"Only occasionally," Paige answered.

"I was there last week, and I took the opportunity to visit my old friend the Tyrannosaurus rex in the Museum of Natural History."

Paige grinned slightly.

"I've been going there for years, actually. I can clearly remember seeing the skeleton of that great beast when I was a child, and I've loved it ever since. It's the greatest goddamned creature in recorded history, without a doubt. Can you imagine how the female of the species must have felt when her guy came home after having a few beers with the fellas? As big as he was? Good God!"

Paige laughed at the ridiculous notion.

Becker's eyes were blue and deep set, alert and intense. His expression suddenly softened. "The real reason I go there is to think about things like perpetuity," he said slowly. "And survival. And adaptation. I'm forty-four years old and I run a billion-dollar-plus company, which also happens to carry my name. With all I've got, you'd have a tendency to think I've got it dicked, right?"

"Not necessarily," Paige answered with a shake of his head.

"Correct," Becker said, smiling. "My friend who left behind his skeleton just went away one day, just faded away. Until somebody dug up his bones and pieced him together, nobody knew a whole hell of a lot about him." Becker's expression quickly turned more serious. "I won't have my company end up like that. I won't allow Becker International to become a billion-dollar dinosaur. And I won't tolerate anyone on my management team who doesn't share those exact same sentiments, and with an almost religious-like fervor. We've got to understand that we have to do whatever's necessary to survive, to adapt, to move ahead, to put the right people in the right places. *That's* the challenge," Becker said with a nod and a jab of his finger, adding, "and that's why I keep visiting my old friend in the museum. And," he said with a hard look at Paige, "that's the reason I'm talking to you this evening."

Becker seemed to stare at Paige for what seemed an eternity before finally and abruptly asking, "Do you think you could run a company like Becker and Associates, produce a minimum of a twenty percent return on invested capital, a twenty-five percent growth in fees, a plan to gain national market share, then international market share, and take a major role in building a dynamic, world-class consulting organization?"

Becker watched carefully as Paige sorted the stipulations and considered the rapid-fire questions one by one. Paige's eyes remained locked on Becker, and in every way he appeared composed and in deep deliberation. If Paige had flinched or laughed or in any other way made light of the situation, Becker was prepared to call for the check and politely draw the evening to a close.

Paige finally gave a resolute nod. "The firm's infrastructure seems sound, based on what I've been able to gather on Becker and Associates. The professional skills, the test-lab capability, the client base, the image— presumably it's all there. If it's indeed there, then all the better. If it's not, then it'll take more time. But it can be fixed. It's all a matter of creating a good plan, finding and keeping good people to execute it, having the guts to stay the course, and demanding the very best from every employee, every process, every vendor, every day. Yeah, I could get those results. Absolutely. Positively."

Paige had another of those grimly determined Gentlemen-Start-Your-Engines expressions on his face. Only after Becker smiled did Paige break into an impish grin.

"I think we may be on to something here," said the delighted Bob Becker as he summoned the waiter for more coffee. "Let's chat a bit more, shall we?"

Opportunities, Paige thought again for what seemed the hundredth time since he had spoken with Becker by phone. The word now seemed to hang onto Paige like flypaper. And here was Becker in the flesh, one of the full-fledged Captains of Industry, obviously attempting to recruit him for his own team as much as if Paige were a star quarterback. The only decision to which Paige pledged himself while in Becker's presence was that he would make no decisions. At least not yet. Not tonight.

They later left the restaurant and found an all-night diner in Midtown where they drank coffee and talked until two in the morning.

There were no offers and consequently no acceptances. There was, however, very much a clear understanding on Paige's part of what Becker meant when he used the well-traveled term *opportunities*.

CHAPTER FOURTEEN

Atlanta's stifling heat oozed off the concrete and asphalt, drifting upward in undulating blurs as if seeking a return to its solar source. The tall downtown buildings seemed to conspire in trapping the heavy air at just the right level for the pedestrians moving about on the sidewalks. A sticky humidity didn't help matters, either.

It was Wednesday.

Paige walked along Peachtree Street with his tan jacket slung over his shoulder. Beside him, in shirtsleeves and with tie loosened at the collar, was Mike Petrovic. Paige and Petrovic were close friends, the latter having succeeded the former several years earlier as manager of the Pittsburgh Branch, a position still held by Petrovic.

The tall, olive-skinned, dark-eyed Petrovic had arrived in Atlanta the previous evening. Paige had been waiting at the airport, and from there they had enjoyed dinner at a cross-town Buckhead restaurant. Afterwards, they had visited Richardson's, where a late finish had ensued, typical of their days together in Pittsburgh when neither had been particularly adept at calling it a night much before dawn. Unlike the old days, however, the ability to function normally after such a session was no longer a given.

"Feeling better?" Paige asked as they jaywalked in front of the Peachtree Center complex.

"Yeah, some. Jeez, I must've had five gallons of water already today."

They entered the Peachtree Center South building and caught the elevator to the twenty-first floor. They were alone except for a pizza delivery boy.

Petrovic elbowed Paige softly. "The waitress in Richardson's. Have you had some time alone with her, D.P.?"

"Chrissie?"

"Yeah, her. The one with the fantabulous caboose."

"No, Mike. I haven't."

"She was really coming on to you, man. If Valerie's given up her rights to your body, how come you're not wearing Chrissie like a Brooks Brothers suit?"

The young delivery boy with the large, flat box was cackling when the elevator door opened.

"Because," Paige replied as he walked past the receptionist after checking for messages.

They went back into Paige's office and closed the door. Petrovic slumped in a chair, still at something less than his best.

"Your secretary's got some fabulous hooters, Dave."

Paige shot Petrovic a quick stare.

"So, how is she in the sack?"

"Dammit, Mike, I have *no idea*! Now don't ask me that again."

Paige returned two telephone calls while Petrovic glanced through a trade magazine. It was Petrovic's first visit to Atlanta in some time, but it was the first such visit in which Valerie Paige had not been there to prepare him a lavish Italian meal and to press him for all the latest Pittsburgh gossip. Sensing a strain, Petrovic had downplayed the entire matter of the split after explaining to Paige that he had neither seen nor heard from Valerie since her own return to Pittsburgh.

Married and the father of two teenage sons, Petrovic sometimes felt himself to be the only fortysomething who still remained paired with his original spouse. Especially among the Elerbee Engineering bunch.

Paige hung up the telephone. "Okay, killer. Where were we?"

"You had gone over some of the projects in St. Louis."

"Did we finish?"

"Yeah, we did. It's a good mix. I think it has lots of potential."

Paige nodded. "Okay, then. Are you clear on what I need done out there?"

"Yep, I am."

"Then do you still want the job as Branch Manager, St. Louis?"

"Yep, I do."

"Then will you *take* the job as Branch Manager, St. Louis?"

"Yep, I will."

"You're an easy sell, you old whore," Paige said with a wink and a boyish grin. "Welcome to the Central Region, Petro."

"Thanks, Dave. How long a stench do you think I'll do out there?"

Paige grinned. "You mean 'stint,' don't you?"

"Yeah, that."

"Two or three years, I'd guess. Is that workable?"

"Sure. Just so I can tell the old lady. When do we meet with Ogden?"

"I'll handle Ogden alone. I've got you scheduled to meet with the marketing gurus next. And I want you to talk to Hal Mortensen. He's gotten the administration squared away in St. Louis, and he just came back last night. Spend some time with him, pick his brain, and find out what's what. And if you need him to come back when you get out there, call me and I'll have him on the next plane."

"Okay, you got it. But are you sure you don't want me around when you talk to Ogden? I might be able to add some authentricity to it. Know what I mean?"

"Approximately. But this one's between me and Ogden."

Petrovic grinned and gave a thumbs up. "Okay then. Good luck, boss."

Jim Ogden had an utterly astonished look on his face when Paige bluntly announced the transfer of Mike Petrovic from Pittsburgh to St. Louis. They were across the desk from one another, behind Ogden's closed office door.

"You have *got* to be shitting me! You don't have the friggin' authority to do that. Who the hell do you think you're friggin' kidding, anyway? What do you friggin' think this is? A goddamned *fraternity* or something?"

"You're upset, Jim. I can tell."

Ogden exploded. "You're friggin' *right* I'm upset!"

"It's a done deal," Paige replied with a straight face. "We even shook on it."

"Your *ass* it's a done deal."

Paige nodded firmly. "It's a done deal. Period."

"That's bullshit, Paige. He works for *me*. You can't friggin' *do* that."

"I already did it. We can't go back now."

"I'm not letting you get away with this. You're *way* out of line this time."

"I really didn't think you'd mind, Jim, I swear."

Ogden took a deep breath. His face had become blood red, and he fought to maintain what was left of his self-control. "Undo it, goddammit, that's all there is to it. I'm going to see to it that you play by the rules for a friggin' change. So just go get your ass back out there and undo it."

"It's already done, Jim. I can't undo it. I *won't* undo it. Too many things have already been put into place."

Ogden swallowed. His eyes bulged and darted quickly from side to side. He swallowed again. His breathing was shallow and quick, and Paige noticed the accelerated heart rate showing in Ogden's temple. Paige considered for a moment that Ogden might very well be on the verge of a stroke, but then he could barely contain himself when he saw how completely dumbfounded and provoked Ogden had become.

"Does Jeff Wylie know about this?" Ogden finally managed to say with a tongue thick with emotion.

Paige shook his head. "No, but I didn't think he'd mind, either. Honestly, I didn't think either of you would mind."

Ogden's emotions finally got the better of him. He upset a full cup of coffee when he slammed his fist down on his desk. "You've definitely screwed up now, Paige. *Definitely*!"

Jeff Wylie showed little emotion when the three of them, at Ogden's insistence, gathered in Wylie's large office. The calm, composed Paige sat alongside Ogden, facing Wylie, and in stark contrast to Ogden's visible agitation. Little time elapsed before Wylie picked up on the hot anxiety that Ogden was radiating like a blast furnace, and soon both men began to appear ill at ease. When Ogden launched into an emotional summary of the incident, Wylie became fidgety to a point that he could hardly remain seated in any one position for much beyond twenty seconds. He shifted, straightened his tie, thumped his fingers, and then shifted again.

"I told him the deal's off, Jeff, and that he could get on with undoing everything he's done to this point," said Ogden, looking for approval. "No way can this be allowed to stand. It's, it's, it's goddamn insolence, that's what it is."

There was a long, heavy pause when Ogden finally concluded his remarks and sat back heavily.

Wylie turned to Paige. "Did you really think you could get away with something as grade-schoolish as this?"

Paige remained expressionless. "I only did what I thought would be best for the company, Jeff," he answered. "I didn't consider it grade-schoolish."

"That's *ridiculous!*" Wylie exploded. "You know the approval chain for the naming of branch managers. What the hell are you trying to pull, anyway?"

"Yeah, I'd like to know that, too," echoed Ogden.

Paige said nothing.

"Are you trying to make fools of us?" Wylie said, his voice rising again. "Do you think of this as some sort of joke? I'd certainly like to hear your rationale. I'd like to know what makes you think you can operate as you please, outside conventional procedures, in any way you see fit, with a different set of objectives and a different set of rules to go by. Your *own* goddamned rules, apparently. I'd like to hear the whole thing from you. And I want to hear it now."

Jeff Wylie's eyes were suddenly aflame.

Paige sat up straight and cleared his throat, then nodded. "All right then, gentlemen. Here's the bottom line: The St. Louis Branch is one of the most important operations in our company. The St. Louis Branch is also in need of a strong leader. Mike Petrovic is one of the strongest branch managers in our company. I would have to spend very little time with Mike because I've worked with him in the past. Plus, Mike is a native of St. Louis, and he knows the territory. Therefore, based upon the needs of the firm and the close fit with Mike Petrovic, I took it upon myself to offer the position to Mike and to close the deal as soon as he accepted."

Wylie shook his head in disgust.

"Then," Paige said quickly, continuing, "I made arrangements for Mike to call all the major clients in the St. Louis area and tell them of his appointment, and then to schedule separate meetings with each one beginning week after next. While he did that, I called all the key members of the branch staff and broke the news to them, asking them to remain quiet until I could announce it more formally later on."

"Jesus Rodriguez Christ!" Ogden shrieked, bolting upright.

Paige continued. "Then I followed up with phone calls to those same St. Louis clients and told them that Elerbee Engineering was sending one of its very finest into their area, that we were serious about the St. Louis market, committed to it for the long haul, and that I just wanted them to hear it from me personally before a letter was sent out later making the formal announcement. And finally, the formal-announcement letter under my signature went out in this morning's mail."

Wylie got up from his chair and walked to a corner of the office, his back to the others and his hands clasped behind him. "Will you excuse us, Jim?" he said without turning around.

Ogden, who continued to glare at Paige, appeared mad enough to throw a punch. He finally got up and left the room with a loud bustle. The only words Paige could identify from the string Ogden mumbled under his breath as was leaving was, "We'll see about that, you stupid bastard."

Wylie returned to his chair. He was outwardly more composed, though Paige did notice the tight muscles in his jaw. Wylie sat up straight, his hands on the table and his head erect.

"I should terminate you outright for such a stunt," Wylie said, a note of finality in his tone. "I certainly have the grounds to."

Paige stared at Wylie and said nothing.

"Is that what you want? Do you actually *want* me to fire you?"

"Of course not."

"It certainly seems that way to me."

"I can't help that. You see things one way, I see them another. We've known that about each other for some time now."

"Your grasp of the obvious is truly stunning, I have to confess."

"Thank you."

Wylie nodded. "Okay, fine. Why don't you tell me what you think I should do. Put yourself in my place. Let's hear what you've got to say."

Paige paused before finally speaking, "The decision's yours, Jeff, not mine. You decide."

Wylie exploded and rose from his chair. "Things would go a lot smoother around here if you would just clean out your desk and get the hell out of here. Vamoose, disappear. I don't have any more use for you than you have for me. And for the life of me I really don't see what keeps you here. You're not a factor anymore; you're not a player on this team— *my* team—and you never will be as long as I have any goddamned say-so in this company."

Wylie again walked to the corner window and stared outside. "And I plan on having a say-so in this company for a helluva long time to come."

"Okay," Paige said, uncrossing his legs and preparing to stand.

"Okay what?" Wylie snarled, turning around.

"Okay, I hear what you're saying."

"And?"

"There's no 'and.' I only meant that I had heard and understood the points you were making."

"Shall I take that to mean you're not resigning?"

"That's correct. I'm not resigning."

Wylie edged closer to Paige. "I intend to include a description of this entire affair in your personnel record, along with a letter of reprimand from me which will state that any further abuse of established policy or procedure or protocol by you will result in your immediate dismissal. As long as I'm in charge here, I will not permit you to go off on your own and operate any way you damn well please. Not today, not tomorrow, not ever. Do you clearly understand that?"

"I do."

"You have been warned, Paige. Consider yourself on notice from this day forward. I will not hesitate to terminate you from this firm if you deviate from this understanding. You're on very thin ice, sir, and I would advise you to conduct yourself accordingly. We will *not* have this conversation again."

When Wylie turned away again, Paige took that to mean the meeting had concluded. He got up and left.

Paige was returning to his own office when, at the far end of the long hall, he spotted Mike Petrovic standing in the hallway and chatting with a mid-level marketing executive. Petrovic immediately stopped and gave Paige a somber, searching look.

Paige grinned ever so slightly, and then flashed a waist-high thumbs-up to his friend.

Petrovic grinned back and raised a triumphant fist into the air.

"What time's your flight?" Paige asked Petrovic once they were together again near the end of the long day.

"A little before seven."

"Is there a later flight?"

"Yeah, I think so."

"Then get Sherry to change it."

"Does that mean we're retiring to the bar?"

"It does."

"Shall I invite Sherry? She's got some fabulous knockwursts."

Paige shot Petrovic a harsh glance from across the desk.

Petrovic raised both arms in surrender. "Okay, boss. I was just asking."

Petrovic hovered over Sherry's desk like a grinning wolf until she had called and made the requested change in his flight. But then he remembered Paige's nasty look and promptly left her desk the moment they were finished.

Richardson's was unusually crowded. There were no available seats or tables, so Paige and Petrovic were forced to stand and call their orders to the bartender. The speakers were turned up loud to the old familiar *A Whiter Shade of Pale.*

"My, my," Petrovic remarked over the music.

Paige turned and noticed three attractive females seated at a nearby table. The brunette who was facing in their direction occasionally aimed a not-too-subtle look of invitation at them. Paige smiled; she smiled in return. She was well-dressed in dark blouse and white slacks; a cute face; short, curly hair; mid-thirtyish; no wedding ring; available. She smiled again, with full lips, even though Paige concluded that her mouth was about a size-and-a-half too small in relation to the rest of her face.

More people trickled in and stood near the bar. Chrissie walked by, tray in hand, to place an order for a round of drinks. She wore a blue shirt with *Braves* across the front, nipples protruding conspicuously, with jeans so tight that Paige was certain her circulation was being impaired. She called out to the bartender, then stood and waited patiently. She was oblivious to Paige's presence in the crowded chaos around the bar.

Paige stepped around several others and moved beside her. "How are you, dear Chrissie?" he said, leaning near her.

"Oh hi, Dave," she said, smiling sweetly. "Why aren't you over in the corner?"

"No tables."

She raised her eyebrows in amazement. "Really! Isn't this incredible? Um, I suppose we're becoming like, one of 'the' places downtown."

The drinks were placed on her tray. "Will you be here a bit?" she asked.

"Yeah, I think so."

"Then I'll see you," she said, staring a moment before picking up the tray. "Bye, Dave."

Paige followed her with his eyes as soon as she stepped away and moved out onto the floor. She's gorgeous, he thought to himself amid the pleasurable images swirling inside his head. And she's young. And she's—

"Hey Dave!"

Paige turned and noticed Petrovic seated at the nearby table, in the midst of the three women.

"Hey, c'mon over, Dave."

Paige waved, grinning politely but shaking his head in decline of the offer. The brunette smiled invitingly. Petrovic had seated himself beside the redhead in the group, his apparent favorite. The third, a bleached blond, puffed on a cigarette and tried hard to appear ambivalent.

The brunette smiled again.

Nope, he thought. Not with all the Elerbee people in the crowd. The stories of his womanizing would probably be in the company gossip circuits by early morning if he started hitting on the brunette.

"C'mon over, Dave."

Paige looked away. No, not this time. Not here. Not on the very same day that he'd been told by his boss that he was to be the recipient of a "letter" in his file.

"Dave, c'mon, man."

The brunette hadn't taken her eyes off him in several minutes. Nope, Paige thought again. Somewhere out there, some young Elerbee employee is watching to see how a senior member of management conducts himself in public. But the brunette did appear to have a nice body. And she looked clean, almost antiseptically so. And she had a decent smile, undersized mouth notwithstanding.

"Dave, we have an empty seat at our table," said Hal Mortensen, Paige's assistant. Mortensen held a mug of beer, and his tie was loosened. He stood directly in front of Paige. "We'd be pleased to have you join us."

Paige glanced quickly at Petrovic, who was busy wooing the redhead. "Sure, why not," he answered, motioning Mortensen ahead.

The brunette flashed a look of contempt when he walked by the table. The brassy *Spinning Wheel* was blaring through the speakers.

Paige joined Mortensen and his two contemporaries for the better part of the next hour. The three directed dozens of probing, insightful questions at Paige, questions dealing predominantly with company goals and operating principles. The young men were intelligent and informed, and they thoroughly enjoyed their chance to hear from someone of Paige's organizational stature, especially on the topics that helped to better define the corporate culture of Elerbee Engineering.

The conversation eventually came to an end when the three young men left together after paying their bar tab and thanking Paige for his company. Across the room, Petrovic remained seated beside the redhead. The two other women were conversing with two men who had joined them at the table. Paige sat alone and watched from afar.

Some were singing along to *Saturday in the Park*.

Chrissie happened by eventually. "Your friend requests your presence at the other table," she said, smiling coyly as she removed the empty mugs.

"Tell him I'm leaving for dinner in ten minutes, and if he doesn't plan on joining me then he'd better get his stuff out of my car and find his own way to the airport."

Chrissie giggled. "I'd hate to disturb him when he seems to be like, doing okay for himself, ya' know?"

"Then I hope he's not hungry."

"What time's his flight?"

"Ten."

"Are you coming back here?"

"Not tonight," he said, winking.

Chrissie's divine body and overpowering perfume suddenly reminded Paige of something else. Earlier in the day he had received a call from Diane Tresvant, who had returned to the city from an out-of-town assignment. She had suggested a quiet dinner together, but Paige had begged off in favor of using the time to cover a few final details with Petrovic. She had then suggested meeting later for a nightcap, but Paige had already committed to drive Petrovic to the airport, and it would be late before he could get back across town to a bar near to where Diane lived. When she had become silent on the other end of the line, as if the rejection had chafed her, Paige had quickly suggested that if she were to agree to wait up for him, then he'd more than make it up to her by personally delivering the nightcap. A long silence had ensued before she had responded with, "White wine will do nicely."

Paige grinned at the thought.

Petrovic showed up nine minutes later. He had a bored expression on his face. "What's for chow?" he asked.

"How about Chinese?"

"I'm game," Petrovic said with a shrug. "Cantonese or Setchgone?"

"Szechwan. That okay with you?"

"Sure. It's all the same to me."

"What about your friend with the red hair?"

Petrovic shook his head. "Nah, no way. She uses the word 'relationship' too damned often. It's every other word out of her mouth. Gives me the heebie jubbles, man. And she's got all those business buzzwords, too. She manages a temporary-help agency, and she was constantly saying stuff like 'touch base' and 'proactive' and 'results-oriented' and 'customer-driven' and 'plenty of runway left.' You know, like she's really hip or something. But that 'relationship' stuff was like a red light going off over her head."

"What about the relationship with your wife?"

Petrovic cleared his throat and looked carefully at Paige. "I was just speaking with her, my good man. *Speaking*, that's all. Speaking of speaking, do you want me to give Valerie any messages when I get back?"

"No," Paige said quickly. "It's over between us. Might as well leave it go."

Petrovic shrugged. "Okay, man. Thought I'd offer."

"Thanks just the same."

"Then would you mind if I called her up and asked her out? The secret's out, man: Valerie was always crazy about me, and that's no kidding. And there's no need keeping it under wraps any longer. We're destined for some proactive, results-oriented, customer-driven lovemaking."

"So you want to do a deep dive on my ex?"

"I'm just trying to make this a value-add conversation," Petrovic said, grinning.

"And I suppose you want me to give you a quick download and onboard you about all her key drivers?"

"Sure, even though I know it wouldn't make you a happy camper."

"Actually, I don't know if I have enough retained capital left with Valerie to get your project run up the flagpole."

"At the end of the day, you're still one of the key stakeholders. Just keep me in the loop."

"I will, as long as I have enough bandwidth left."

They both laughed.

"Let's continue our other game, shall we?"

"Fine," Paige said with a nod. "Give me a category, please."

They'd been playing the game for years, originating inside their two heads at some Pittsburgh bar on some cold night at some ungodly hour. Petrovic mulled it over a moment before finally announcing, "Okay, give me three Hates."

Paige deliberated only briefly. "I hate it when someone hums that little godforsaken four-note tune to 'The Twilight Zone.' I hate it when I can see a little thing of spit fly out of my mouth when I'm speaking in front of a group and everyone else sees it, too. I hate it when some kiss-ass repeatedly says 'Great Question' during the Q & A after a presentation, when in truth some of the questions could have been better constructed by a ten-year-old."

Petrovic smiled. "Nine point six."

"Nonsense. That was at least a nine point eight," protested Paige. "That was certainly as good as the one I did in Ninety Six when you gave me a nine point eight."

"I'm sorry, Dave. The mark stands. Next category, please."

Paige gave a vindictive look. "Okay, then. Give me three Don'ts."

Petrovic took a quick breath. "Don't wipe your hand underneath someone else's chair or you might get something crusty or flaky on it. Don't ever shout 'Over my dead body!' when airport security asks if they can inspect your briefcase. And don't ever, *ever* offer a job to another guy's employee without first getting the permission of that other guy."

Paige roared with laughter. "A ten, unquestionably."

They both laughed and then high-fived.

Paige raised his glass. "In spite of your arrogance, you sorry prick, here's to the best branch manager in Elerbee Engineering."

"The best *ever*," added Petrovic.

"No dammit, the best *now*."

Petrovic touched his glass against Paige's and nodded graciously. "And to you, my old and dear friend," he said, speaking softly, "the someday, someway, by the grace of God soon-to-be Executive Vice President of Elerbee Engineering."

CHAPTER FIFTEEN

The Wylie home, perched along the banks of the Chattahoochee River in fashionable North Atlanta, settled atop a hilly rise in a neighborhood of exclusivity. It was a single-story brick home with a wide front porch, and behind the glass windows the sparkle of living-room lights shone through to the outside world. Inside, the crowds gathered in the den, in the living and dining rooms, the library, sometimes even the kitchen. The sumptuous menu—Beef Wellington and vegetables—had been expertly catered. A bartender quietly served in a corner of the den.

The occasion for the gathering was a dinner party in honor of Larry and Dot Collier, and the guests were a virtual Who's Who of Elerbee Engineering. All of the members of the Board of Directors were present, together with various other corporate officials. Holly Wylie carried out her role as hostess with elegance, enthusiasm, and efficiency. Likewise, Jeff Wylie seemed to say the right things at the right moments. With humility and sincerity, the emotional Colliers accepted the praise, the reminiscences, and the collective warmth from all who gathered there.

It was late June, and Collier's retirement was close at hand.

After dinner, Paige circulated among the groups, making certain to exclude no one and paying particular attention to the four members of the Board who were not employees of the firm. Attorney John Brice, banker Marshall Wilkinson, and professor Lawton Alford were in attendance with their wives. Mrs. Langdon Elerbee, widow of the company's founder, was also there.

The other members of the Board were also present, to include vice presidents Ron Steinkempf, engineering; Vincent Kincaid, finance; and Edward Webb, marketing. Ralph Boudreaux, a retired engineering technician who represented the company's hourly workface, rounded out the field of twelve who, with Wylie, Collier, Ogden, and Paige, comprised the Elerbee Engineering Board of Directors.

Jim Ogden had arrived with his wife, Mary, and wasted little time in casting his line into the abundant political waters.

The Board was scheduled to convene in New Orleans in less than two weeks. The rumor mill was active, and there were at least a half-dozen hypotheses on the potential outcomes. Seemingly everyone in the company was speculating—in offices, hallways, conference rooms, conference calls, break rooms, mail rooms—such that significant amounts of productivity were being burned away like the fuel of a jetliner awaiting takeoff in a long queue. Everyone knew it, but no one would dare admit it.

The conspicuous absence of Valerie Paige was a bit awkward for those who had grown accustomed over the years to seeing the Paiges together. Valerie had been an accomplished political operative, always charming and attractive and otherwise extremely valuable in her role as Executive Wife. She had always known what to do and say, and her witty, sometimes earthy comments were always enjoyed. For Paige, it was strange without her, almost uncomfortably so, and it took a stiff drink before he finally jettisoned the odd sensation of working the room alone. He even crossed paths with Ogden once, nearly bumping into him in the process.

"Heard anything from Valerie lately?" Ogden asked in a whisper when they were alone. "Wow, I miss her pretty face at these things."

Paige gave him a hard glare which immediately prompted an innocent Who Me? expression from Ogden.

"Actually, I don't hear much from Valerie these days," Paige answered. "I trust the lovely young Nina is doing well."

Ogden gave an embarrassed laugh and looked away, wishing that he'd kept his mouth shut and silently wondering how the hell Paige could've known.

Ed Christoff, burly, sloppy, and a brilliant technical specialist in metallurgy, ambled across the room and took up a place beside Mary Ogden. Christoff was a fixture in the Atlanta Branch where, as a senior consultant, he commanded one of the highest hourly rates on the fee schedule, nearly eight-hundred dollars per hour. His work was considered by those in the industry to be of the highest caliber, and ranged in scope from consultative engagements to expert testimony in court cases, and involved numerous writings for technical journals. He loved his work; he also loved his play. He never missed a party, always arriving slightly tipsy and departing thoroughly wasted, and always by taxi. He meant no ill will and rarely caused any. Christoff was a happy drunk, harmless and endearing, and the Elerbee people had long ago learned to put up with him.

"Greetings, young lady," Christoff said, leaning and kissing Mary's hand.

Mary, a pleasant but mostly plain, subdued woman, smiled and blushed, saying, "Oh, hi."

Christoff shook hands with Paige and Ogden, and then slid his arm around Mary's waist as he inched closer to her. "When do you want to leave Jim and run away with me to some remote Caribbean island?"

Mary glanced at Christoff's considerable paunch, then at his full drink. "Are you sure you could make it on bananas and rainwater?"

Christoff, Ogden, and Paige all laughed loudly. For his part, Christoff backed away and slapped his thigh amid his bellowing, managing in the same motion to spill most of his drink onto the thick pile carpeting.

"Oh damn!" Christoff roared when he eventually noticed his empty glass.

Mary leaned over and blotted at the stains with a paper napkin.

"I'll be hung out to dry for sure now," Christoff said with a noticeable slur. "I've made an overture toward Jim's lady and I've spilled whiskey on Jeff's carpet. Good God, I'm toast. Stick a fork in me, boys, I'm done."

He turned and lumbered away toward the bar. "Might as well take on more preservative, in that case."

Paige thought about Christoff's brilliance, and how he had probably sacrificed more brain cells with his years of heavy boozing than had been consigned to most people in the first place. Paige laughed at how even the remnants of Christoff's prodigious brain would likely be plenty enough to get him through the rest of his life in good standing. His liver, however, might be a different story.

Meanwhile, Grace Elerbee remained discreetly off to the side, politely greeting her friends and making benevolent small talk about children and grandchildren and vacations and assorted other minutia. She was short of stature, trim, silver-haired, and fashionably attired in a blue dress with white scarf. She wore a solid gold necklace and bracelet in contrast to several other women who were far more heavily jeweled. Naturally refined, she had an altogether pleasant but reserved manner. She allowed the attention to focus upon the Colliers, though she was unmistakably the most important of the guests. As the largest stockholder and most influential member of the Board, she had remained vitally interested in the company since her husband's untimely death. Her business acumen was considerable, as was her knowledge of people. She had wisely left the job of managing to the professionals, but she never failed to ask a steady stream of pertinent and insightful questions when she met with the other members of the Board. She understood much about the company and the industry in which she had spent the better part of a lifetime, albeit indirectly. And she was respected not only for her name and her ownership, but for her obvious talents in stewardship and executive evaluation.

"Good evening, Mrs. Elerbee," Paige said after eventually making his way to her side.

"Well, a good evening to you, too," she said with an agreeable, gracious smile. "I've been hearing nice things about the firm's successes, so I take it that you've had a role in at least some of that."

"Maybe a little of it," Paige said softly, grinning. "But probably very little."

"I'll bet the percentage is far higher than you're willing to let on," she said admonishingly.

Paige laughed. "So I'm shy and retiring."

Grace Elerbee laughed softly. "I didn't necessarily mean that. After all, I do know you."

Paige had hoped to chat a bit longer, to have enough time to tell her how much her late husband had meant to him; how he now treasured the experience of having worked with him; how he missed him and yearned for his guidance and leadership and friendship. He wanted to be able to tell her that he could help complete what her husband had started, that he had the same vision, the same goals, even much the same style. He wanted to let her know that there was an alternative to Wylie and Ogden—to nothingness—and that she had it within her power to help change things for the better.

Instead, Holly Wylie called out for the guests to gather in the next room.

"It's great to see you again," Paige said warmly, taking hold of her hand.

Grace Elerbee smiled, her eyes twinkling. "And I'm delighted to see you, Dave. We'll meet again when we have more time."

Paige nodded his agreement. "I look forward to it, as always."

In the large living room, the Colliers were standing alongside Jeff Wylie in the center of the room. Several wrapped presents were stacked high on a nearby table. There was an expectant hush when Wylie raised his arm and cleared his throat.

Collier slipped his arm around Dot's waist.

"If I might have your attention for a moment," said Wylie as he looked over the crowd of forty people. "I'm going to ask Dave Paige to kick things off and say a few words about our guest of honor, so at this time I'll yield the floor to Dave."

Paige hadn't been told beforehand that he'd be called upon to speak, so he hesitated a moment before stepping forward to the center of the room. He glanced quickly at Wylie, as if to thank him for attempting to portray him as an inept bungler in front of such an august group. He then drew a deep breath and fixed his eyes upon Larry and Dot Collier.

"We've all gathered here to honor one of the real pioneers in our firm's young but rich history. We're honoring a man who has given our company a length and a quality of service that truly stands apart from all but a few, in this or any other organization. We're honoring a man whose excellence in his chosen profession, whose value to his community, and whose dedication to his company and his family, stand as examples of the very best in the American character. Here is a man of integrity, of honor, of loyalty, who has set an example that younger contemporaries could and did follow with great success of their own. I am one of those who followed Larry's example, and I feel grateful that our paths crossed and our friendship developed into what is, for me, one of the great blessings of my life. I'm reminded of the Chinese proverb that says, 'One generation plants the trees, another gets the shade.' A lot of us will be working in the shade of the trees planted by this man, and for that we are thankful. The shadow he casts is considerable, and we have been blessed to have shared a portion of our lives with him. Let me also add that we're honoring a wonderful, lovely lady who has stood by and supported her man throughout their many years together."

After a brief applause, Paige drew another breath and continued, extemporaneously citing his friend Collier's career highlights.

"Larry, our hope is that in some small way, our influence on you has helped to improve you as a person because, without any doubt, your influence has darned well improved each of us. And I know of no higher compliment to pay a friend and business associate than to say that he's leaving our organization a lot better off than when he first joined it."

This time there was sustained applause. Wylie stood aside and forced a smile. He took the floor only after the Colliers had stepped across to embrace Paige.

Wylie then thanked Collier for what he termed, "A body of work that would be the envy of any and every employee in our firm, especially the younger ones who view Larry with such high regard."

The gifts came next. An all-expense paid vacation, with two round-trip tickets to Banff, in the Canadian Rockies; an engraved bracelet for Dot; box-seat tickets to an upcoming series between the Braves and Collier's beloved Dodgers; and finally, a photographic montage of the buildings and equipment and people of Elerbee Engineering that represented each of the locations where Collier had served during his career. Holly Wylie had enlisted the aid of several branch managers and their secretaries in combing the firm's archives for usable material, eventually finding enough to piece together this special gift.

The Colliers were deeply moved.

"Speech," someone called after more applause.

Collier declined at first, but was eventually prodded by Wylie into saying a few words. He paused a moment, collecting his thoughts and emotions and reaching for Dot's hand. He gazed out at the faces of his dearest friends, and a stream of warm, pleasurable memories collected over many decades came rushing at him in clusters. He smiled, but his mouth and face were strained from the obvious sentiment that was on the verge of overtaking him. He took a long, slow, calming breath.

"Dot and I thank you, Dave and Jeff, for those generous words. And we thank every one of you for all the gifts and all the love," he said thickly. "I'm a fortunate man tonight. I have a wonderful wife and family, wonderful friends, a lifetime of wonderful memories. But the truth is, I've been fortunate for a mighty long time. I was fortunate to enter a grand profession—the engineering profession—of which I am proud beyond measure. And I had the singular good fortune to join a young firm where there happened to be a giant of a man named Langdon Elerbee," Collier sought and made eye contact with Grace Elerbee, who smiled and nodded graciously. "My God, what a rock he was. I consider myself privileged to have known him, and will never forget him. And I've been fortunate to have worked with people like all of you, and so many others along the way."

Collier stopped to brush a handkerchief beneath his nose. He glanced at Dot and grinned nervously. "I'm not sure how to do this since I've never retired before."

The laughter eased the tension.

"I thank you for what you mean to me, to us," he said emotionally. "I thank you all from the very bottom of my heart."

There was a final round of applause, and then came handshakes and more embraces.

The crowd began to thin afterwards, and Paige sought once more to sequester Grace Elerbee for a few final moments before the evening ended. At one point he noticed Jim Ogden with her, the two of them huddled in a far corner. When he looked again, Ogden was laughing and politicking with a few remaining Board members.

And Grace Elerbee was gone.

Afterwards, Paige drove home in a misty rain. He arrived at eleven o'clock to a dark, empty condo. He was anxious to sleep off the effects of having crisscrossed the Midwest earlier in the week on a busy trek to a half-dozen branches. Wylie had at first refused (out of spite, Paige was certain), then finally relented to his use of the company jet, and several of Paige's branch managers had begun referring to his arrival as the Rock 'n Roll Jet Patrol. Almost as an afterthought, Paige checked his recorder for messages. There was one from Bob Becker, explaining that he needed to talk to Paige ASAP; one from Diane Tresvant, requesting a return call; then another from Becker, requesting Paige's presence at an odd 2:00 a.m. meeting at the Fulton County Airport on Atlanta's west side.

Paige was ready to dismiss the whole thing as a joke until Becker called again. He was in Philadelphia, and would be leaving within the hour for Atlanta. And he needed to meet with Paige immediately upon arrival.

"You're kidding, right?" Paige said in his fatigue.

It was urgent, Becker said. And no, he wasn't kidding. He even managed to slip in that word again—*opportunities.*

"Jeez, two o'clock? Are you sure?"

"It's urgent, Dave. It can't wait."

"Okay," Paige said, glancing at his watch. "Two o'clock. I'll be there."

This had better be good, he thought to himself as he hung up the phone. This had better be *really* good.

CHAPTER SIXTEEN

Jim Ogden had been busily packing a suitcase when he suddenly stopped and reached for the notepad in his open briefcase at the foot of the bed. He jotted down a telephone number, then passed the sheet to Nina, who was fully dressed and sitting in the middle of the bed, drinking a diet soda.

It was Sunday.

"I'll be at the Baltimore Branch. If the attorney who's handling Derek's case calls here, get the details and give me a ring on my cell phone," he said in reference to his son's drug-possession charge. "Or have him give me a call direct, whichever suits his fat lawyerly ass."

"When will you be back?"

"Tuesday."

"Then what?"

"I'll be in town until it's time to go to New Orleans."

Ogden resumed his packing. There was a sly grin etched across his face, as if he were the sole proprietor of an internationally important piece of information. Nina took one final sip of her soda and then crushed the can in her hand.

"How do you know Dave Paige's gonna leave?" she asked.

"He won't work for me. It's as simple as that."

"And you'll move the guy in from Baltimore to take his place?"

Ogden turned around from the closet and winked at her. "You got it, baby."

"Will that guy Wylie go for it?"

"That guy Wylie," Ogden said, smiling, "goes for everything I bring him. When Paige resigns, Wylie won't waste five bloody minutes before calling me in and asking me for a recommendation."

"And you'll be ready."

"I'll be ready," he said, his eyes twinkling.

"That's really neat," she said admiringly. "How long have you been planning all of this?"

"About a year."

"It's all falling into place, just like you said it would." She leaned back and muttered a soft, "Wow."

"Yep. The Becker situation was the clincher. Everything was going perfectly as it was and then all of a sudden here comes this incredible bonus, right out of the blue. I couldn't believe it."

"There's no way they wouldn't select you now. I mean, it's all sealed, right?"

"Right, especially after the comment at the party."

They laughed knowingly. Ogden raised his arms into the air in the manner of a triumphant prizefighter. He walked over and kissed her. "Be a sweetheart and get me a beer," he said, pulling her off the bed.

Nina dutifully returned a few moments later with a bottle of beer for Ogden and a granola bar for herself. She climbed back atop the bed and sat with her legs crossed. She took a bite from the granola bar, then smiled broadly at Ogden's seemingly brilliant coup.

"So we'll still buy a house after New Orleans, right?"

"Right," Ogden called from the bathroom where he was packing his toiletries.

"Then what?"

"Then I'll go after Wylie's job."

"With us, I mean."

"We'll see," he said without much enthusiasm as he emerged from the bathroom.

"But what if Dave Paige decides to stay? What then?"

"He won't stay. I know him too well to misjudge him on that one. He'll resign before he leaves New Orleans."

"Will anybody tell him why he wasn't selected?"

"If Jeff doesn't, I will. He'll see there's nothing left for him at Elerbee, and he'll leave quietly. I guarantee it."

The phone rang. Nina reached for the receiver on the nightstand, answered it, and then passed it to Ogden. "Ten minutes, my man," he spoke before hanging up.

Nina took a sip of her drink. "Who was that?"

"Don Burroughs, the HR honcho. He's driving me to the airport."

"I could drive you to the airport."

"Nina honey, we've got some business to discuss," he said with faint irritation. Ogden then remembered that Paige had beaten him to the company jet when he had requested it for his trip, the thought of which made him even more irritable.

"What will you do tonight when you get there?"

Ogden zipped his shoulder bag closed. "I'll be going over some of the things that will be discussed tomorrow. It's always a good idea to do a little advance work. Takes the rush out of things, you know?"

"Sure you won't be shacking up with some foxy lady?" she asked, grinning playfully.

He leaned and kissed her on the tip of her nose. "You're the only foxy lady in my life."

When she made an attempt to pull him toward her, he stiffened and moved away.

"Baby, Don Burroughs is on his way here."

"But I won't have you for two long nights."

"You had me for two long hours this morning."

"That's not enough. I'm a young, vibrant woman with wants and desires."

Ogden laughed and went to the closet for his blue blazer. He slid the airline ticket into the inside pocket, dropped his coat at the end of the bed, and then took a seat on the bed beside her. He faced her away from him and began massaging her shoulders and neck. Her head fell forward, relaxed, as he moved his soothing fingers over her.

She moaned softly.

He heard a car door outside, followed moments later by a ring of the doorbell. He pulled her to him, turning her and kissing her. He then got up and reached for his things. He started toward the doorway, stopping and glancing back at her.

"See you soon, baby," he said, winking.

"So what did you end up doing to the reports?" Ogden asked, staring across the front seat at Don Burroughs.

Burroughs swallowed. "I did as you asked, Jim. I've doctored the data on your region's affirmative-action profile, its safety performance and days-lost summary, its minority recruiting results, and the numbers of minorities and women promoted in the past six months. It's all ready to hand out to the Board members."

Ogden nodded. "So where do I rank now in those categories?"

"First among the three regions."

"And where would I rank without putting the different spin on the numbers?"

Burroughs swallowed again and announced, "Last, I'm afraid."

Ogden gave a raucous laugh.

"Jim, I don't feel good about your putting me in such a position," Burroughs said in a whiny tone.

"Oh bullshit. Paige will never know."

Burroughs gave Ogden a quick disbelieving glance. "Oh, he'll know. His region's way ahead in all categories. He'll know the data's been fabricated the minute he sees it."

"It won't matter because he won't see it. But even if he does, it'll be too late."

"Does Jeff know that we've," Burroughs paused and cleared his throat nervously, "that we've 'put a different spin on the numbers,' to borrow your phrase?"

Ogden laughed again. "Jeff knows everything, my man. Why, Jeff's God," and then added under his breath, "for the time being, anyway."

Ogden smiled and glanced about the interior of Burroughs' new BMW. "That kind of stuff won't stand alone, but you combine it with my region's fee and profit improvements, along with my friends in high places, and it's all over but the shouting. There should be no question."

The traffic was moderately heavy for an Atlanta Sunday afternoon as they sped along the interstate toward Hartsfield International.

Ogden snickered at first, then broke out in full laughter. "Don, when's the last time you came across some strange?"

Burroughs gave a puzzled look. "Beg your pardon?"

"Strange, Don. When's the last time you stepped out on your old lady?"

"May I invoke the Fifth?" Burroughs asked with a self-conscious smile.

"No, you may not. I've seen how you look at the chicks."

Burroughs toyed with the radio, as if his search of the digital display would somehow distract Ogden.

"How old was she?"

Burroughs gave a thoughtful pause and finally answered, "Thirtyish."

"Too old. Next time try twentyish. You do that, and you'll sure as hell age more slowly."

Burroughs gave his passenger a quick, curious glance. Nothing was sacrosanct with Jim Ogden. He looked again at Ogden. "What's Paige going to do? There are all kinds of rumors floating around that he's up to something."

Ogden glanced at his fingernails and then said softly, "Yeah, I've heard. But the fact of the matter is, he's finished. And he damn well knows it."

"Are you sure? He seems to have a way of emerging out of the smoke and ashes."

"Hell yes, I'm sure. He's on the last leg of his ninth life this time. There's no more magic left in Dave Paige. He's a spent son of a bitch."

"I hope to God you're right, Jim."

Ogden nodded confidently. "His little CPA friend will be sweeping up his bloody pieces after he walks into the buzz saw that's waiting for him in New Orleans," he concluded with a wicked little laugh.

"What 'little CPA friend' are you referring to?"

Ogden smiled. "Nothing, Don. It's not important."

Several moments passed with only the muted sounds of the road and the radio's smooth-jazz melodies.

"It seems that everything's in place, then," Burroughs said after a while.

"That's right, my man. Wylie's absolutely sold on my proposal for a new organization that'll divide the country into nine regions, instead of just three. All the regional-manager slots will be open with Paige and Collier out of the way. I figure I should be able to hand pick at least six of the nine. That ain't too shabby, huh?"

"Certainly not."

"Kincaid's worked out the necessary financing to buy out the old lady and get her the hell off the Board. That'll leave another open seat."

Burroughs shot a quick sidelong glance at Ogden before returning his attention to the road.

"I'm almost certain I can get you on the Board," Ogden said. "That's what we've talked about, and that's what I'll be lobbying to get."

"Are you certain Mrs. Elerbee will sell?"

"I'm sure, yeah. She wants to travel before she shrivels up and croaks, so this way she can cash in all her chips and go on an African safari, or some such."

"Does Jeff Wylie really want her off the Board?"

"Oh my God, yes! She holds almost thirty percent of the shares; Jeff holds maybe fifteen percent; the other Board members hold another ten percent, or so. The rest is held by a large number of other employees, and in reasonably small increments. It's her equity that bothers Jeff the most, plus the fact that she can be the world's biggest bitch at times."

"What happens to her shares if she agrees to sell? What happens to the stock?"

"I have a proposal for that, too," Ogden said smugly. "All of the repurchased shares should be kept in the treasury until everything cools down, for six months, say. Then, the top management should be given options on enough of those shares to be able to keep a strong position. The rest of the crumbs could be sold off in a special offering to the regular schmucks."

Burroughs smelled a kill. His senses were heightened, and his imagination was speeding out of control. He wanted admission to the Board of Directors in the worst way, for it meant the ultimate corporate seal of approval. He wanted the privilege it afforded, including the potential for significant monetary gain. He wanted it all very badly, and Jim Ogden was his ticket.

"What are the odds, Jim?"

"Of what?"

"Of all of this happening, just like you've been saying."

"Well," Ogden mused, "let's break it down. I'd have to say that my being promoted to Executive Vice President is easily a ninety-nine point-nine percent probability, maybe even a few decimal places higher; on my being able to stack the regional-manager slots with at least six of my own people, ninety-six percent; on the old lady selling out and going on a world tour, ninety-five percent; on my being able to get you on the ballot for nomination to the Board next April if the old lady does leave, ninety percent."

Burroughs liked what he heard. "Those are high enough odds to make it all a reasonably sure bet."

It would be simple enough to get Burroughs nominated and on the ballot, Ogden knew. But getting him *elected* would be an altogether different matter. Burroughs was hardly revered by Elerbee's engineers, and in some quarters he was downright despised. Ogden quickly calculated that Burroughs' realistic chances of being elected to the Board were less than twenty percent, if even that high. The thought amused Ogden, and he decided then and there that he would save himself the embarrassment of placing Burroughs' name in nomination simply by firing him at the first available opportunity.

Ogden smiled. "Yep, that's exactly the way I see it, my man."

Burroughs was plainly ecstatic. They each laughed, and then executed a front-seat high-five.

It was dusk when the Boeing 757 touched down at Washington's Reagan National Airport. Ogden walked through the terminal, bag and briefcase in hand, and weaved his way to the exit doors. He twisted awkwardly to get a glimpse at his watch. It was a little past six.

His business in the morning would take him into Baltimore. First, however, there was a matter to be handled in Alexandria.

The glass doors opened and Ogden walked out into the sticky evening heat. He wore the blue jacket over a red knit shirt, with faded jeans and white sneakers. He glanced around the outside, declining a taxi ride and stepping out into the street. When he heard the sudden beep of a car horn, Ogden turned to see a copper-colored Nissan 350Z. He walked toward it, almost stepping directly into the path of another vehicle whose driver braked suddenly and gestured at Ogden. The driver of the Nissan got out and opened the back. Ogden tossed his belongings inside, and then climbed in on the passenger side.

"I've missed you, Claire," he said as he leaned across and kissed her moist, painted lips.

"I've missed you, too," she replied.

They kissed again, more deeply. A horn sounded from directly behind them. A passing patrolman called out, "Move it, people."

"Take me to Alexandria and screw me to death," he said in a low voice.

She smiled. Claire Boyette was a former administrative assistant at Elerbee Engineering's Baltimore Branch, and a longtime acquaintance of Jim Ogden. Their romantic past had been instrumental in nearly cracking Ogden's otherwise model marriage, and for a time they had even considered marriage for themselves. But Claire's new career in commercial real estate had suddenly taken off, thus making her reluctant to follow Ogden to Atlanta. They still saw one another no less than once every couple of months, since Ogden managed his schedule to the point that trips to the Baltimore Branch often became "necessary."

Claire dropped the sporty car into low gear and lurched away from the terminal area. "So tell me how you've been," she said after she had cleared the airport area.

"I've been great. How was your week?"

"Not enough hours in the day, Jimbo."

She wore white shorts and a red blouse that was only nominally buttoned. She was tall, in her mid-thirties, richly tanned, and full-featured in every sense. Her hair was reddish-brown and curly, long enough to fall over her shoulders. When she leaned forward to shift, Ogden could look across and see her left breast almost in its entirety.

He ran his hand along her smooth, bare leg. "Pull off the road," he said gruffly. "I can't wait."

Claire laughed and moved his hand away. "You'll have to wait, big boy."

"Aaaahhhh," he said, tilting the seat back and relaxing with his hands behind his head. "This is gonna be the start of something good."

CHAPTER SEVENTEEN

It was officially designated the Management Development Seminar. The brainchild of the late Langdon Elerbee, its purpose was to identify young managers of exceptional promise and bring them to the Atlanta headquarters for what amounted to a week-long Elerbee Engineering finishing school. The course was conducted only once a year, and the group size was typically small—twenty or so individuals selected by branch or other senior managers and representing the talent pool from which Elerbee would likely fill the future management needs of the firm. It was a fast-paced learning experience for the young executives, and it also provided the senior management with a names-and-faces recognition of the fast-trackers in the ranks.

The week started with an overview from Jeff Wylie, and proceeded through a series of detailed sessions with the heads of human resources, finance, engineering, quality, marketing, and data processing. The students were taught everything from financial-statement analysis to the handling of sexual-harassment complaints. In addition to the sometimes overwhelming scope and pace of the sessions, the students were exposed in no small way to the operating philosophies and the corporate culture of Elerbee Engineering. The net result at the end of the session would presumably be a more informed and more deeply committed group of individuals when they left to go back to their places in the Elerbee structure. Too, the seminar was in many ways a badge of distinction, and the competition for selection was always keen.

The session's final day was reserved for the traditional group photo, an award-of-completion certificate, lunch with Jeff Wylie, and a question-and-answer opportunity with the three regional vice presidents.

The luncheon with Wylie was over by early afternoon.

Ogden, Paige, and Collier were seated together at a cafeteria table to the front of the twenty students, who were seated in two rows of chairs. Don Burroughs, who usually made the arrangements and coordinated the activities, was also present at the front with the regional executives. The format was open, and the students could ask questions of whomever they pleased. Burroughs presided, and the regional vice presidents were free to add follow-on comments to the answers of their colleagues. The students were encouraged to use the opportunity to tap into the collective wisdom of the three senior managers.

And tap they did.

Student: "I'd like to ask Jim Ogden if he thinks the business climate will start picking up anytime soon."

Ogden: "I would think that by early fall, the worst will be over. There are lots of encouraging signs that business activity is picking up."

Collier: "Maybe by mid-to-late fall."

Paige: "The economy's plenty resilient, but there are some structural changes underway. And some of the problems are deeper than what we've seen in the past. The airlines are bleeding cash, and the public still isn't traveling at the pre-September 11 levels. There's an unhealthy level of suspicion about business people and their ethics that seems to me to be at a higher-than-normal scale. The U.S. economy is and will be influenced by the economies of China and India, and the huge amounts of capital flowing there. We're still not certain what the E.U. effects will be, and we're going to be fighting this war against the terrorists for a long time, I think. Having said all of that, and the uncertainty that clearly exists, I believe the business climate will improve significantly over the next two quarters. Inventories are under control and productivity remains high. There's little inflation. Many of the signs are good, so I think we'll see some improvements."

Student: "For Larry Collier—Will the management structure change dramatically because of Mr. Elerbee's death?"

Collier, grinning: "I certainly hope not. The people you've seen and heard from this week will still be running this company in one form or another. If there are dramatic changes ahead, I can only hope they're for the better, although I'm not aware of the specifics of any particular dramatic change."

Ogden: "That's right. What you've seen is what you'll get, in a manner of speaking. There's plenty of experience in place, and the changes will be more of a tweaking. Jeff may shift some things around, but I seriously doubt that anything major will result. Why screw with a winning formula, right?"

Paige: "I have nothing to add."

Student: "I'd like to address this question to Dave Paige—Dave, how did you manage to turn around the Central Division so quickly?"

Paige: "Multi-vitamins and black coffee (laughter). It was largely the basic stuff—finding new clients, keeping the old ones happy, and changing the entire mind-set of the Elerbee Engineering people who were running the branches and engineering the projects. And that usually takes time, so to turn things in a hurry we had to have everybody understanding exactly what's needed, what their role was in relation to that bigger whole, and then doing everything with a sense of almost warlike emergency. And if anyone showed any hesitation or lack of grasp of what we were trying to do, then we found them another role. And of course, if it involved a lack of commitment, then I'm sure you know what happens there. You start with a plan, then you staff to it, measure the results and give constructive feedback, and by all means stay close to the client and give him the best top-to-bottom performance that can be found anywhere. A consistency eventually develops where people expect to achieve winning results as a matter of course. And the client sees that consistency, as well. When you have all of that come together, then you've got the right ingredients. But once you have all that in place, you're not finished; you're merely ready to begin. You have to make darn sure you know your business, how it changes, how you must anticipate and adjust. Otherwise, you'll simply be driving a well-oiled machine off a tall cliff. (Pausing) I hope that answers your question."

Same student, nodding: "It does. Thanks."

Student: "I'd like to follow-up on Dave Paige's comment that the problems in the economy are deeper than in the past. Could you elaborate, Dave?"

Paige, after a brief pause: "It seems to me that America's ability to compete on a worldwide basis has been seriously undermined with a lot of problems that are essentially of our own making. We've got problems with education; with imbalances in many companies between what management people are paid and what value they actually contribute to the organization; with the perception even among our own people that the quality of some of our goods is inferior. We're going to put a giant strain on the social security and healthcare systems as the Boomers retire, which isn't being addressed by our political leaders. There have been some knocks on the work ethic of the American worker, but in my judgment that work-ethic thing may be more a reflection of rotten management than anything else. Things aren't so gloomy that they can't be corrected, and I firmly believe that our bigger ailments will be reversed, but it's going to carry a price tag with it. And that price may be painful before we're out of the ditch and back up on the road. (A pause and a grin.) We'll get there, and what's more we'll be counting on many of you to stay the course once it's set. You good people and others like you are going to play a big role in the turnaround. So please understand that although the problems are big and difficult and complex, our history as a nation suggests to me that we'll eventually wake up and get off our asses and do something about it. And in the end, I foresee a far greater requirement for individual responsibility on the part of business and political leaders. But that will be resisted, I'm quite sure, until voters and stockholders finally get a belly full and insist on a more demanding standard. Then we'll see things change for the better."

Collier: "I agree with Dave wholeheartedly, and I'll be watching this group with interest in the coming years."

Paige smiles and turns to Collier: "From the banks of the fishing pond, that is."

(Laughter.)

Student: "Larry, what's the biggest change you've observed in Elerbee Engineering in the past ten years?"

Collier: "The growth, no question. A technology-driven company like ours has to grow to remain vital, but growth like we've experienced puts a strain on all the resources, especially human. Elerbee Engineering outgrew its small-company persona, out of necessity, certainly, but some of the old hands like me miss the ways things were way back in the Stone Age."

(Laughter.)

Student: "Question for Jim Ogden—Are any specific companies or technologies being examined for possible addition to our current mix?"

Ogden: "None at the moment, but we're always keeping our eyes and minds open."

Student: "Dave, how far out is the planning you do for your division?"

Paige: "Generally in the range of twelve-to-eighteen months, in some cases up to two years. I have a five-year forecast that I guide upon, but the more detailed stuff comes in the closer-term range."

Same student: "So does that mean the longer term, strategic planning is done by Jeff Wylie? And if so, how far out?"

Paige: "That's right. Jeff handles the long-term planning, in the two-to-five year range, sometimes longer."

Ogden: "Jeff's amazingly good at strategic planning, I might add. He's one of the best strategists alive. He didn't get to his level without being able to plot a course for the future and then mobilizing the resources of the company to get there. I'm certain that he's spending a lot of time plotting our new course, even as we speak."

Ogden glanced quickly at Paige, who grinned slightly and said nothing.

Student: "Jim, what qualities will managers in this new decade need to have to be successful?"

Ogden: "Good technical knowledge of their industry, good understanding of financial principles. Hell, you just may need to be part engineer, part accountant, part lawyer, and part politician. And you have to be willing to do whatever it takes to be successful. It's all about delivering results."

Collier: "Stay close to your clients."

Paige: "Managers create value for clients, and in so doing maintain or enhance the value of the firm to its stockholders. That part hasn't changed, and won't change. It's still much the same as Adam Smith described it: Human skill creates social wealth; social wealth in turn defines government's responsibility. But the separation's breaking down. Managers will be forced to spend more time and money educating and training. There will likely be more, not less, governmental regulation and taxation—potentially much more. Managers will still have to deal with uncertainty; with the challenge of allocating scarce resources; with the need to develop human beings. So the more things change, the more they stay the same. My advice to you is to never settle, never accept the status quo as inviolable. Keep pushing, stay hungry, and love what you do."

Student: "Is there any other area we should become proficient at?"

Ogden: "Apart from those we've mentioned, you mean?"

Student: "Yes."

Ogden: "I don't think so, no."

Collier: "No, I can't think of any other."

Paige (pausing): "I would suggest that personal and professional ethics be something you consider as a cornerstone, as critical to you as, say, your technical expertise. Business leadership is an honorable and noble profession, in spite of what many write and say about it these days. Sure, we in the business world have our share of scoundrels, no doubt, but the presence of unethical people is a condition of life and by no means limited to business. Be quick and unyielding about smoking out those of low integrity and shallow ethics and sending them packing. Be proud of who you are and what you do; be ethical in how you do it. Do it well; do it right. You're a credit to this firm, and we're all counting on you."

Their time expired, and after a round of applause from the students, the session was ended so that the late-afternoon flights could be met. Everyone agreed that more time for questions should be scheduled in future sessions.

Paige sat facing Jeff Wylie in the latter's office. Wylie's expression was hard and unbending, and he stared across the desk at Paige as if he were an errant schoolboy.

"I've got it on good authority that you're planning some sort of insurrection at the Board meeting. Something about your making a play with the other Board members to unseat me as being unfit to serve, and dragging Jim into it as my accomplice. Is that essentially correct?"

"I don't know what you're referring to when you use a term like 'insurrection.' Could you explain?"

"You know good and damn well what I mean. Don't play word games with me, goddammit."

Paige nodded. "I understand all but the 'insurrection' part. It has a grimy, third-world, revolutionary connotation to it and I'm having a hard time applying it to an American corporate board meeting of well-paid, mature, middle-aged adults."

Wylie took a long, deep breath and regained his composure. "Do you or do you not have an agenda that's outside the normal Board proceedings?"

"No more so than you yourself, Jeff," Paige answered quickly.

"I would like a simple yes-or-no answer, please: Do you have a plan whose results will interfere with the normal functioning of the Board when it meets in New Orleans?"

Paige hesitated a moment before answering, "Anything that happens between me and the rest of the Board in New Orleans will be done to enhance its normal functioning, not interfere with it."

Wylie shook his head with obvious displeasure. "That's not what I'm looking for, dammit."

"I really have nothing further to say, Jeff."

"Then do you have anything to say about your meetings with the Becker people?"

Paige winced slightly and swallowed. "Nope, nothing there, either."

"Or about Diane Tresvant?"

"What about Diane Tresvant?" Paige asked after a short pause.

Wylie sensed a direct hit. "You've been seeing her?"

"So what if I have? That's certainly none of your business, and I suggest you leave Diane Tresvant out of this."

"She's a consultant engaged by this firm to perform a service—a very expensive service, I might add. Issues of fraternization between the project leader and the project consultant cause me serious concern. So, no, I will not leave her out of this."

Paige's eyes narrowed. "You know damn well that any contact I've had with Diane outside this office has had absolutely no bearing on her or anyone else's project activities."

"Is her boss aware of this, uh, romantic interlude?"

"I have no idea *what* her boss is aware of, and I don't especially care for your description. If you think that because I've seen her a few times outside the office that we're romantically involved, then you're—"

"Then I'm what?"

Paige took a deep breath and fought back the almost overpowering urge to lash out at Wylie.

Wylie straightened and leaned toward Paige. "I intend to telephone her boss, Dick Deluca, who incidentally is an old friend, and have her immediately re-assigned. In view of the circumstances, that's the most reasonable course I can come up with. I'm certain he'll go along with it once I give him my reasons. And if that were to have any negative implications on her career with the firm, well, it is what it is."

"That's unnecessary. It would be petty and vindictive on your part, and besides, it would be counterproductive to the project. I'm surprised you'd even contemplate something like that."

Wiley took a deep breath, looking away for a moment. "Well, the fact is that she's apparently too tempting."

"She's a damned good project manager, that's what she is. And she's done nothing to deserve being taken off the project. I resent the hell out of the fact that you're suggesting otherwise. Besides," Paige said, pausing and staring hard at Wylie, "it's not like I'm taking advantage of a company employee. Diane is not an employee, so there's no direct reporting relationship, and thus no fraternization issue here. I trust that you can see that distinction."

Wylie stared back at Paige, then finally smiled and leaned back with his hands folded across his lap. "So what would you suggest?"

"I would strongly suggest you stay out of this. It's my project; leave it to me."

"I will not stay out of this matter. It has important implications for this firm."

"Then wait until after New Orleans," Paige said after a quick deliberation. "Let's see what happens there. Things could change to the point that nothing further would be needed."

Wylie gave a confused look. "Change? How?"

"Oh come on, Jeff. You know things will change within our organization. I'm sure things will be a great deal different when we get back. After all, I might not have the same responsibilities."

Wylie frowned. "No dice. She still has to go, regardless."

"She does *not* have to go. And I won't stand idly by and let you get away with making a big mistake here."

Wylie sniffed and glanced to the side, out the window. "Of course, if you were to end up after New Orleans reporting to Jim Ogden, then I—"

"I'll never work for Jim Ogden," Paige snapped.

"I see," Wylie said, measuring his words. "Then I take that to mean you'd resign if things didn't work out for you as planned."

Paige grinned slightly "So what are the terms, Jeff?"

"Terms?"

"The terms of the deal you're ready to strike."

"I've made no mention of any deal."

"Let's make the deal and be done with it. Let me hear your terms."

They stared at one another briefly.

"All right. I see it shaping up something like this," Wylie said after sniffing and glancing at his fingernails. "If you end up reporting to Jim after the New Orleans meeting, then you promptly resign. In exchange, I leave Diane Tresvant on the project and make no mention of the previous matter to anyone, as if nothing ever happened."

"Agreed. But in the event that things were to somehow turn out differently in New Orleans, then it's my call."

Wylie smiled contemptuously. "Let's concentrate on our original scenario, shall we. However, if things did happen to turn out differently, then I'll agree to leave it up to you how you'd want to handle it as long as one important condition is fully met."

"Which is?"

"As long as your behavior at the Board meeting is constructive and not out of order."

Paige stood. He drew a deep breath, exhaled slowly, and finally said, nodding, "It's a deal," before turning and walking out of Wylie's office.

CHAPTER EIGHTEEN

"Is he traveling this week?" Ogden asked.

Wylie frowned. "No, of all weeks. I'd sure as hell like to have him out of here so I can circulate with the Board members on a little more 'intimate' terms."

"Any place you can send him?"

"Like where?"

"I don't know. Anywhere."

"He's gone most of the time, as it is. There's hardly a place I could send him that he hasn't recently been."

"But you're right. It would be good to have him out of the office this week."

The phone rang.

Wylie motioned to Ogden to remain seated after the latter had stood and prepared to leave. Ogden could tell from Wylie's raised voice that the caller was outside the country. And when Wylie offered, "Good to hear from you, Trevor," Ogden knew immediately that the party on the other end was Trevor Mansfield, a British architect/engineer with whom Elerbee Engineering had previously collaborated on several joint-venture projects in Asia-Pacific and the Middle East.

Ogden listened.

"Thanks for returning my call, Trevor ... Yes, it's about the project we spoke about last week ... We'd certainly like to have a part in helping with the proposal preparation ... I'm sure arrangements could be made for someone from my staff to attend ... In London, you say? ... On Thursday and Friday? ... Of this week? ... It's a bit sudden, but I don't see that as a problem, not at all."

Wylie glanced at Ogden and winked.

"You've met Dave Paige, Trevor. Right? ... Splendid. I'll have Dave contact you directly about the necessary background for the meeting ... That's right. You book him a room over there and we'll arrange for everything else on this end ... So, today's Monday; he can leave tomorrow night and be over there Wednesday morning; use Wednesday to recover and be ready to meet Thursday and Friday. Does that sound workable? ... Excellent. Might I suggest that you use Saturday to perhaps show Dave the city, and he could then schedule his return on Sunday ... Sounds good, Trevor. I can't tell you how good it is to hear from you. ... Brilliant. Dave will be in touch soon. Cheerio."

Wylie hung up the phone.

"Is this our lucky friggin' day, or what?" said Ogden.

"It would seem so, yes."

"What's up?"

"Trevor's chasing a shopping-complex project in Kuwait. I asked him to let us help develop the soils part of the proposal."

"Paige's not gonna know anything about that partnership."

"So? He can learn, can't he? Now's as good a time as any to give him a little more international experience."

Ogden shook his head in amazement. "London, for crissakes. What a well-timed break."

Wylie nodded. "Almost as if it were preordained to happen that way."

There was only a short pause before both men erupted in laughter.

CHAPTER NINETEEN

Dave Paige leaned to his left and glanced outside the aircraft's window. Below was the southeastern tip of England, with the reddish-brown of the coast, the green inland, and the shimmering blue-gray of the English Channel. He glanced at his watch. It was eight o'clock in the morning London time, but after having spent most of the past eight hours sleepless in his aisle seat, his body clock was still languishing five hours behind.

Thank you, Jeff Wylie, he thought as the Boeing-767 jet banked sharply on its approach into Gatwick International. Thank you for all you do for me, including the chance to leave the new world and see the old one.

Under the present circumstances, especially.

Beside him was daughter Sara, who was covered with a blanket and only semi-comfortably wedged between her seat and the bulkhead. Sara had chosen to sleep through breakfast, but Paige had kept a croissant and glass of orange juice waiting for her on his tray. She soon stirred out of a deep sleep, groggy and stuffy, as she sat up and yawned and then ran her hand over her unruly hair. Her eyes were puffy and bloodshot as she glanced first at her father, then out the window. "We're here," she said in a raspy voice. "Look down there, Dad. There's someplace really green. Is that England?"

"That's it, sweets. Better hurry with the food and drink. We're not far from landing."

It had worked out well, Paige thought. Sara had been able to leave Pittsburgh on short notice, fly to Atlanta, and join him for the trip across the ocean. Overseas travel would undoubtedly benefit her, he thought. Deepen her appreciation. Broaden her horizons. Extend her awareness of the world's rich diversity. She would be the better for it, no question. And besides, it would give them quality time together. There was at least some consolation in knowing that one of the two traveling Paiges would benefit from the trip. Damn Jeff Wylie, he thought again. Damn him!

Trevor Mansfield's office was located in Hatfield, a suburb twenty miles to the north of London. Trevor had selected a quaint inn in nearby Hertford in which to house his guests and hold his meeting. It was an old two-story structure, and the upstairs conference room was small and confining, with creaky floors, metal folding chairs, and open windows to assist in ventilation.

Otherwise it was a peaceful, pastoral setting. There were hardwood trees and a lovely flower garden, and the busy chirping of the birds was rarely obscured by a passing motor vehicle. Sara was staying at Trevor Mansfield's home in Hatfield, in the company of Trevor's wife Jean and their seventeen-year-old daughter, Jennifer. The ladies would keep busy on their own with shopping, touring local points of interest, and dining out, while the guys carried on with their business.

The next morning and afternoon Dave Paige sat in a stuffy room with a Frenchman, two Englishmen, and a Kuwaiti. On the other side of the Atlantic, however, Jeff Wylie was busily counseling the inside members of the Elerbee Board of Directors on exactly what, in Wylie's considered opinion, would constitute a productive Board meeting.

It was Thursday.

The Frenchman, Claude, who spoke decent English, reviewed with the others the scope of the project, and referred to the maps and charts he had brought along attached to an easel. The two Brits, Trevor and his associate, John, tended to dominate much of the discussion with their questions, elaborations, and humor. The Kuwaiti, who was referred to as Ahmad, was actually the client in this case, and to whom Claude and the two Brits were exceedingly deferential. Ahmad spoke excellent English, but he said little and made copious notes in a spiral notebook, chain-smoking his way through the presentations.

As the discussions dragged on through the day, Paige felt out of place and useless. He couldn't imagine why Claude or Trevor would want to involve Elerbee Engineering when a dozen or more European firms could surely be engaged far more economically and pragmatically. What Paige didn't know was that Trevor had suddenly concluded that he had no intention of working for either the French firm, for whom he had little regard, or the Kuwaiti developer, whom he considered unreliable. He now intended only to go through the motions of showing a proper professional interest.

By Friday, Paige had had enough. At one point in the morning session there was a brisk discussion taking place between Claude and Trevor's assistant when Paige suddenly raised his hand and silenced the room.

"Trevor, I've got to confess that I find myself totally without conviction for this project, and therefore I suggest that I leave it to you gents to finish hashing it out," Paige said, rising to his feet. "Forgive my boorishness, but I believe the best thing for me to do would be to take my leave and let you all get on with it."

"Does that mean we should look for another soils engineer?" asked Claude, seated beside Ahmad.

"Yes," Paige answered. "No hard feelings, I hope, but you'd be much better off to hire a firm who can set up shop on the job site. The logistics burden would be greatly eased, and I'm sure that'd be reflected in the overall cost of the project."

Claude nodded but said nothing further.

With that Paige gathered his briefcase and started out the door. Ahmad quickly stood, extended his hand to Paige, and spoke in perfect English, "Maybe we can do business at some future time, Mr. Paige."

After staring for a moment at Ahmad's smiling face, Paige smiled in return and responded, "Yes, maybe so."

Paige then nodded to the others and left.

Trevor followed Paige out the door and escorted him to a nearby lobby. "I hope it's nothing I said," Trevor remarked with a grin.

"No, Trevor," Paige said, also grinning. "The problem's not with you. It's just not a good project for Elerbee Engineering, that's all."

Trevor gave a resigned sigh. "And you had to come all the way across the bloody pond to find that out."

Paige chuckled. "Funny, but those are my exact sentiments."

"You must be a bit of a thorn to someone, ole boy," Trevor said with a slight grin. "Somebody must've decided that they'd be better off with you in the U.K. doing nothing than back in the States doing *something*. That about it, mate?"

"I'd say that's pretty darn close, Trevor."

"And that somebody wouldn't have the initials of J.W., now, would they?"

Paige laughed but offered no response.

Trevor shrugged. "Right. So what now?"

"Are we still on for touring London tomorrow?"

"Absolutely." Trevor edged a step closer to Paige. "If you'll stick around for an hour, I'll be rid of the lot of 'em and we can jump in my car and find a spot for some good English beer."

Paige grinned and nodded. "I'm game."

"Brilliant," Trevor answered, holding up one finger. "Give me one hour and I'll ring you in your room."

Paige went back to his nearby room and sprawled out on the bed. It was clear what Jeff Wylie was doing, had been all along. And while he had seriously considered leaving immediately to return home, he had eventually concluded that there was little consequence in remaining in the U.K. for the additional day. Besides, he wanted Sara to see London, and the opportunity to have a pair of knowledgeable tour guides in Trevor and Jean was an additional benefit. So he would stay over and dine with Trevor and the ladies, then spend the next day touring London. And on Sunday he and Sara would get on a plane and return home, just as Jeff Wylie had orchestrated it.

On Monday, he grimly determined, he would fight the jet lag and do some serious orchestrating of his own.

CHAPTER TWENTY

"Good morning, Atlanta. It's Monday, it's six-thirty, and it's gonna be a beautiful day. Temperatures are expected in the high eighties today, with no rain in the forecast. The freeways are moving nicely, and no major delays are being reported. Here's one to get things rolling this morning, called *City of New Orleans* . . ."

It was a busy morning at Elerbee Engineering.

The members of the Board of Directors were scheduled to convene in New Orleans on the following day. Afterwards, the branch managers and other corporate officials would gather for the company's leadership meeting that would take place on Wednesday, Thursday, and Friday morning. The agenda called for general sessions at the beginning and end of each day, with several smaller, more specialized meetings in between. Wives were invited, and the meeting schedule was liberalized to allow for ample free time to enjoy New Orleans. A party on Wednesday night and a formal dinner on Thursday night would highlight the affair.

Larry Collier's retirement would commence on Wednesday, after the Board meeting, although he and Dot planned to remain in New Orleans for one last Elerbee-sponsored fling.

Collier, meanwhile, along with Wylie, Ogden, Paige, and other key executives on Wylie's staff, sat in the Atlanta headquarters conference room and studied the financial statements that represented the month just concluded as well as the first six-months of the year. The company's fees had dipped below quota in June, the first such reversal in nine months. The year-to-date results were nevertheless satisfactory—102% of plan—but the momentum of the previous months had been halted. Ogden's Eastern Region had encountered a sudden softness in its billings and had thus retarded the progress of the entire company. Paige's Central and Collier's Western Regions had exceeded their respective quotas, though only barely. Profits were also below plan in roughly the same proportion as fees.

Clearly, Ogden had not anticipated such a development. He appeared confused and distracted as Wylie summarized the results. Something was dreadfully wrong, and Ogden's face showed it.

"We've got some work to do, admittedly," Wylie said, glancing at the managers seated around the big conference table. "But a hundred and two percent of quota year-to-date is nothing to scoff at. The results are following on down to the bottom line, and our return-on-investment is just about where it ought to be. So I'd have to conclude that, despite a bad June, we're still on schedule."

More to the point, a bad June in Ogden's Eastern Region, Paige thought to himself as he looked across the table and noticed Ogden's escalating discomfort.

"Gentlemen, if there are no further questions, then I need a few minutes with Larry, Jim, and Dave," Wylie said, dismissing the others.

The door was closed. Wylie removed his glasses and sat back in his chair. He rubbed his eyes, drew a deep breath, then sat up straight.

"I won't keep you long, gentlemen, but I do want to make a few comments before we meet again in New Orleans," Wylie said as he stroked his chin and fidgeted with some papers to his front. "You three no doubt understand that firms sometimes make decisions of such importance that they have to be supported and accepted by the key members of that firm, whatever one's personal feelings may or may not reflect. There will be those types of decisions made this week, decisions that will affect each of you in this room, including myself. Larry, you'll be affected to the extent that you'll be involved *in* the decisions, whereas Dave and Jim will be involved in and be affected *by* those same decisions. And I can assure you that the entire process will be done with great care, with a sense of propriety, because the results will be widespread. There will be those who will be satisfied and those who will be disappointed. But no matter the degree of either, the top management of this firm *must* be in accord once things have taken their final shape. There just isn't any room at the top for discord, and I will not tolerate any. Not for a minute."

Wylie paused and stared at Paige for a moment, then cleared his throat and once more began shuffling the papers to his front. "I wish each of you the best of luck, and I'm counting on and expecting your continued support."

Wylie stood, and the others immediately followed.

"See you in New Orleans, gentlemen."

"I want a transfer," Sherry said, studying the stoic but seriously jet-lagged Paige. She touched the eraser of a pencil to her lips and cocked her head slightly to the side.

Paige didn't bother looking up from his laptop where he was reviewing his presentation to the branch managers. "And just where is it you'd like to be transferred?"

"I want to work for the Executive Vice President."

Paige glanced up. "Fine with me, but you'll probably need to get Jim Ogden's final approval."

There was an instant smirk on her face. "There won't be any need to ask Jim Ogden diddly squat. My money's on you."

"Oh yeah?"

"Yeah. Jim's history."

"How so?"

"I just know, that's all."

"Exactly what is it you profess to know, my dear Sherry?"

She grinned. "I know that you've somehow found a way."

Paige's eyebrows raised. "Oh you do, do you?"

"I do indeed."

"And you're ready to take that to the bank?"

"Imminently ready."

Paige laughed. "We've really not sat down and discussed what the impact may be on our respective careers if New Orleans turns out to be a bust, have we?"

"There's no need. I know you've found a way. We're both safe and sound, good to go."

Paige gave a yawn and a loud sigh. "May I ask again how you profess to know all of this?"

"You certainly may, but I won't answer." She leaned forward slightly and said in an animated British accent, "I've got me reasons, ya' know."

Paige smiled slightly, then coughed and sat up straight, looking serious. "Okay then, Ms. Painter. If it so happens that I do indeed move elsewhere in this building, then I'll be happy to accept your application for a position on my staff."

Sherry stiffened, eyebrows raised. "Mr. Paige, if you do indeed relocate elsewhere on this floor," she said formally, nodding in the direction of the empty office down the hall, "then I will damn well expect you to take more than my *application* with you."

"You're on," Paige said, grinning boyishly. "I move, you move."

"Good," she said, mostly satisfied. "We can discuss the matter of my increased compensation at a more opportune time."

"There was a huge error on the first run of the financial statements, Dave," explained Paige's assistant, Mortensen. "Jim's guy Ezell somehow forgot to tell him, and when the error was corrected on the next run, the Eastern fees were only ninety-two percent of quota instead of the one hundred and one percent figure from the first run. My God, what a fiasco."

"What happened?"

"All I know is there was some confusion in accounting about two journal entries, that they were keyed wrong, and it affected the Miami and the Cleveland fees. Jim must've relied solely on the first-run data—the screwed-up numbers—because when he came out of the meeting with you guys this morning, he was so bent out of shape that he called Ezell in and fired him on the spot. His door was closed, but a couple of guys who walked by said they could hear Jim screaming at Ezell at the top of his lungs. Ezell's face was really pale when he came out of Jim's office, like he'd just witnessed a plane crash or something. It was awful, Dave."

"That's unfortunate," Paige offered, nearly biting off the tip of his tongue.

"Yeah, it really is. The dude was really trying hard."

"Is he any good, this guy Ezell?"

"He's outstanding. It was just an honest mistake, that's all. It could've happened to anybody."

Paige waited until the stunned Mortensen had left his office before giving in to a wellspring of laughter. He later instructed Sherry to telephone Ezell at home and suggest that he contact Paige after the New Orleans meeting.

Sherry smiled. "I *knew* it!"

It was almost noon. Paige opened his *Laws of Business* and reached for a pen.

> *Corporations are created to serve customers, as per Drucker, and are owned by a multiplicity of owners, in some cases much like a passbook savings account. They are, in the broadest of senses, profitable or not profitable, which predominates in the setting of value to outsiders.*

*Unlike passbook savings accounts, corporations are measured by insiders in ways other than profitability; such yardsticks include loyalty, morality, culture, and ethics.

*Don't ever give up; don't ever give up; don't ever, ever, ever give up. The other guy just might fumble on his own goal line.

He closed the book, and then left the office and proceeded out of the building. He walked across the street to Macy's where he purchased a 4-ounce bottle of expensive French perfume, a pair of gold earrings in the form of seashells, and an attractive, peach-colored maillot that he felt certain would be the perfect fit. He then found a humorous card and wrote to Diane Tresvant that he looked forward to being with her again, and included an invitation for her to join him for a Florida vacation after the New Orleans meeting (adding parenthetically that an airline ticket would soon follow). After he had the items boxed and wrapped for shipment, he took the package back to the office and had Sherry send it to Diane's office via courier, along with another package of work-related systems documentation that Paige had seen fit to withhold for several days.

Larry Collier dropped in on Paige during the late afternoon. They spoke fondly of the old days of the firm, and several of its previous characters of infamy. They laughed plentifully and easily, although Paige couldn't help but notice that Collier was bothered by something.

"When are you leaving for New Orleans?" Paige asked after the reminiscing.

"Tomorrow morning, early. What about you?"

"Later tonight."

Collier glanced quickly at the doorway to make sure they weren't being overheard. "Wylie's been using a helluva lot of behind-the-scenes leverage to get his boy Ogden approved. He really took advantage of your being out of the country."

Paige smiled but remained silent.

"Some of the company insiders on the Board are scared shitless that if they vote for you, they'll have to answer to Wylie at some point. The outsiders aren't a hell of a lot more independent, either. If it wasn't such a highly politicized atmosphere, I'm not sure but what you wouldn't be approved hands-down, like you were the first goddamn time. As it is, though, nearly everybody will be voting with an eye toward Wylie. It's enough to make me sick, I swear to God."

Still, Paige said nothing.

"Maybe Grace Elerbee will have some influence on things. If she asserts herself, then the others will follow like so many sheep. I plan on having a talk with her, anyway."

"It'll work out," Paige said confidently.

Collier nodded slowly, thoughtfully, as he stared across the desk at Paige. "There are rumors, you know."

Paige grinned slightly. "Is that a fact?"

"It certainly is, my friend. I swear there's a clear majority on the Board who much prefer you, who'd follow you in a heartbeat if they thought you'd survive."

"Real troopers, aren't they?"

Collier smiled.

Paige took a deep breath. He yawned and scratched his head, then his chin, then sat up in his chair. "Just hang in there with me, Larry. That's all I can ask for now."

A moment of silence settled over them.

"You got it, pal," Collier said, nodding.

Paige grinned and winked.

"I just hope the light at the end of the tunnel isn't really the exhaust of an approaching Scud missile," said Collier.

Paige shook with laughter but otherwise said nothing.

"I still care about this firm, dammit, even though I won't be a regular for much longer. I think it's terribly important that Elerbee Engineering stay above this corporate-incest thing, and let the best possible people rise to the top. Otherwise, we won't be able to keep anybody who's not in The Club. And these goddamned cliques have a way of fostering a lot of incompetence once the infrastructure's been built. Anyway, I plan on having my full say about it in New Orleans, for sure." Collier smiled. "After all, what the hell can they do? Retire me?"

Paige's eyes twinkled. "I'm grateful to you for being my friend," he said with obvious emotion. "And I'm thankful for how you've made my life better."

They both stood. Collier smiled graciously, then reached over and slapped Paige on the shoulder.

"Keep the faith, Dave, no matter what happens."

"I will, sir. And thanks again."

The end of the day was near. Paige had taken calls from several of his branch managers—mostly wishing him good luck in the upcoming Board meeting, and pledging their support whichever way things turned out. There had also been calls from his good friend Ted Haygood; from daughter Sara at Penn; from Diane Tresvant, who called in her best wishes from a client's office in Cleveland; and, finally, from Bob Becker, who said only, "Knock their dicks in the dirt, Dave, and give me a call when it's all said and done."

Paige glanced at his watch. It was nearly six. He was tired, yet he was on edge, alert and filled with great anticipation. Events such as this, he reasoned, would undoubtedly be stored forever in his brain's vivid-memory file. He thought of the past, all the way back to his engineering-student days—the trig and calculus courses; fluid dynamics; rock mechanics; the incessant labs; the Dean's List; the football games against Notre Dame. Then there was the Marine Corps. Then came Elerbee Engineering and a young engineer's excitement over the opportunity to finally close ranks with his chosen profession.

Paige smiled as the pleasant memories warmed him like a fine wine. He swiveled around in his chair and looked out the window, toward the southwest, in the direction of Louisiana.

It might very well be his time.

For certain, it wouldn't be much longer now. It would be decided within the next forty-eight hours, as if everything he had ever done in his life was suddenly about to be measured. And if found deserving, then reward would follow. But if found otherwise, well, there was always risk in life and love and business.

Yeah, right.

Whatever.

In any case, it would all happen soon.

He had not only remembered but heeded the advice of Paula Markham, the psychologist acquaintance who had advised him to conduct an objective assessment of his situation, prior to constructing his plan of action.

And he had done exactly that. While Sara had watched movies and read magazines on their return flight from London, Paige had made copious notes of his strengths and weaknesses and how those findings matched the opportunities and threats that now stood before him. He had agonized over the assessment, long and hard, just as Paula had so adamantly suggested, and he had validated much of what he already knew about himself. Most of the results were positive, encouraging, and reaffirming, but not all. He found he needed some additional personal growth, a level of maturity he should have acquired by now at this stage of his life, a key finding for which he knew he needed an improvement plan. He decided to review his assessment with Paula and seek her advice on how to proceed. When he had sent her an e-mail message and briefly outlined his assessment and his need for a specific area of improvement, he asked if she thought she could help.

Paula had returned his message within minutes with a short, terse, "CAN DO!" response.

First, however, would come New Orleans.

The Battle of New Orleans, he thought with amusement.

Victory or defeat.

Glory or humiliation.

A beginning or an end.

In any case, it was now time.

CHAPTER TWENTY ONE

Jim Ogden and Don Burroughs poured themselves some strong coffee, then proceeded to hash out a few final details in preparation for the Elerbee Board meeting scheduled to start the following morning. They had arrived in New Orleans that same evening, and had retired immediately to Ogden's suite in the Canal Street hotel that would also host the Elerbee contingent and several of the associated activities.

Ogden had shed his pinstriped suit in favor of jeans and t-shirt, while Burroughs remained in business attire. The hotel suite was spacious, and the glass doors permitted a scenic view of the river bridge and the Mighty Mississippi's legendary brown waters flowing beneath it. Burroughs' wife and Mary Ogden had earlier opted for a shopping foray into the nearby French Quarter. Nina, Ogden's girlfriend, had decided at the last minute to remain in Atlanta to photograph a wedding for the niece of a wealthy client.

Burroughs sat in a chair, notepad in hand, and faced Ogden who was shoeless and sprawled lengthwise on a couch, his head propped by a cushion.

Ogden leaned toward a nearby table took a sip of his hot coffee. "You're having dinner with Ed Webb and Vince Kincaid, right?"

"Right," Burroughs answered.

Ogden checked the two names off the list on his yellow legal pad. "Keep trying to get Ron Steinkempf in that group, too. He told me he would be in town this evening, so leave him a message at the desk. He needs to be in that group."

"Right. Who's in your group?"

"Marshall Wilkinson and John Brice, along with Jeff Wylie. I think Wilkinson and Brice are in the bag. If your three come our way, we're home free," Ogden said, slapping the pencil against the pad. "Hell, I think we're home free anyway, as long as Grace Elerbee does what she's supposed to do."

"Will she speak out against Paige?"

"You're damned right, she will. She's an Elerbee; she'll speak out."

Burroughs smiled. "That should put the finishing touches on the Dave Paige story, as we know it."

"Right on."

"She's that upset, huh?"

"When I made the comment to her at Collier's retirement party that I was afraid we were going lose Paige to the Becker organization, she puffed up and her eyes turned cold as steel, like a cobra. She asked me if he was talking to them, and when I said that yes, he most certainly was, she asked me what evidence I had. I told her that I had a contact at Becker—a guy in Philly I had gotten to know and trust when Becker was my client in Baltimore—who had called and asked if I wanted to be considered, and if I did, that I'd better hurry up. It seems that Bob Becker and Dave Paige were really hitting it off, getting to be real tight. I told her that I had declined, because the truth is I'd never go to work for Becker, that I'd rather get out of the business altogether than work for those people. Well, she didn't say a word, but she took one of those long, deep breaths like chicks take when they're on the verge of being out-of-control pissed. She didn't say anything, but I could see it in her eyes, man. It was all over but the shouting. From that moment on, I'll guarantee you that Dave Paige went to the very top of her shit list."

"Is that the way it actually happened, that the guy called you and told you about it?"

"Of course not. I called him and told him to dig out the goddamn story, no matter what. And that's what he did. It ended up costing me two field-level tickets to a Phillies-Mets game, that's all."

"She'd buy all of that without asking Paige directly?"

"On that subject alone, yes. She's got one blind spot: Anything involving the goddamned Beckers. Anything else, you're right, she goes straight to her boy Paige."

"Why so much animosity toward Becker?"

"Langdon Elerbee and Charles Becker, Bob's father, were the bitterest of enemies. It went way back, forty years or more. They fell out over a project when Elerbee was a young engineer with the State of Illinois, and Becker was a young building contractor. It was a state building, and there were problems with the work and the budget and the union and so forth, and those two went at it tooth and nail. It always amazed me how they could so detest one another, but allow their two firms to continue to work so closely over the years. Anyway, I'm sure the old bird thinks it would be unbearably disloyal for an Elerbee Engineering executive to seriously entertain an offer from the Becker camp, especially when that same executive was being considered for bigger and better things with our own firm."

"And when she goes to the Board meeting and speaks out against Paige, the rest won't dare cross her if they place any value on their employment," Burroughs observed.

Ogden smiled. "Exactly. They already know how Jeff feels. He's made no secret of the fact that he wants me in that position. So, it ought to be clear to everyone that if they support Paige, then they'd better be ready to fly with his raggedy ass right into the mountainside."

"Amazing," Burroughs said, grinning.

Ogden sat up and sipped his coffee. "This time tomorrow," he said, wiping his mouth with his hand, "I'm in the catbird seat and Dave Paige's history, along with his buddy, Larry Collier."

"Anybody still with Paige?"

"Collier, for sure, the old fool. Maybe Ralph Boudreaux. Ralph's such a simple bastard that he doesn't understand but maybe half of what goes on in the meetings. We'll get him off the Board in due time. One or two others are iffy, like Professor Alford and Ron Steinkempf."

"Any chance of anyone else defecting to Paige?"

Ogden grinned devilishly. "Very little, especially if they want to stay on the payroll."

"Amazing," Burroughs said again. "Simply amazing."

There was a knock on the door. Ogden got up and let Jeff Wylie into the room.

"Greetings, gentlemen."

Burroughs rose. "Good evening, Jeff."

Wylie was dressed in slacks and open dress shirt. He didn't bother to take a seat. "I assume the dinner arrangements are in place."

Ogden nodded. "Everything's all set."

"Any questions, Don?"

"No," Burroughs answered, shaking his head. "It's all covered."

"Perfect," Wylie said, smiling and turning toward the door. "And the champagne? I assume it's on ice."

Ogden laughed and slapped Wylie on the shoulder, then shot a quick glance at Burroughs. "Right, and as it happens, that's not the only thing on ice in New Orleans."

The three enjoyed an orgy of self-congratulatory laughter. Wylie finally turned toward the door.

"Well, let's get this thing moving, gents."

CHAPTER TWENTY TWO

Jeff Wylie stood at one end of the long table, referring to the array of charts and graphs placed on easels to either side of him. At the opposite end of the table sat Mrs. Langdon Elerbee, composed and unsmiling.

All twelve members of the Elerbee Engineering Board of Directors were present in New Orleans. Also in attendance was Stephen Caudill, the corporate Secretary, who was there to record the minutes. They were gathered in a private room on the mezzanine level of the large Canal Street hotel. Most had arrived the previous evening; a few others, Larry Collier included, had that same morning hurriedly summoned an airport taxi after an early morning flight from Atlanta.

The agenda was full.

The minutes of the April meeting were confirmed, ratified, and approved in the opening moments of the meeting.

Wylie then launched into his review, rattling off the numbers and the analyses with ease and confidence. Although the string of consecutive revenue increases had been broken in June, the year-to-date results were nonetheless impressive. The firm, Wylie stressed, was on sound footing. And the data largely supported him.

Dave Paige sat between Ed Webb and Vince Kincaid and directly across from Larry Collier. His mind began to wonder as he glanced around the room at the gathering of these successful colleagues. He could look across and see that Collier was already filling with emotion on this the last day of his working career. He watched as Collier sat up, cleared his throat, and reached for the bottle of water at his fingertips, his eyes misty from what Paige judged to be the flood of memories evoked by the faces and circumstances.

Vince Kincaid, Vice President-Finance, followed Wylie with a detailed report on the financial condition of the firm. Elerbee Engineering's basic conservatism in its financial practices yielded a balance sheet with few shortcomings. There was adequate cash flow, the receivables were collectible, and all the ratio measurements were favorable. Lines of credit were in place with major banks in Atlanta, New York, and Chicago. Idle funds were being invested wisely, with an eye toward liquidity. In short, the ongoing operations were generating a sufficient enough stream of capital to meet the near-term requirements at the projected rate of growth.

Next came Ed Webb, Vice President-Marketing, who made a largely unimaginative presentation concerning Elerbee's current market position. Webb concluded that Elerbee's stake in the marketplace was indeed strong.

Well no kidding, Paige thought to himself. Thanks for that, Ed.

Marshall Wilkinson, a top executive in a large Atlanta bank and Vice Chairman of the Board's Audit Committee, reported on the committee's meeting which had taken place at an earlier date. The Audit Committee had met with several representatives of the firm's outside auditors and produced a letter stating that there were no material weaknesses in any area, and that access to accounting records and documents had not been restricted in any way during the year-end audit process.

Questions by members of the Board were answered during these sessions, and a report containing the fee and profit data on each of the firm's branches was then distributed to each individual. When the meeting adjourned at noon, the Board members gathered in an adjacent room for lunch.

After lunch and a short break, the meeting continued.

Seated beside Jeff Wylie near the head of the table was a smartly dressed, mid-fortyish man with thick eyeglasses and a receding hairline. Two thick manila folders were stacked neatly to his front. He was erect and stocky, his nose flat, his brown eyes magnified behind the lenses. He nodded and smiled at those in the room with whom he made eye contact. He wore a dark pinstriped suit of high quality, with white shirt and red silk tie.

It struck many of the Board members as odd that a visitor would be introduced during the afternoon session, just prior to the all-important business of naming an Executive Vice President.

"Let's come to order," said Wylie, quieting the group.

Paige noticed the evident change in Wylie's expression, in his tone.

"We have quite a bit of unfinished business at hand, so we'll need to move on," said Wylie. "At this time, we're going to review with you an unpublished agenda item. And while it's unpublished, it's certainly not unimportant."

Wylie hesitated. He glanced at Mrs. Elerbee, at the far end of the table. The room was silent in its anticipation, as if a deep, solemn voice had suddenly broken in on a television show and announced, "We interrupt this program . . ."

Wylie cleared his throat nervously. "The gentleman to my left is Hilton Wynn. Mr. Wynn is an attorney, and he has some information that will be of interest to you. But before I turn the floor over to him, some background information is in order. Just a few weeks ago, I was approached in Atlanta by Mr. Wynn regarding his representation of a Mr. Peter Halloran, a Boston businessman. Mr. Wynn proceeded to advise me of his client's interest in acquiring sole ownership of Elerbee Engineering."

Wylie hesitated again. A collective astonishment swept over and around the table like an electrical current, though the quiet still prevailed.

"I informed Mr. Wynn that Elerbee Engineering was not for sale, nor had any consideration been given to a future change of ownership. Mr. Wynn informed me that, because of Mr. Halloran's deep interest in our firm, perhaps we'd be kind enough to at least meet with his client and hear his proposal."

"And," Wylie said, dropping his head, "that's what we eventually did."

Paige glanced around the table at the others. Only Grace Elerbee sat calmly, staring ahead at Wylie. Most of the others appeared confused, some pale even, as if they were on trial and awaiting a judge's sentence. Larry Collier's scorn was evident to all.

"In late June, just a few weeks ago, Mr. Halloran and Mr. Wynn met in Atlanta with Mrs. Elerbee and myself, along with our counsel, John Brice. As a result of that meeting," Wylie said, pausing suddenly as if he might be in danger of hyperventilating, "as a result of that meeting it is my duty to inform you that an agreement in principle has been reached for the sale of Elerbee Engineering to Halloran Investments, Incorporated, Boston, Massachusetts."

A perceptible buzzing was immediately released into the room, as if everyone had exhaled on cue. Several turned and looked in Mrs. Elerbee's direction, hoping for some sign, some assurance of her refusal to permit such a travesty.

"Your attention, please," called Wylie.

There was no such signal forthcoming from the founder's widow.

"*Please*. I *must* have your attention."

Paige glanced at the alternate ends of the table. Wylie seemed severely rattled by the reaction while Grace Elerbee remained aloof to the bewilderment and anxiety. Paige then looked across and noticed Jim Ogden's anguished expression. What in the holy hell is *this*? he seemed to be asking of Paige, without words.

"Please, allow me to continue," Wylie begged. "There will be time for discussion, I assure you. I must ask you to hold your comments and questions until then, please. Now, if I may go on," said Wylie, clearly unnerved.

The room finally came to order. Paige could see that Jim Ogden appeared to be in a state of shock, and that Ogden, who sat to Wylie's immediate right, seemed torn between either bursting into tears or overturning the large table in a fit of primordial anger.

Or both.

"As I have stated, an agreement in principle has been reached with Mr. Halloran. The agreement stipulates a purchase price of twenty-eight dollars per share, contingent upon a two-thirds vote of the Board of Directors in approval of the sale, and subsequent ratification by a majority of shares. This offer is quite generous when considered in the context of the current book value of twenty-one thirty-seven. The agreement further states that business will be ongoing, and that the actions of the Board in selecting an Executive Vice President and such other organizational matters will continue on as planned."

"Good God, Jeff!" Collier said in what was nearly a shout. "How can you tell us that—?"

"Larry, please."

"Please? Hell, *I'm* the one who feels like asking 'please,' for crying out loud."

"As I mentioned, there will be time for—"

"For what? For a vote to validate this nonsense?"

"Mr. Collier," Grace Elerbee said sharply, "you may express your views at the appropriate time."

Collier sighed loudly.

Wylie nodded his appreciation to Mrs. Elerbee as the sulking Collier sat back heavily. "To continue, let me say that, in my opinion, this agreement is one of fairness and completeness. Mr. Halloran owns several other companies, as Mr. Wynn will discuss, and Elerbee Engineering will be a strong addition. And the strength of Mr. Halloran's existing organization will likewise be a positive situation for Elerbee Engineering."

You slimy son of a bitch, Paige thought as he watched the performance of Wylie.

Wynn looked up at Wylie.

"Mr. Wynn, why don't you take a moment and acquaint us with your client."

Wynn smiled slightly and then cleared his throat. When he stood and quickly glanced over some handwritten notes, Wylie promptly took his seat and reached with a trembling hand for the glass of water to his front.

"Thank you very much, Jeff," Wynn said with a nod toward Wylie. "I can assure you gentlemen that when Mrs. Elerbee and Jeff invited me to come down here to be with you, I had serious misgivings about barging into your meeting with news such as this. At the same time, however, I knew what an exciting opportunity this is, and will be. And so I wanted to be here, in the absence of my client, to convey to you, first, the deep and abiding respect for Elerbee Engineering that Mr. Halloran holds; and second, how important this relationship can be for both Elerbee Engineering and Halloran Investments."

Wynn glanced at his notes again, and then adjusted his glasses. "Let me begin with the first statement. For years, my client has followed the engineering-consulting profession, particularly as it relates to soils and materials engineering and consulting. You see, Mr. Halloran is not just an investor. He's also an engineer—a P.E.—whose technical understanding of the industry gives him a unique insight."

Many of the members of the Board, especially the employee members, began to feel as if they were witnessing the execution of a family member, and with no available recourse. They were crestfallen and embittered. Here was the smooth lawyer with the rich Boston accent speaking to them about an outsider owning and controlling what had only moments before been theirs.

"You'll be joining an eight-hundred-million dollar concern that includes a transportation company, a medical-equipment distributor, and a data-processing consultant group. You'll have at your disposal a virtual reservoir of resources— financial, data, and human. You'll be an important cornerstone in the foundation of the organization. You'll run your own business as you have in the past, as you do now. In short, the only change will be in the ownership. Of course," Wynn said, grinning slightly, "there might be another addition to the Board."

There was little laughter, and none of it was heartfelt.

Jim Ogden had such a bitter look on his face that Paige interpreted it as meaning, Ha-ha-ha yourself, you goddamn asshole lawyer!

Paige listened to the usual prattle as it went on,

The attorney Wynn talked about "synergies" and extolling the virtues of the sale, about how "we're excited about it" was mentioned several times with little more passion than if Wynn were discussing the latest legal developments in Sri Lanka. There was also emphasis on the "great fit" between the two companies, about how "one plus one will equal three," and the reference to the Elerbee Engineering executives as the "best in class."

"I wish to thank you for so graciously giving of your time," Wynn said with a confirming nod. "And I want you to know how great my client's desire is to become a part of Elerbee Engineering."

With that, Wynn took his seat.

Wylie stood and cleared his throat. He nodded toward Mrs. Elerbee. "We will now open the floor for discussion," he said, after which he took his seat. When no one spoke up, Wylie looked toward Collier. "Larry, care to start things off?"

All eyes in the room quickly settled upon Collier. There was a long, agonizing silence in which there was an abundance of coughing and shifting by the Board members.

"I sure as hell don't understand it," Collier finally said. "I mean, we've been running this firm successfully for a bunch of years. It's not like we're inept or stagnant or undercapitalized, or anything of the sort. I'm sorry, but I simply can't comprehend the need for this."

"Neither can I," added Ralph Boudreaux, a retired engineering technician. "It don't seem right to me. If it was improving the company, then yeah, I'd go along. But it's not doing that, or at least I can't *see* where it is. It's just improving those who'll get twenty-eight bucks a share out of it."

"Ralph's absolutely right," added Collier. "We're talking about breaking up a tradition, a family. That's not worth twenty-eight bucks a share to me."

Ogden and Paige kept glancing at one another, though neither spoke. And while there was additional discussion from the others, Mrs. Elerbee remained cool in her detached silence. Wylie said little, though he did attempt to guide the discussion. The other insiders on the Board, those vice presidents who, regardless of the outcome, would still get their marching orders from Wylie, were naturally tentative and restrained in their comments. Likewise, the banker and the attorney who sat on the Board as outside members also moderated what little they dared to volunteer. Only Lawton Alford, the engineering professor, expressed a measure of doubt over the proposal.

"Will we have a chance to meet Peter Halloran in the near future?" Ed Webb asked of the attorney Wynn.

"If the vote of the Directors is favorable, Mr. Halloran will be here in New Orleans on Friday to meet with you and begin to get to know you."

"Are there any more questions for Mr. Wynn?" Wylie inquired.

There were none.

"If not, then I'll excuse Mr. Wynn with our thanks for his having joined us."

Wynn and Wylie stood. They shook hands, and then Wynn turned toward the others at the table.

"Thank you again for your time and attention. I foresee great things ahead for Elerbee Engineering—tremendously exciting things. By the way, I'll be staying over in the hotel, so if there's anything I can do for any of you, please don't hesitate to call on me."

With that, Wynn nodded and took his leave.

Wylie returned to his seat and immediately noticed Collier shaking his head in disgust. "Let's continue the discussion, shall we?" Wylie said in a crisp, assertive tone.

Collier sat up stiffly, arms folded across his chest, and glared hard at Wylie.

"Any further discussion?" asked Wylie, turning away from the hostile Collier.

"Why wasn't the Board apprised of this beforehand?" Collier demanded in a steely tone.

"There wasn't time," Wylie snapped. "Larry, I can assure you that all of this happened rather suddenly. There just wasn't time."

"My circumstances are obviously quite different from most of the others in this room," explained Collier with a glance toward Mrs. Elerbee. "I can speak my piece today without having to worry if I'll be working tomorrow."

"So what's your point?" Wylie pressed.

"My point is, I think this whole deal is being shoved down the throats of the governing body of this firm. A *fait accompli*, as it were. There's no choice in the matter, given your and Mrs. Elerbee's preference to sell out."

Wylie became irate. "Larry, there is *no* attempt by *anyone* to shove *anything* down the throats of the members of this body. There is free choice in the matter, as there is in all others. And I resent any suggestion that something otherwise is taking place."

Paige could stand it no longer. "Something otherwise most certainly *is* taking place," he said, glancing at Ogden for a moment to see if he, too, wanted to jump in, which he did not. "It seems to me that it's fundamentally a question of either voting 'yes' or catching the next bus out of town. Only to that extent, Jeff, are you correct in saying there is free choice in the matter."

Wylie glared hard at Paige.

"Let's consider something else," interjected professor Alford. He squinted thoughtfully and ran his hand through his silver, crew-cut hair, then straightened his red bow tie. "A company owned by its employees, substantially or perhaps even partially, tends to view its performance a bit differently than in the case where the ownership resides exclusively outside the executive, and even the employee, ranks. My friends in the public corporations might argue differently, but I've seen it time and again in many of the firms I've consulted with in the past. That being the case, might there be an eventual erosion in the level of care administered by the technical staff?"

"Yes," Collier answered quickly.

"No!" countered Wylie.

"Frankly, I must admit to some concerns," Alford said. "Let's say that, at first, there's only a slight, almost imperceptible deterioration in the technical quality. After all, now the firm belongs to someone else, an outsider. It's his company, his money, his risk, and so on. The question thus becomes, does the slight deterioration then lead to a major degeneration? Will the technical managers who review the work, who before might have taken extra care, now be satisfied with less, even if it's only very slightly less? And if so, how long before a technical error or omission comes back to kick the 'new' firm squarely in the seat of the pants? These are real issues, my friends; issues that need careful thought; issues that aren't measured easily in dollars and cents, at least not initially."

Wylie thumped his fingers impatiently on the table. Ogden slumped down in his chair, looking worn and exhausted. Paige toyed with a peppermint candy, sliding it on the table between his thumb and forefinger.

The others sat still.

"So," said Collier as he opened another bottle of water. "Where do we go from here?"

"Do you care to discuss the matter any further?" Wylie asked.

"Jeff, I don't think there's any mistaking my position. I don't like it and I obviously don't want to see it happen. Frankly, I'm concerned that the company will lose its soul, that it'll be different than before. Not better, mind you; just different. And that's not something I'd vote to accept. My God, this company holds a warm place in a lot of hearts, and they're not all here to get in their two-cents worth. But if they were here, I feel certain that they'd tell you—they'd *beg* you—to leave it alone. There's a special quality about this firm that attracts and keeps the types of people that we have, and that attraction won't be as strong if this thing goes through. And if those same attractions aren't there anymore, then the firm's going to change, and not for the better."

"You're being a sentimentalist, Larry," spoke Vince Kincaid. "You're being blinded by your emotions. Look at it in realistic terms." Kincaid then gave a quick glance toward Wylie at the far end of the table. "Try to look at it objectively."

"I'm afraid, Vince," Collier said, slowly turning toward Mrs. Elerbee, "that I can't look at it as being anything other than what it really is."

Grace Elerbee stiffened. "And what is that, Mr. Collier?"

Collier could feel the stares from all directions as surely as if the lines of vision were charged with tiny particle beams. He took a sip of water to moisten his gluey mouth. He then turned toward Grace Elerbee, who was staring at him in aggravation. "It's the end of Elerbee Engineering as we've known it for all these years. And, as best I can determine, all for a few bucks for you and Jeff Wylie."

No one dared speak, and hardly anyone moved, breathed. It was one of those extraordinarily rare gems—a moment of unqualified corporate candor. Mrs. Elerbee's icy stare met Collier's equally determined look.

"Mr. Brice, as our general counsel, would you be so kind as to review with Mr. Collier a few of the facts of life surrounding ownership in a privately-held corporation," she said, glancing at the attorney.

"That won't be necessary," Collier said quickly. "We're already getting a case-study just by being in this meeting."

"I have a question," said Ron Steinkempf, Vice President-Engineering.

"Go ahead, Ron," said Wylie, happy to wrest the floor from Collier.

"This guy Halloran's an engineer, right?"

"Right."

"But it's an eight-hundred-million dollar company already. He won't be *that* close to our operation; he couldn't be. So, what kinds of people will we be dealing with?"

Wylie shrugged. "He has a big staff, Ron. They didn't get that big and that successful without some quality people at the top."

"They're business people, right?"

"Yes, of course."

"Then I'm opposed," Steinkempf declared, sitting back in his chair and noisily tossing his pen atop his notepad.

"Why the problem with the business people?"

"Jeff, we go to great lengths, *expensive* lengths, to make absolutely certain that the quality of our service and the technical training of our people and the maintenance of our reference materials are not restrained for any reasons, including profitability. Don't get me wrong—I'm certainly not anti-profit, by any means; I understand those relationships, believe me. But I don't want to tamper with the mechanism that allows us to *generate* those profits. We've always charged higher fees because we've always spent more to maintain what I consider to be our technical preeminence, along with our ethos of staying very close to the client. My fear is—my *horror* is—that the twenty-five-year-old bean counters won't even *begin* to understand that. All they'll know is that the history of this firm started on the first day they pranced through our doors. Or, if somehow they do understand it, they'll allow it to be compromised for the sake of short-term profits. And *that*, gentlemen, is something I just can't swallow."

"Bingo," said Collier.

"I think your worries are misplaced, Ron," Wylie said.

"Thank you, Ron, for being kind enough to give us the facts of life surrounding short-term profitability in a privately-held corporation," said Collier with a brazen glance at Mrs. Elerbee.

"Mr. Collier!" snapped Grace Elerbee. "Your sarcasm is not only out of line, it's also counterproductive to the discussion we're attempting to have here."

"No ma'am, it's not," spoke Ralph Boudreaux in a respectful tone. "Larry's only saying what some of us feel but don't have either the eloquence or the courage to say for ourselves."

"I agree," said Ron Steinkempf.

"Well, I *disagree*," said Vince Kincaid, with vehemence.

"So do I," echoed Ed Webb.

Wylie stood. "Let me have your attention, please," he ordered. The room became quiet. Wylie glanced at his watch. "Let's take a twenty-minute break, then we'll meet back in here to complete our discussion. I remind each of you that nothing is to be said outside this room concerning any of the material under discussion here."

The group broke up quietly. Some remained in the meeting room and gathered near a table stocked with coffee and soft drinks. Others ventured outside. Most were still dazed, as if they were soldiers in a once proud and victorious army that had inexplicably just been offered up for an unconditional surrender.

Paige and Collier caught the elevator to Collier's room. There was a note from Dot, that she'd be back from shopping at three-thirty. Collier searched his things and then realized to his enormous chagrin that he'd forgotten his travel flask. He could remember no other time in his life when a stiff drink would have been more welcomed.

Collier plopped down upon the bed and stared at the ceiling while Paige took a seat in a nearby chair.

"Everything's going to hell in a handbasket, Dave," Collier said with a sigh. "And at a blindingly high rate of speed."

Paige nodded. "I know."

Collier propped against the bed's headboard and lit a cigarette. He inhaled deeply, and when he exhaled, he did so slowly. "I never thought it'd come to this; never, in my wildest dreams. God, they're willing to barter away one hell of a great company, and I just can't believe that I'm actually hearing it."

"Don't let it get to you, Larry," Paige said in an almost fatherly tone. "Remember, there's a two-and-a-half million dollar spread between the current book value and the offer from Halloran for the old lady's shares. Before this, she was all set to sell out at twenty-one thirty-seven, but now she's got an offer on the table of twenty-eight bucks."

Collier took another long puff. "I suppose so."

"Your own shares will be worth more, too. I assume you've considered that?"

"Yeah, I have. I've considered a lot of things lately." Collier crushed out his cigarette. He glanced at his watch and thought again how nice it would be to have a drink. A feeling of exhaustion seemed to hang heavily upon him like a wet bedspread.

Paige sighed, and then shrugged. "The buying and selling of companies happens every day, Larry. If it improves the company, fine. But we shouldn't get too hung up on that point; that's only an incidental consideration. The real crux of the matter is that there's some quick money to be taken here, and so the takers are going to goddamn *take*. And who the hell can blame them. They've got theirs now; let the others freeze in the dark. It's as contemporary American as mom and apple pie. Elerbee Engineering was nice while it lasted, at least as we knew it. Now it'll be something else—maybe something good; maybe not. We're not going to determine that today. That'll probably take a while. So don't take it so personally. Just roll with it."

Collier shook his head and sighed in utter resignation. "Elerbee Engineering has always been something a person could believe in, in a world where there's a growing scarcity of such things."

Paige smiled and nodded. "I suppose we're down to mom and apple pie."

"It would seem so," Collier said, staring off into the distance.

"Let's come to order," said Wylie, seated in his usual place. "We have quite a bit to cover, so we'll need to press on. Is any further discussion needed on the proposed sale of Elerbee Engineering to Halloran Investments?"

There was silence until Ron Steinkempf, the firm's chief engineer, muttered a soft, "Yeah."

"Fine, Ron. Go ahead."

Steinkempf, tall and thin with medium-length salt-and-pepper hair which grew with no discernible sense of direction, sat up straight in his chair. The knot of his oft-stained polyester tie was slightly left of center and partially hidden beneath the collar of his white shirt. His eyes were dark and probing and alive with energy.

"I have a counterproposal."

Wylie's expression immediately changed. "I thought we were discussing the original proposal."

"We were, and we are. My proposal would be to—"

"Ron, we are discussing the original proposal."

"But what I have may—"

"The *original* proposal!"

Steinkempf gave off an angry look. He then turned toward Collier, then Paige, and then Mrs. Elerbee before finally lowering his head and saying nothing further.

"Gentlemen," Wylie said firmly, "let me be frank. I believe it to be in the best interest of this body to bring this issue to an immediate vote."

Wylie paused and made eye contact with each of the Board members, with prolonged emphasis on the inside members. "And the sooner the vote is taken, the sooner we can get on with the business at hand. You've heard from the representative of the purchaser. You've heard the subsequent discussion around this table. I think it's time now to decide upon this important matter. I move that the resolution before you, which sets forth the terms and conditions of the purchase of Elerbee Engineering by Halloran Investments, Incorporated, be adopted."

The motion was quickly seconded by Vince Kincaid.

"All in favor so indicate by a raising of the right hand," Wylie ordered.

The hands went up: Wylie, Mrs. Elerbee, Kincaid, Ed Webb, attorney John Brice, banker Marshall Wilkinson. Paige glanced across at Jim Ogden who, after quickly surveying the others, looked back at Paige with a strickened expression on his face. Collier, Ron Steinkempf, Ralph Boudreaux, and professor Alford all kept their hands noticeably upon the table. Only at the last possible moment did Ogden finally creep a tentative hand into the air, and then only after Paige had raised his.

"The resolution is hereby adopted."

Paige glanced at Grace Elerbee, who remained expressionless.

Collier let out an audible sigh—a groan, almost.

"Before we move on to the Executive Vice President issue," said the immensely relieved Wylie, "I think we should take a moment to discuss the timing of the announcement. My plan at this point is to break the announcement on Friday morning, first thing. Mr. Halloran will be here to say a few words, and then we can adjourn and go back home. Anyone have any thoughts on this?"

Collier laughed out loud.

"What's so funny?" Wylie asked sharply.

"Why string it out? What don't you do something unusual for a change and be absolutely straight with everyone?"

Wylie became furious. "Larry, I resent that!"

"That was most certainly out of order!" said Grace Elerbee.

"C'mon, Larry," said Ed Webb. "That's not helpful."

"I agree with Larry," called Ron Steinkempf.

"So do I," voiced Ralph Boudreaux.

"The end of the meeting would be better," asserted Vince Kincaid. "It'd create fewer wrong impressions than by doing it at the beginning."

"That's malarkey," argued Steinkempf. "All of you know how the rumors will circulate if we don't deal with it right away. The meeting will then become secondary, and we definitely don't want that."

"There won't be any rumors if nobody discusses it," said Webb.

Attorney John Brice held up his hand and asked for the floor. "Jeff, if I may," he said, clearing his throat.

Wylie nodded. "Yes, John, please."

"There might be a tendency for some to view the timing of the announcement as an ethical issue, when in fact it's nothing of the sort. Ron was right on target when he spoke of the tangential effects. Let's think in those terms rather than when one time or the other might be morally or ethically better. I happen to think a Friday announcement would be better because it'd likely staunch what might otherwise be a lot of unnecessary confusion and consternation, which would hardly be productive. Make the announcement when Peter Halloran is here to emphasize to everyone that it's still business as usual. Peter's a very convincing man, and he'll greatly ease the shock quotient of the whole thing. Friday's the best option, in my opinion."

Wylie nodded his appreciation to Brice.

"Nicely said, counsel," said Grace Elerbee, who then got up and excused herself from the room.

"As it stands now," Wylie said firmly, "we'll announce on Friday."

The bottle of Dom Perignon was opened within moments of the telephone call. It had been Grace Elerbee on the other end, calling from downstairs to report that the Board had given its stamp of approval to the deal.

"Splendid," said Peter Halloran, his glass raised in triumph.

"To a job well done," Hilton Wynn added, his glass also raised.

Halloran sipped. "A fitting end to a productive day, indeed. Especially so for a man who's supposed to be in Boston."

"Will you be staying over for dinner?"

"Afraid not," answered Halloran, his pale blue eyes squinting as if he had been suddenly reminded of something. "I have a full day tomorrow. I'll need to be leaving soon."

"What about your return?"

"Thursday afternoon. If they change their minds and try to announce before Friday, quash it. Tell 'em I'm unavailable before Friday morning, and that I strongly urge that it be done then."

"All right," said Wynn with a dutiful nod.

"Give Wylie the standard assurances, and find out who they're promoting to Executive Vice President. Call me with that first thing in the morning."

"Right."

Halloran savored the last sip of the bubbly. He got up and walked to the full-length window where he scanned the length of Canal Street from his top-floor suite. Below, the auto and pedestrian traffic streamed in either direction. Halloran ran his hand through his silver hair, and then straightened his navy-and-white silk tie.

"This fella who's retiring, what's his name?" Halloran asked as he fidgeted with a gold cuff link while staring at the street below.

Wynn slumped in a chair, his tie loosened and his vest unbuttoned. "Collier. Larry Collier," he answered. "He goes way back, as I understand it. Almost to the firm's very beginning."

"Will he take a drink?"

Wynn smiled. "Anytime, anyplace, or so I'm given to understand."

"Fine, then. Buy him and his wife a meal at the Commander's Palace. As for Wylie, he'll lay low, I'm sure. And the old darlin' is leaving town tonight. Give this Collier fellow a nice going-away present, and I'll do the rest on Friday."

"Shall I use September first as the target date for the closing?"

"Yes. The sooner, the better."

"Then I'll have a full schedule for several days to come."

"Work quickly, Mr. Wynn, because you sure as hell don't work cheaply."

Wynn chuckled. "You're only paying me what I'm worth, sir."

Halloran stared out the window, beyond the streets and buildings and out into the gray distance. "I've spent the better part of my adult life, Mr. Wynn, in a deliberate attempt to trade dollars for value, and vice versa. Sometimes there's an imbalance, because sometimes there's a misjudgment. But it all comes down to control, mostly."

Halloran turned to Wynn. "My daughter calls me a 'control freak,' whatever the hell that means. Compulsive, I suppose. But I do know that the stronger the preparation, the better the control, and thus the smaller the size of that little sphere of things over which absolutely no control can be exercised. So, as long as the little sphere stays little, and hopefully turns out to have a neutral or even favorable influence, why, Mr. Wynn," Halloran said with a wry smile, "I'll inevitably gain a victory."

Wynn nodded slowly, thoughtfully. "Not unlike the way I view the practice of law, sir."

The fifty-year-old Halloran gave Wynn a measured stare. "And that's why I pay you what you're worth."

Wynn smiled in admiration of the older man. He had been associated with Halloran for nearly eight years, through a multitude of successes and a handful of setbacks. In each of the deals, however, he had never failed to discover a different side to Halloran, a new wrinkle in a multi-faceted character. Halloran was adaptable, a convenient by-product of his originality and his insatiable curiosity. He was bold and decisive, seemingly fearless. And he possessed just the right combination of instinct and raw intelligence so that his moves were often studied by fellow entrepreneurs with admiration and occasional wonder.

Halloran poured himself another glass of champagne. "You know, I've always wanted my own engineering firm," he said, his eyes twinkling.

Halloran and Wynn both began to laugh.

After a short break, Wylie introduced the proposal to reorganize the company into nine regions. The plan called for accounting and data centers, each headed by a regional vice president, to be located in Atlanta, Boston, Columbus, Dallas, Denver, Los Angeles, Minneapolis, St. Louis, and Seattle. The Board members were given territory maps with each branch highlighted within the proposed regional boundaries. Wylie then spoke of the timing of the move, explaining that a minimum of ninety days would be needed to have everyone and everything in place. He also made conspicuous mention of Jim Ogden as the author of the reorganization plan.

The reorganization was approved by a majority vote after an examination of the projected costs.

"Now then," said Wylie, jotting some quick notes onto the outside of a manila folder. "We've come to another very important point in our meeting." Wylie glanced quickly at Ogden and then Paige. "We will now address the naming of an Executive Vice President."

Wylie then launched into a lengthy monologue on the reasoning behind the creation of the position, its attendant duties, and the assertion that the position be filled with an individual already within the organization. Wylie went on to maintain that he and Langdon Elerbee had always assumed that the person selected should come from one of the three regional vice-president positions. That, of course, led to Dave Paige and Jim Ogden.

Wylie then mentioned how the changing needs of the firm had necessitated that the original award to Paige be re-visited. "In the normal course of things, I would have made the appointment and come to the Board for its approval. However, given the rather unique circumstances that now exist, I would prefer that the Board consider the choices and make a final selection."

Collier spoke up, saying, "In the normal course of things, Dave Paige had already been named. Why is this being re-visited when the choice had been previously made by Langdon Elerbee himself?"

"Larry, as I've mentioned, there are some unique circumstances in play now. I consider it altogether proper to have the Board look at this again."

Collier shook his head in disgust and said nothing further.

"I therefore move that the two gentlemen who head our Eastern and Central Regions be exclusively considered for appointment to this position," said Wylie.

There were no other objections.

Paige and Ogden were then dismissed from the proceedings and advised by Wylie to remain outside the room until the matter had been fully discussed and voted upon by the rest of the Board. Once outside, Paige and Ogden walked away in opposite directions, each making calls on their cell phones.

A long evaluation process thus began that included biographical information on each candidate, copies of the previous three annual Executive Performance Reviews, and comparative information on each region's year-to-date performance in a number of categories. Each of the Board members quietly studied the data, some making occasional notes or underlining certain words or phrases on some of the sheets in the half-inch stack of papers to their front.

Refreshment service was brought into the room, filling it with the aroma of fresh coffee. Fifty minutes passed before everyone had completed their review.

Wylie then handed out a single sheet of paper to each member which outlined a broad listing of the duties and responsibilities of the Executive Vice President.

"Before we begin our discussion," Wylie said as everyone glanced over the paper, "I think it's appropriate for us to review the job description so we can be satisfied that our choice of individuals matches the requirements for the position. Please note that the Executive Vice President will be responsible for directing the regional vice presidents who, as we've decided today, will total nine. Our selectee will be principally involved in the day-to-day running of the firm. The other key staff positions, as you can see, will still report to me as Chairman and Chief Executive Officer."

Wylie paused. "Are there any questions, then, on what it is we're talking about with regard to this position?"

Ron Steinkempf spoke up. "I have the impression," he said, shrugging and shaking his head, "that none of what we're doing here will matter once Halloran steps in and starts to want things his own way."

"We have the word of Peter Halloran that we'll continue to run this business as we have," said Wylie. "Beyond that, Ron, if you're asking me if we all have guarantees of sustained employment, I think the answer to that should be obvious."

Larry Collier stared blankly at the pencil he was rolling back and forth across a notepad. He felt drained and exhausted, the way he imagined marathon runners must feel when they fall out after reaching the finish line. Good thing it wasn't already Christmas, he thought. That would only be another dose of cruelty. Ho, ho, ho, you've all been sold.

"Any more questions about the job specs?" Wylie asked.

No further questions or comments were forthcoming.

"Very well," said Wylie with a slight grin. "Then let's get on with the naming of an Executive Vice President."

Everyone seemed to straighten with anticipation, even the languid Collier. The meeting was running longer than planned, and the selection had been scheduled as the final item on the agenda.

The time had finally come.

"The floor is hereby open for nominations."

CHAPTER TWENTY THREE

Paige reached for the canned soft drink on the table beside him. His hand quivered slightly, his mouth dry and sticky, his palms moist. He sipped once, and then leaned back on the sofa and waited.

Wylie sat in an armchair and sipped a martini. He glanced at a legal pad propped on his lap, then jotted some additional notes in the margins, all without looking or otherwise acknowledging Paige's presence. The hotel suite was spacious, the glass-door curtains pulled open, permitting a view of the large bridge spanning the river and the cars moving steadily across it. Holly Wylie was away again, shopping in the French Quarter with a group of Elerbee wives.

"What was the vote?" Paige asked, breaking the silence.

Wylie cocked his head slightly. "Do you really want to know?"

"Yes, I do."

"Eight to four," Wylie answered with a note of finality.

Paige winced.

"Right. It was a pretty convincing confirmation for Jim, I have to say."

Convincing enough, Paige thought. Jim Ogden was the new Executive Vice President of Elerbee Engineering.

Paige rose. He stepped toward the glass doors and looked out at the river. He stood quietly for a moment with his hands in his pockets, his shoulders rising and falling with his slow, steady breathing. "Then you'll have my resignation on your desk when you get back to Atlanta," he said, exhaling slowly. "I'd like thirty days to be able to clear up a few things before I turn the branches over to someone else. Is a thirty-day arrangement agreeable to you?"

Wylie remained expressionless. "I'll agree to thirty days, yes."

"And I'll be expecting you to honor your end of the deal we made in Atlanta concerning Diane Tresvant."

"You needn't worry about that."

"Anything in particular swing it Jim's way?"

Wylie hesitated before answering, "In my view, it was simply an example of the Board using sound judgment and making a good and responsible business decision."

"Bullshit," Paige said, turning and facing Wylie.

"I beg your pardon?"

"You heard me, that's a bullshit answer. The Board didn't decide anything of the sort. Eight people decided only that today they wanted to survive."

Wylie smiled. "That's both good and responsible, given the circumstances. Their acting in their own best interests also caused the best interests of the firm to be reached. It worked exactly the way it was supposed to work."

"I'm sure it did," Paige said as he started toward the door. He then stopped and turned back toward Wylie. "Just out of curiosity, who drove the sale of the company?"

Wylie gave a strange look. "Just exactly what do you mean?"

"I mean, who pushed for accepting Halloran's offer—you or Mrs. Elerbee?"

"Those negotiations were a private matter, and for that matter are still private."

"Was it you or her?"

"You heard my answer," Wylie snapped indignantly. "The matter's closed."

Paige grinned. "I'm an officer and a stockholder, you know."

"The Board dealt with the matter, you will recall. There was a successful vote after a diversity of opinion was considered."

"The Elerbee Board of Directors under Jeff Wylie," Paige said, feeling his cheeks flush with anger, "has never been one to foster a diversity of opinion among its members, but only to suppress any inclination there might have otherwise been to do so. And I'd say on that count, you've been a smashing success."

"Are you finished?" Wylie snapped.

Paige stared at Wylie for a moment, then suddenly laughed. "It would appear so," he said as he turned away and prepared to leave.

"Just a minute," Wylie called.

Paige hesitated just as he was reaching for the doorknob.

Wylie stood and placed his drink glass on a table. "Were you planning on joining the rest of the staff and myself for dinner this evening in the Quarter?"

"You've got to be kidding," Paige said calmly, after which he opened the door and left.

The telephone's message light was blinking when Paige got back to his room. The desk clerk told him that something had been left for him, that it would be brought to his room immediately. Moments later, Paige was handed a fifth of Jack Daniels with a note reading, "To a worthy competitor. Enjoy with my compliments, Jim Ogden."

Paige considered for a moment the idea of drinking the contents of the entire bottle and then showing up at the staff dinner and promptly vomiting the results all over Ogden, right after the appetizer and just prior to the main course. Nope, he thought. That wouldn't help. Then he considered remaining in his room alone that night, drinking the contents of the entire bottle and then barfing in complete privacy. Nope, he thought. That might help, but then the other nighttime pleasures of New Orleans would go to waste. Finally, he considered sending over to Ogden a bottle of champagne with a note reading, "Congratulations, and now go screw yourself. Love, Dave." That'd definitely help, he decided, but then again Ogden might go to dinner and proceed to spew the contents all over the staff, and under the current promotion methodology he might then become President Ogden or perhaps even Chairman Ogden.

Finally, the reality of it all came back to him. Neither Dave Paige nor Elerbee Engineering would ever be the same as before.

Paige took a seat on the bed. He stared at the bottle, finally deciding that the last thing he needed at this point was a belly full of booze. Things had changed, were changing, and the less he dwelled on it, he concluded, the better off he would be. He couldn't resurrect the old Elerbee Engineering, the same way he couldn't resurrect Langdon Elerbee, or his own failed marriage to Valerie, or the nice fit he had so enjoyed in the old world in the old ways. It would forever be different, he knew, but not necessarily forever worse. To the contrary, there was always reason for hope. And hope was something he preferred to be filled with. At least for now, anyway.

He smiled softly and put the bottle on the dresser. It wasn't his choice of beverage, and he knew he would now forever associate that particular brand with this particular time and these unique circumstances. And, of course, with Jim Ogden.

The bottle remained atop the dresser. Maybe some other time, he concluded.

CHAPTER TWENTY FOUR

"Good morning, ladies and gentlemen."

Jeff Wylie stood at the podium in the hotel ballroom. It was Wednesday morning, and the Elerbee contingent was gathered in full.

The leadership meeting was officially underway.

"Welcome to New Orleans. I trust that this year's meeting, like the others before it, will be productive and beneficial. We've got a great deal to cover in the next two-and-a-half days, so we'll begin this morning with comments on the overall state of the company, followed by our group sessions. We'll gather back here at the end of the day for a wrap-up, and then start again in the morning, here in this room. At this time, I'm going to ask Vince Kincaid to come up and give a summary of our financial position through the first six months."

The group applauded politely as Wylie moved aside and Kincaid stepped forward and pulled up the PowerPoint slides on his laptop.

Seated together on the front row were Ogden, Ed Webb, Ron Steinkempf, Don Burroughs, and several other Atlanta headquarters people. Larry Collier had yet to appear, but the circumstance of his retirement made his absence from the morning sessions understandable. Conspicuously absent, however, were all of the outside members of the Board of Directors, including Grace Elerbee. Those same members had, in years past, typically been present for the opening of the meeting.

Paige took a seat in the back, alone.

Ed Webb followed Kincaid with a few slides on the activities of the corporate marketing effort. Webb was, in Paige's opinion, the quintessential corporate fat cat. Webb was lazy and grossly overpaid for the quantity and quality of services he rendered to the firm. Some consolation existed in the fact that he was an unusually likeable person, but not enough to offset his organizational worthlessness. Beyond that, Paige could only guess that Webb's relative passivity and his sycophancy had been responsible for keeping him on Wylie's staff for so long. Ed Webb could play the inside corporate game adroitly, and what's more he wasn't a threat to anyone.

Don Burroughs made a presentation on the changes taking place in Elerbee's program of medical insurance. Burroughs spelled out the woes resulting from the dramatic increases in the costs of healthcare, especially hospitalization, and the resultant harsh impact upon the company in its funding of the majority of the premiums. He went on to explain that a sizeable portion of the rate increases would consequently have to be born by the employees in the form of higher payroll deductions. Additionally, Burroughs advised, the coverage would now carry higher deductibles, resulting in an even greater overall cost to the employee.

"That's swell, Don," someone commented from the middle of the audience. "Sounds like we negotiated a real astute package. This ought to go over well."

A sprinkling of laughter followed.

"Then go back and tell 'em not to have so many claims," Burroughs shot back, immediately regretting it when a chorus of moans and hisses instantly came back at him.

Paige smiled. Branch managers could sometimes be an unruly lot, especially when the speaker was an administrative figurehead with a tendency toward arrogance and pomposity.

"Let's move on," Burroughs said in an attempt to regain control. "Are there any other questions?"

"Yeah, Don," came a voice from the side of the room. "Have you looked at any other alternatives, such as changing insurance carriers or HMOs, or whatever?"

"Yes, we have."

"Well?"

"You can be assured that we've studied the problem thoroughly from all angles."

"You and Hillary?"

Again, scattered laughter.

Another voice, that of Mike Petrovic, chimed in. "And the results are in, ladies and gentlemen: Higher premiums and reduced coverage, along with specific instructions from corporate headquarters expressly forbidding so much ill health. And it's all for you, our valued employee."

The room shook with laughter. Wylie managed to catch Burroughs' attention and promptly signaled to him to bring his remarks to a close.

Wylie then rose and approached the podium. Paige could see and hear the whispering and the muffled conversations to his front. The entire room seemed to be stirring with energy, as if everyone awaited the results of a beauty contest.

"Ladies and gentlemen, as you are no doubt aware, the Board convened yesterday to take under consideration a number of issues, one of which included the naming of an Executive Vice President. That process has been completed, and it's a great honor for me to announce that Jim Ogden has been appointed as the new Executive Vice President of Elerbee Engineering, effective immediately."

There was a pause at first, as if the audience was somehow waiting for more. Only when Wylie turned and summoned Ogden to the podium did the applause begin, quickly receding from the front of the room to the rear like the passing of a cloud's shadow.

"I just want to say that I'm honored to have been selected by the Board for this important post, and that I'll do my best to earn the trust and confidence that has been bestowed upon me," said Ogden, mostly looking down. He then turned and shook hands with Wylie, and again drew only moderate applause when he returned to his seat.

Wylie leaned toward the microphone. "So, welcome to all of you. We're excited about having you here because you're the finest group of managers in the industry. 'Nobody does it better,' as the song goes. And that follows for all our technical people, as well. We're the best because you're the best. And we're certainly glad you're here. Enjoy yourselves while you're here in New Orleans, and let's have a great meeting."

When the assembly was dismissed, nearly all proceeded to a group of nearby, smaller rooms in accordance with a prearranged list of people and places. As everyone busied themselves with collecting their belongings and leaving, many of the corporate staffers—Wylie and Ogden included—kept their distance from Paige, almost as if to do otherwise might expose them to an infectious disease. Meanwhile, the crowd around Ogden became thick with well-wishers. Others, especially those downcast Central Region branch managers who reported to Paige, stole only quick glances at their fallen leader as they filed out of the big room. Paige, as was brutally apparent, was toxic.

It wasn't until Paige was outside the ballroom that Mike Petrovic intercepted him and requested that Paige join him at a nearby hotel coffee shop.

"You aren't going to the session?" Paige asked.

"Screw the session, Dave. We've got to talk."

"Yeah? About what?"

"We've got to talk, man. C'mon, let's get the hell away from here."

As they left, Petrovic walked quickly, as if under a deadline. The coffee shop was out of the way of the meeting rooms, and was half-filled with business types and elderly tourists. Petrovic pointed to a corner table, and they each ordered coffee when the waitress arrived moments later. Petrovic's expression was grim, and his eyes were swelled and soupy red. His coffee remained untouched.

"How in the name of God did this thing degenerate to this level, man?" Petrovic asked in a tone saturated with astonishment.

Paige sipped from the cup, and then grinned slightly. "You want to be a little more specific, Petro?"

"You know what I'm talking about. How the hell did the Board manage to screw up such a simple task as choosing between you and that limp-dick Ogden?"

"It wasn't that close, pal."

"Get *outta* here!"

"That's right. He had the votes; I didn't. It's as simple as that."

"How'd you find out?"

"Wylie told me afterwards, after the meeting had adjourned."

Petrovic frowned, wrinkling his brow. "Tell me who voted for that asshole."

Paige looked away for an instant. "It's not important, Mike. Better just to leave it at that."

"Wylie, sure. And maybe Kincaid. And Ogden himself. And Wilkinson and John Brice, those pricks." Petrovic paused a moment, searching Paige's eyes for a clue. "That's five. Who were the others?"

"Mike, c'mon, this won't change any—"

"Dammit, Dave, tell me who the others were."

Paige took a deep breath and exhaled slowly. "What the hell," he said with a shrug, knowing that the details of the Board meeting would soon enough become common knowledge. "Grace Elerbee went for Ogden. After that, Ron Steinkempf and Ed Webb caved in."

"Grace Elerbee?"

"Yeah. I was surprised by that one."

"What the hell came over *her*, for crissakes?"

"I haven't had a chance to talk to her."

Petrovic squinted. "That left Larry Collier, Ralph Boudreaux, and Lawton Alford with you."

"Right," Paige said with a nod. "It wasn't even close."

"Those gutless sons of bitches."

Paige laughed softly. "Don't worry, man. We'll have our day sooner or later."

"Aren't you upset? Aren't you big-time pissed?"

"No," Paige answered, sipping again.

Petrovic sighed. "Well, I'm pissed to the point that I'll polish up my resume as soon as I get home. This thing's coming unhinged and about to go into free fall. No, man, I don't like the way it's starting to smell."

"No," Paige said sharply. "Don't do anything foolish. Sit tight for a little while. It may be okay yet."

"Yeah, right."

"It's not over, Mike. Believe me."

"Sounds like it's all over to me, what with all the other shit that's going down."

"What other shit?"

"There's a rumor that the firm's being sold," Petrovic said to a surprised Paige. "Something about Wylie and the old lady cashing out and giving up the firm to some bigshot dude from New England. Give it to me straight, Dave. Is it true?"

Paige smiled again, shaking his head. "Unbelievable. It's simply unbelievable how the information flows in this company."

"Well, dammit, is it true?"

"Yeah," answered Paige with a nod. "That's all the more reason to sit tight until everything shakes out."

"Who's the buyer?"

"Guy named Halloran, out of Boston."

"What's he like?"

"I have no idea. He'll be here on Friday when they formally announce it to the others. See for yourself."

"Will it have any effect on you?"

"Yes, but I'm not sure of the full extent just yet."

"Jeez," said Petrovic, sitting back and becoming even more disgusted. "I think I'll just skip out on the rest of this bullshit and hop a flight for home like Larry Collier did."

Paige looked surprised. "Larry left?"

"He and his wife left the hotel last night."

"Why?"

"I don't know. I was in the lobby with a branch-manager friend when I saw Larry and his wife walk by, and a porter was right behind, hauling all their stuff. They went out the door, and I assumed they were leaving town."

"Hmm," Paige said, still weighing the Collier issue. "I'd better see if I can reach him at home."

Petrovic reached out and touched Paige lightly on the arm. "Two other things, Dave."

"Okay, shoot."

"Are you staying through the end of the meeting?"

"No," Paige said with a quick shake of his head.

"Okay. Then are you staying with the firm?"

"I can't answer that yet," Paige said quickly. "Just sit tight, please, no matter what the reaction is to the announcement on Friday. Just stay cool. It'll work out somehow, Mike, I swear. And when it does, I'll damn well need you there with me."

"How?"

"I can't say just yet. But trust me. Please."

"You're not screwin' with me, are you?"

"No, I'm telling you straight. It'll work out, and when it does, you'll be one of the first people I'll be counting on to help me."

Petrovic paused a moment, then finally shrugged. "You got it, boss."

Paige sipped the last of his coffee and then dropped three dollar bills on the table. "I gotta run, babe. Keep the faith and I'll be in touch soon."

Petrovic waited until Paige had disappeared before he got up and went searching for a Bloody Mary.

Paige went directly to the hotel's Assistant Manager and confirmed that the Colliers had indeed checked out the night before.

"The Colliers are no longer our guests in the hotel, Mr. Paige."

Paige thanked the man and then placed a cell-phone call to Collier's home in Atlanta, only to get a busy signal. He waited two minutes and dialed again. Busy, still. He then placed a call to Diane Tresvant at her Atlanta office which lasted six minutes. When he re-dialed Collier's home, it was still busy.

Paige then went back upstairs, located Wylie, and after requesting a private moment outside one of the meeting rooms, announced to Wylie that he had decided to leave New Orleans immediately for a badly needed vacation in Florida. "It's your call," Wylie said, showing neither disappointment nor encouragement.

One more attempt was made to reach Collier as Paige quickly packed his things in his room. When it again registered a busy signal, Paige proceeded downstairs to check out of the hotel and hail a taxi for the airport.

New Orleans was over. All that was left was a grizzled old taxi driver inside a dinged-up cab with cloudy windows and an odor of dirty feet, and whose radio blared a tear-jerk country song.

"So how's your week been so far?" asked the driver once they were underway.

"Interesting," Paige answered with a slight smile. "It's been very interesting."

CHAPTER TWENTY FIVE

Larry and Dot Collier had just finished their lunch of vegetable soup and ham sandwiches and were relaxing downstairs in their comfortable den when the mail was delivered to their home. Dot retrieved it and immediately began reading over the glossy promotional material on the Canadian Rockies that had finally arrived from the travel agency. Collier, meanwhile, concentrated on the user's manual for the new desktop computer he had just that morning purchased and installed.

"We're gonna make a billion in the stock market with this little jewel," he commented from his easy chair. "These are the best graphics I've ever seen."

"We don't need a billion, dear. Just make sure you don't lose everything we've got."

Collier glanced up over his reading glasses. "What, no confidence, dear?"

"As an engineer, yes; as a financier, no comment."

Collier laughed and closed the book. He reached for the cup and saucer on the small wooden tray beside his chair. "I'll just keep the budget and let the bank worry with the investments," he said, sipping the lukewarm coffee.

"That's a relief. Now maybe I'll have some spending money for the trip."

Collier lit a cigarette and inhaled deeply. "How does it look?"

"The area around Banff is absolutely gorgeous. Here," she said as she passed one of the brochures to him. "Look at those magnificent mountains."

Collier admired the photos of the rugged mountain peaks, the green lushness of the eighteen-hole golf course, the hiking trails, and the beautiful blue, crystalline waters of the surrounding lakes. "Ought to be some great fishing," he said as he studied a picture of a fly fisherman in the waist-high waters of a clear mountain stream.

"And what about the resort? Doesn't it look fantastic?"

He leaned over and passed the brochure back to her. "Looks great," he said half-heartedly. He placed the cup and saucer back on the tray and then reclined in full with his hands clasped behind his head.

Dot peeked at him over the reading material she was holding. "Feeling okay, dear?"

"Just a little tired, is all. No big thing."

"You're still upset, aren't you?"

"Ah," he replied with a wrinkle of his nose. "It's nothing. Everything's fine."

"Why don't you plan on taking it easy for the next couple of months? You're looking exhausted, and you could certainly use the rest."

He grinned. "I'm officially retired, as of today. I suppose that means I can do absolutely nothing for the next few months and be entirely in character."

"So you'll rest. That's an order."

He saluted obediently.

Dot got up from the sofa and reached for her cup on the nearby coffee table. "Fresh cup of joe, dear?"

"Sure, why not."

Dot was right on the mark about needing some time off, Collier thought. He was tired, especially after the strain of the previous day's Board meeting. He had been looking forward to New Orleans for many months, but now his disillusionment over the outcome greatly clouded his judgment. There was an uncharacteristic bitterness welling deep within him, and the more he thought about the events leading up to the previous day, the more bitter he became. Dwelling on it only exacerbated it, he knew, for it was a vicious emotional circle, one he was better off in avoiding completely, at least to the extent possible. His career was now a thing of the past, if only for a day. But it was over—his association with Elerbee Engineering; indeed, even the Elerbee Engineering itself that he had known and grown to love throughout his adult life. It was strange and emotional and, he thought, most unfortunate. But in its wake would come a new phase of his life, a new beginning. All was not lost; all would not go to waste. He would make sure of it by living each day, each hour of his retirement as if it were a gift for all the toil that had preceded it.

He was ready for the onset of the fulfilling inner peace he hadn't known in months. The mind and body were incredibly resilient, he surmised. A few days and he'd be as good as new, ready to get on with the rest of his life. He took a deep breath and exhaled slowly, deliberately. His new toy—the personal computer—was connected and ready for action. It filled the room with the smell of an exciting new electronic device, that same odor which suddenly brought back the memories of cherished Christmas mornings years ago when the kids were small and the hour was early and the toys were all unwrapped and neatly arranged about the room.

He smiled softly. Things were already getting better.

"Here you are," said Dot, entering the room and gingerly holding two steaming cups. "Careful, it's scalding."

Collier sat up and accepted the coffee. Dot, meanwhile, took her seat on the sofa and plopped a magazine onto her lap. She lit a cigarette and left it in the ashtray. Collier glanced over and quietly studied her as she flipped the glossy pages amid a continuously rising column of smoke.

"Why don't we agree on a time and we'll both give up the cigarette habit," he suggested.

Dot looked up, squinting. "What brought that on?"

"We both agree we need to stop," he said with a shrug. "The doctor chastises us every time we go. Let's pick a mutually acceptable date and just do it."

"Okay. What about September first, then?"

"September first of what year?"

"This year, silly."

"All right. September first of this year, it is. That'll give us a little time to get ready."

"We'll quit for good this time. And we'll both be glad we did."

Dot returned to her magazine and made small talk while she enjoyed the final few puffs of what would presumably be one in a diminishing number of cigarettes left for her.

"Yep, we'll make it this time," she declared, almost in a mumble, as she crushed the butt into the smoked-glass ashtray. "We'll make it just fine."

It was at that moment she heard the crash of Collier's cup and saucer.

The uncharacteristically grim expression on the face of her husband startled her. He was sitting up, hunched slightly forward, his arms drawn up into his chest. The hot coffee had spilled on him, drenching him. The ceramic cup had broken into several large pieces, most of which still remained in his lap. But it was his facial expression that concerned her the most.

"Larry?"

He offered no response, his eyes staring straight ahead, unblinking, his facial color suddenly gray and translucent.

"Larry!"

Dot got up and moved quickly to him. His trousers were soaked from the hot spill, yet he remained motionless.

"Oh dear God, *Larry*!"

"Call 911, dear."

His forehead had become moist with perspiration. His breathing was labored, and his expression was clearly registering the discomfort and uncertainty he was feeling.

"*Hurry*, dear."

"Larry, hang on, *please*!"

The emergency rescue crew was in the Colliers' den within nine minutes from the time of the call. They sped away in the red-and-white ambulance, siren wailing, toward a North Atlanta hospital. Dot sat beside her husband, silently commanding him by the force of her own will to remain conscious. Collier's eyes were open and his pulse kept a strong register. He lay on his back in the ambulance gurney, fitted with an oxygen mask, staring up at the vehicle's ceiling, his face contorted, his eyes straining to focus, as if there was something up there he needed to see.

It was Wednesday, a little past one o'clock.

The telephone rang inside the Collier home. It was Dave Paige, calling from the airport in New Orleans.

Paige badly needed to talk with his good and trusted friend Collier. He wanted information, perhaps even a little guidance, or maybe just a chance to talk with someone who would undoubtedly make his day more tolerable, his mood more hopeful. And Larry Collier would help with that, Paige knew, because Larry Collier would tell him the whole truth, and nothing but.

What was wrong? What had happened? Why had the Colliers left so abruptly?

Paige wanted their assurances that everything was okay, and then hear Collier give a laugh and make a joke about the meeting and the sale and the entire sordid affair.

But there was no answer, still.

CHAPTER TWENTY SIX

The 757 arriving from Atlanta touched down at Tampa International Airport at one o'clock on Friday afternoon. According to a flight-crew announcement, the temperature was a sizzling ninety-six degrees. From the window near his first-class seat Paige could look out and observe the heat waves billowing off the concrete apron.

Wednesday and Thursday had been long days for Paige as he had returned to Atlanta to ponder and then plot his future course. He had also been concerned over Larry Collier's unexpected departure from New Orleans, and was stunned when Collier's son answered his dad's cell phone early Friday morning at an Atlanta hospital as Collier awaited triple-bypass surgery. The son, himself a medical-school student, explained that his dad's heart attack had been relatively mild, thankfully, and that subsequent tests had uncovered the major areas of blockage. There was every reason to be optimistic, albeit cautiously, that Collier's recovery would be full after the bypass procedure.

Once Paige was in the Tampa airport, a rental-car reservation was waiting in his name. It was a silver Town Car, and it had the strong interior odor of fresh deodorizer with just a hint of stale cigarette smoke. He left the airport complex and drove the twenty or so miles to the Tarpon Springs area, to the northwest, where he eventually located a sign for Laurelbrook, the golf and tennis resort. He then turned toward the east, past Lake Tarpon.

The Laurelbrook community had been developed on three-hundred acres of virgin Florida woodlands. It was recognized as one of the leading resorts of its kind in the entire nation, and it offered first-rate recreation and living accommodations. Guests were always plentiful at Laurelbrook—if nothing else a testament to its popularity with the corporate crowd as a meeting and convention spot. The gardens, lakes, and rolling hills had such a refreshing, rejuvenating quality that the considerable expense of such an excursion was always made a bit more palatable.

Paige turned into the entrance and came to a stop at the rustic, glass-enclosed gatehouse. A uniformed guard presented him with a temporary permit and provided instructions on reaching the reception area. Paige then proceeded ahead along a winding, two-lane paved road that took him past long fairways, grayish-blue lakes, and lengthy lines of pine, palm, and cypress.

He wheeled the Lincoln into a parking spot adjacent to the large clubhouse area. At the registration desk Paige was handed a room key and a note in a white envelope. The bellman, a man in his sixties who spoke softly and moved easily, loaded Paige's bags onto the back of a motorized cart and then drove a short distance along walkways lined with flowers and shrubs. They soon arrived at a cluster of condominiums where the use of automobiles was prohibited, and thus access to the nearby units and amenities required either walking or bicycling. Paved streets and individual parking were found only at a group of units on the property's northwest fringe.

"But not this part," said the bellman, grinning broadly. "About the only thing that'll run over you here is me."

There were lots of walkers who seemed quite content at being out and about, even in the searing heat. The cart rolled past a large outdoor swimming pool which was crowded with young adults. Paige noticed several healthy and barely concealed young women in thongs.

"My goodness," Paige said softly, prompting a mischievous laugh from the bellman.

The bellman turned the cart toward a block of three condos and stopped at the entrance to the unit in the middle. "This is it. Number 1021."

The buildings were two-story structures, all of wood-frame, each with outdoor patios or balconies. Paige's room was a one-bedroom suite on the first floor, complete with king-size bed, kitchen, bath, and living room. The patio could be reached from either the bedroom or the living room.

Paige smiled. Diane Tresvant had arrived the night before from Atlanta, and her things were everywhere.

"Hope you enjoy your stay here at Laurelbrook, sir," the bellman said once Paige's bags were stowed.

Paige thanked the man with a ten and then opened the envelope he had received at the desk. It was a single handwritten sheet, and it said only, "D.P.—Welcome to Florida. Beer in the 'fridge. We'll be at the tennis courts. Missed you last night. Best, D."

The note was accurate—there was easily a case of beer in the refrigerator, and he immediately indulged himself. The interior of the suite was tantalizingly cool, and the temptation to stretch out on the sofa was strong enough that he had to consciously resist it. Instead, he unpacked a few things and then changed into shorts and tennis shirt.

He left the condo and walked the short distance to the tennis area where the six courts in the first facility were all occupied. He looked over the players, nearly all female and all strangers to him, before leaving for the other courts. He crossed a cart path and stopped to glance at the nine additional courts, in groups of threes.

There came a call from a far court. "Hey Dave, over here."

Paige walked through an open gate at the far end of a fence which surrounded the courts.

"Hi," called Diane Tresvant, dressed in all-white and standing alone on the far side of the court, facing another attractive lady across the net.

"Glad you could make it," called Bob Becker of Becker International, sitting off to the side with a towel draped over his balding head. Becker's face was red and his shirt was soaked with perspiration.

The game was suspended temporarily as Becker and Paige met and shook hands, after which Becker introduced his wife Sally, who was on the near court across from Diane. Sally smiled and extended her hand to Paige. She was shapely in her ice-blue outfit—an attractive woman with long legs and short, jet-black hair.

Diane stepped up and greeted Paige with a quick buss on the cheek, then returned to the court with Sally. Diane's cheeks were already rosy pink from the exertion and the exposure.

"I can't keep up with either of them," said Becker, reaching into a cooler and producing two beers. "I'll have a goddamn stroke trying to hang with those two in this heat."

Paige and Becker sipped their beers and watched the women play a mostly even set before the younger Diane finally drove a winner into a corner past the reaching Sally.

"Great shot," called Becker as he turned to see where the ball had landed. "Great game, you two."

Sally was tall, taller than Diane and almost as tall as her husband. And her dark good-looks were enchanting.

And the lovely Ms. Tresvant was likewise appealing.

"So what do you think of Laurelbrook so far?" Sally asked as she slipped her warm-up top over her shoulders.

"Fantastic, what I've seen of it," Paige answered.

"The restaurant's delightful," offered Diane.

"Do you play tennis, Dave?" Sally asked.

"Not much anymore, I'm afraid."

"What about golf?" asked Becker.

"A little, yeah."

"Then we'll play a round in the morning. The course is gorgeous. Not very forgiving, I'm afraid, but plenty scenic. That sound okay?"

"Sounds perfect."

"We'll have a nice dinner tonight, and we can take care of business tomorrow. If your schedules allow, you're both welcome to go back with us on the company jet. We could drop you off in Atlanta on Monday afternoon."

Paige glanced at Diane, who smiled slightly.

"Monday's fine, Bob. Thanks."

"Outstanding," said Becker, slapping at Paige's shoulder. "This is going to work out nicely."

Paige glanced again at Diane, who giggled and reached for her towel.

They started back toward the condos. Paige and Becker carried either side of the cooler, while the ladies hauled the tennis gear.

"So how'd your New Orleans trip work out?" Becker asked once they were underway.

Paige stopped and glanced back with an odd expression. Becker immediately threw his head back in a loud belly laugh.

"What I'd give for a photograph of that look," Becker said, still laughing.

There was an interlude of several hours before dinner. Bob and Sally Becker went for a cool swim while Dave Paige and Diane Tresvant relaxed in their condo. When they took time out for conversation, Diane pressed him for details of the Elerbee Board meeting.

"We'll talk about it later," Paige kept saying.

The two couples later enjoyed a superb dinner together at the resort's flagship restaurant. There was plenty of wine and laughter, and it quickly became clear that they all genuinely delighted in one another's company. Afterwards, they stopped at a nearby lounge for a nightcap. It was only sparsely crowded, and after a couple of drinks and a bit of mild prodding by Diane and the Beckers, Paige sat down at the club's piano and launched into a rousing, twenty-minute medley of collegiate fight songs and military marching songs that brought everyone up and singing at the piano, including the barkeep, who told Paige that he should press the management for payment after such a grand performance.

Becker telephoned Paige at six-thirty on Sunday morning. They met for breakfast at seven. By seven-thirty, they were on the practice green, streaking putts across the dew-laden grass. The clubs in Paige's possession came from an extra set belonging to Becker, as did his golf glove, visor, golf balls, and tees. Only the shoes were rentals, due mainly to Paige's larger feet.

"Shall we?" Becker called when their time had arrived.

"By all means," Paige replied, motioning Becker ahead.

They were each on the green in three, with Becker's ball a mere six feet from the cup. Becker made par; Paige took a bogey.

"Diane enjoying herself?" Becker asked as they climbed into the cart and started off across a wooden bridge toward the second tee.

"She's having a ball," Paige said, after which he blushed slightly when Becker roared with laughter.

The par-five second hole was long and narrow. Becker's tee shot rose in an arc and landed safely on the fairway's right fringe. Paige blasted a drive forty yards beyond.

"Damn!"

They each achieved par.

"How about you, Dave. Are you enjoying yourself?"

"Absolutely. The timing was perfect."

The third hole was a short par-three. Becker made par. Paige birdied by rolling a fifteen-foot putt into the center of the cup.

"Damn!"

They were even again.

"You were good last night," Becker said in reference to Paige's impromptu piano concerto.

"You're the second person this morning who's told me that."

Becker roared again.

After trading the lead over several holes, Paige was ahead by one stroke going into the eighth.

"The loser on the front nine buys the beer at the turn," Becker propositioned.

Paige won eight; on nine, they each double-bogeyed. Becker paid for the beer.

They sat in the cart near the tenth tee, awaiting another twosome to get underway.

"The loser on the back nine buys dinner tonight," Becker said after the pair in front of them climbed into a cart and drove away down the fairway.

Paige glanced at Becker, quickly evaluating his partner's golf game and his general physical conditioning. "Dinner it is," he answered after a brief pause.

Becker bit into a Three Musketeers. "Got a question for you, hotshot."

"Okay. Fire away."

"Are you an ethical person?"

"I'm good for dinner tonight if I lose, if that's what you mean."

Becker laughed. "I want to know if you consider yourself an ethical person."

"Sure," Paige said without hesitation.

"Which means?"

Paige shrugged. "Which means I play hard and fair."

"Good."

Becker got out of the cart.

"What was that all about?" Paige called.

"One of the things I've heard about you is that you're an 'ethical' person, whatever that means. Several people I know and trust used that word to describe you."

Paige gave a strange look.

"One thing you need to know about me, Dave, and it's this: I live by the rules of the goddamn jungle. I stay within the law, but beyond that it's knife blades and hand grenades. If they blink, I'm by 'em; if they stagger, I go for the jugular. I don't let anything else get in the way. Business power is like military power or political power—it'll probably corrupt you when you get lots of it, but without it you'll always be weak and subservient. And power doesn't count for jackshit unless you use it when it's needed. What's the point of being muscular, right? We have a financial muscle that allows us to do what's needed to grow and prosper, and we damn well use it. We can outsmart 'em or outflank 'em or simply roll over 'em like an armored column in the attack. Go for the brass ring, I say, and I'm prepared to do whatever the hell it takes to get there, again within our system of laws."

Becker gave Paige a long stare. "I thought that needed to be said. You ought to know how I view certain things. Any issues?"

"Nope," Paige said, shaking his head. "You've chosen me for who and what I am; I've chosen you for the same reason."

"Excellent," Becker said firmly.

After fourteen holes, the lead remained with Paige.

"What about this, Dave: The loser buys dinner tonight and breakfast in the morning. Can you handle that?"

"I accept," Paige said without hesitation.

Becker drew even on fifteen with a spectacular iron shot. He went ahead on sixteen with an equally brilliant bunker shot that ended up a foot from the pin. Paige evened the score on seventeen with a long drive and a nifty eight-iron shot. They were all alone when Paige drove the cart up the slight incline to the eighteenth and final hole.

"This is it, champ. Are you ready?" Becker asked, a towel draped over his head.

"I'm ready," Paige answered with confidence as he looked down the length of the long, straight fairway.

They got out and reached for their drivers. The white, single-story clubhouse was visible through the tall pines at the far end of the long, green, sun-drenched corridor.

Becker leaned on his club and glanced down the fairway. "I'm just about ready to take your meal money, pilgrim." He then took his stance at the tee and squared himself. He paused and turned to Paige. "Incidentally, Diane Tresvant got a call yesterday morning from someone in the Elerbee organization who told her that the word in New Orleans was that your ex-wife had shown up with some high-powered Pittsburgh lawyer looking to renegotiate the divorce settlement, something about it being terribly unfair, and that she had apparently made one hell of a nasty scene at the hotel in front of a bunch of Elerbee people. And your ex even claimed that the reason you had left early was to flee from her. Diane said she was afraid to mention it to you, that she didn't want to ruin your trip to Florida. She was really upset by it, and she asked me to be the one to tell you."

Paige experienced a sudden break in his reasoning circuitry, the result of which left him speechless. Becker turned and blasted what could only be described as a monster drive, the ball starting low and rising at high velocity, dead center in the fairway. When he rose from picking up his wooden tee, he glanced over at Paige with a huge grin on his face and muttered, "Just kidding, Dave."

They played out the round. Paige fell apart and Becker won easily.

Dinner (and the following morning's breakfast) would come compliments of Dave Paige.

Bob Becker was dressed casually and sat at the head of the rectangular table. Paige sat to his left, alongside Diane Tresvant who was dressed in a white cotton sundress and whose bare shoulders were pink with overexposure. The deeply tanned Sally Becker, also in a white sundress and sipping a Margarita through a straw, sat to her husband's right.

Beside Sally was Peter Halloran, freshly arrived from New Orleans.

Champagne was brought to the table.

"Okay, let's hear it," Becker said, nodding in Paige's direction. "Let's hear what you've got to say about our little coup."

Paige grinned widely. "It was just as we predicted. Everything came together exactly like we'd scripted it."

Becker laughed. "Did anyone resist?"

"Yeah," Paige nodded. "Larry covered us perfectly. Once Grace Elerbee and Jeff Wylie were seen in it together, it was all over but the shouting."

"Greed, man. It's the easiest thing in the world to predict, and the easiest thing to work off of," said Becker. "You had them pegged, partner, I gotta admit. When you called me after the meeting, I almost fell over laughing when you told me it went almost exactly like you said it would."

"It was almost painful, in some ways," Paige said with a tinge of sadness. "The way some of the really good people suffered through the whole thing, I mean."

"Screw the 'painful' part, hotrod. They'll be immensely better off when the gallant Pete Halloran turns around and sells the company to us, and then they have you as their head knocker."

Halloran grinned and raised his glass to Becker.

"Yeah," Paige said, smiling broadly. "I almost couldn't resist telling them, especially after I'd told Wylie that I'm resigning. He and Ogden were strutting around like Arthur and Lancelot."

"More like Laurel and Hardy, I would think."

Paige shook his head in utter amazement. What had begun as a lighthearted suggestion to Bob Becker in the wee hours of their first meeting—that purchasing Elerbee Engineering would be a far more expedient way to become a player in the engineering-consulting business than by developing Becker and Associates—was now a fact. Instead of the idea being *cum grano salis* it had been transformed by Becker and his money and his contacts into a *fait accompli*. Becker had been interested in just such a deal for some time, and when he and Paige had sketched out a conceptual framework involving a broker (disguised ostensibly as an investor to entice and eventually hook the big fish, Grace Elerbee, who would never knowingly sell to a Becker), the die had for all practical purposes been cast. For Paige, the dividends were considerable: Presidency of the new firm, still called Elerbee Engineering but absorbing into its structure the vastly smaller Becker and Associates; partial ownership (with the preferential financing provided by none other than Bob Becker); stock options based upon performance incentives; a salary of three-hundred thousand dollars, with potential bonuses equaling another one hundred thousand; a luxury auto; several club memberships; and the other assortment of perks and privileges afforded a ranking member of the Becker inner-circle. Indeed, it was all there—a professional leap so fast and so elevated that every now and then Paige would nearly hyperventilate when he pondered how his life was changing. As for Peter Halloran, there would be a nice fee to make his time and effort worthwhile.

In return, Becker got precisely what he wanted—the right company, the right industry niche, and the right man. Together. Packaged expensively, but no doubt worth it over the long haul.

"God, I can't believe it," Paige said, still in uncharacteristic awe. He was amazed at how things had changed so dramatically, in such a short span, just by looking at things from a different angle, the same way snow changes from white to dark just by looking up instead of out.

"Believe it, my man. The world is full of opportunities for those who have the stomach to stand on the accelerator and not lift in the corners."

There was that word again, Paige thought.

"You're probably thinking to yourself that I use the word 'opportunities' too much," said Becker.

Paige smiled.

"But I see 'em everywhere, every day of my life. And I see the same quality in you, too," Becker said, leaning closer to Paige. "Most people only see the problems, Dave, if they see any damn thing at all."

Halloran, himself no stranger to opportunity, nodded his concurrence.

"Yeah," Paige said with a nod of his own. "If I didn't believe that before, I certainly do now."

Appetizers and the main course were eventually served. Swordfish, bluefish, snapper—it was all wonderfully fresh and satisfying, though not so filling that there wasn't room afterwards for the extravagant pastries.

"This is decadent," Paige said, smiling, as he used his fork to probe the center of a cream-filled dessert.

Coffee followed afterward, and Halloran used the time to tell of his Friday morning session with the stunned group of Elerbee Engineering executives.

"How did they take it?" Diane asked out of curiosity, still fascinated by the entire arrangement.

Halloran smiled slightly. "They had no choice, really. They walked into the room and were told that the company's being sold, period. Then they listened to me. Then they were told that they would be provided with all the details to make the transition a smooth one. Then they were given the brochures on Halloran Investments. And all of this in the last hour of the last session on the last day of their meeting. I'm sure they all left wondering what the hell had hit them."

"I'm sure they were devastated," Paige said with empathy, remembering all the familiar faces.

Halloran smiled. "Your description's right on the mark, Dave. Heck, there were even wives crying in the hotel lobby by Friday noon," Halloran explained, shaking his head in disbelief. "It wasn't a happy ending for them."

Paige remembered how agonizing it had been for Larry Collier, to whom Paige had confessed his plan only a few hours before the New Orleans session had begun. Collier had been sickened at the thought of Wylie and Grace Elerbee's interest in selling the firm, and had joined with Paige as a co-conspirator, of sorts. Collier had even suggested that he resist the sale in the Board meeting, not just for reasons of principle, but to give Paige a look at how the other Board members would react to Wylie's pressure. Paige might find it revealing, Collier had suggested. And indeed, he had.

"How do you feel about all that's happened, Dave," Halloran asked when he saw Paige immersed in thought.

Paige hesitated before finally answering softly, "It's for the best."

Halloran and Becker both nodded, though their own interpretations of Paige's meaning were likely different.

It was nearly noon on Monday when Becker International's eleven-passenger Gulfstream III climbed into the cloudy skies above the Tampa Bay area. Diane Tresvant, wearing a white halter with blue shorts, sat beside Dave Paige, who wore jeans and a black t-shirt with *French Quarter* emblazoned across the front. Facing them from across the aisle were Bob and Sally Becker, also dressed casually. Once the flight was conveniently underway, Sally broke out an on-board lunch of Cuban sandwiches and canned soft drinks that had been delivered at the last minute from an Ybor City delicatessen.

"Here's what I want you to do, Dave," Becker said with his mouth bulging. "I want you to call in tomorrow and tell old Wylie that you've gotta have the week off to sort through some other opportunities. If you have to tell him something—a reason, or whatever—then give him one. Just don't arouse any more suspicion than will be there anyway. Know what I mean? Then get up to Philly so we can get cracking on an operating plan for the 'new' Elerbee Engineering. We've got a ton of work to do, killer, so bring your lunch pail."

"And bring Diane, if you can work it out," added Sally.

"Good idea," said Becker. "We'll put you up at the apartment we maintain near our offices. Bring your lunch pail, too, Diane."

Diane smiled. "Thanks, but I've got a ton of stuff of my own to do."

"Your call," said Becker. "But you're certainly welcome any time you can break away."

Diane smiled and nodded her appreciation.

"I'll be up there sometime tomorrow afternoon," Paige finally said.

"You gave Wylie a resignation notice of what, thirty days?"

"Thirty days, right."

"Good. We'll close again in sixty days, so you'll have a full month in Philly before you go back to Atlanta, in charge."

Diane saw the instant grin on Paige's face. He had already fastened on the "in charge" label and found the fit to his immense liking.

"Anybody you want to save from your staff?" Becker asked.

"Yeah, several."

"Then get the word to them to stay put."

Paige nodded, the grin still attached.

"Super," said Becker, after which he took another bite of his sandwich.

Sally pointed to something out the window, causing Becker to lean toward her for a look of his own. They both laughed, and then Becker kissed her on the cheek. "Great sandwiches," he remarked, taking another bite.

Paige leaned and gave Diane a light kiss. "Did you have a good time?"

"I had a wonderful time," she answered, almost as much with her eyes as with her voice.

Paige and Becker talked on at some length, the issues ranging from continuity and stability to profitability.

"We'll do this thing right," asserted Becker, "and make it even *more* profitable. We'll let Elerbee absorb Becker and Associates, although if I wasn't so damned concerned about continuity I swear to God I'd do it the other way around and drop the Elerbee name altogether. But nah, I won't do that; I'll keep the Elerbee brand. This company will be a superstar, man, you wait and see. I'm paying a freakin' premium, but it'll be worth it."

Paige nodded his understanding.

"Let Wylie and his boys settle everything down for us," Becker continued. "They'll close with Pete Halloran in a couple of weeks, and we'll announce the second sale right after that."

"They'll be appointing some new regional managers soon. Shouldn't we delay that?"

"I've already asked Pete to advise Wylie that all executive-level changes will have to be reviewed and approved by Pete's office before being finalized. We can have Pete sit on anything they send to him."

"Good. I have a feeling that more than a few of those people would come from Ogden's cronies."

Becker laughed. "And you'd prefer to deal with Ogden and his crowd at the proper time, right?"

Paige grinned in agreement. "Exactly."

Becker glanced over at Sally, and then pointed toward Paige. "This guy's a freakin' maniac," he said in an exaggerated, high-pitched voice.

"Then you two should get along famously," Sally replied.

They all laughed.

The pizza was delivered at a little past eight. Paige quickly dressed himself in his jeans and hurried downstairs to answer the delivery boy's ring of the doorbell. The flat cardboard box was warm, and the aroma from inside was absolutely divine, even if he was practically famished. He paid the young man and ran into the kitchen where he grabbed paper napkins and plates, salt and pepper shakers, a soft drink for Diane and a beer for himself. He then rushed back upstairs with everything balanced precariously atop the box.

Diane was sitting up in bed dressed in a black bra and black bikini panties. Paige entered the room smiling.

"Did you check to make sure it's got the right stuff on it?" she asked, her accountant tendencies surfacing.

"No, sweets, I didn't. I'm so hungry that I don't *care* what's on it as long as it ain't crawling."

Diane made a face at such a thought. She was famished, too, and she had wanted pepperoni and cheese and onions and peppers and sausage. But when she got close enough to the box to get a strong whiff, she suddenly didn't care any longer, either. As it turned out, the toppings were exactly as specified.

Several calls came later.

Bob Becker called and invited Paige and Diane to join Sally and himself, along with several other Becker International executives and their spouses, for a weekend at Becker's Cape Cod place for an upcoming August date. The offer was quickly accepted.

Mike Petrovic called from St. Louis and wanted to know if Paige had indeed resigned. "I gotta know, Dave," Petrovic insisted. "I gotta make some plans." Paige assured him that everything was cool, that soon things would work out beyond Petrovic's wildest imagination. Petrovic was eventually calmed.

Sara Paige called from Pittsburgh to ask her father how his New Orleans trip had turned out. "Great," he told her, then promised to give her the full story later, when she would be visiting in Atlanta. "Everything's working out nicely, doll. Just like it was supposed to."

Dot Collier called to report that husband Larry, though still hospitalized, had recovered to a point that was highly encouraging to his team of doctors. Collier's strength was gradually returning, and Dot's hope overshadowed the obvious strain she had endured over the past several days.

It was soothing news to Paige. The situation with Larry Collier had been eating at him for days. He couldn't quite shake it, though he had tried hard to dismiss it as merely an unfortunate confluence of stressful circumstance and ill health. But it still bothered him, even amid the excitement of the deal with Becker and the pleasures of his burgeoning relationship with Diane. It was just there, always there, unceasing, gnawing at him in tiny bits, gnawing and gnawing and gnawing. Collier had given most of his life in honest, dedicated service to the firm, had fought many honorable fights, had always said his piece with courage and clarity when others had faltered, and had thus been rewarded for it all by being emotionally ground into hamburger in the final, arduous week.

Paige knew he wasn't responsible for Collier's state of physical health. After all, Collier's clogged arteries had been years in the making—a function of genetics and lifestyle, mainly. Paige also knew that what he had exposed Collier to at the Elerbee Board meeting might well have served as the trigger—the tipping point— for the clock that ticked once too often and brought forth the time bomb inside Collier's chest. And the troubling, weighty thoughts of that possibility never strayed very far from Paige.

Collier was damaged and on his back, and Paige was standing tall, on top of his world. And the gnawing over the whole gut-wrenching affair continued.

And continued.

CHAPTER TWENTY SEVEN

More than two months passed before the company once again changed hands. As before, the employees of Elerbee Engineering were stunned when the unexpected announcement came. A few were pleasantly surprised when Becker International surfaced as the new owner; a few others, in their more traditional perspectives, were deeply hurt and disappointed, even though Dave Paige's emergence out of the ashes seemed to appease many of those who had fretted over the quality of the previous management. Most, however, had reached the point that they cared little about who owned the firm as long as some measure of stability could come again to prevail. They had begun to feel helpless, much as if their small boat had been caught in a raging sea and all they could manage to do was to hang on and hope for the best. No one enjoyed the uncertainty and the deep emotional drain that always followed a sudden change in ownership.

Thus, Peter Halloran was no longer in the picture. The company was now Bob Becker's to do with as he saw fit. As such, his first official act after the November first closing with Halloran Investments was to bluntly inform Jeff Wylie that David Paige was replacing him as President and Chief Operating Officer. Becker himself was assuming the duties as Chairman and Chief Executive Officer, effectively leaving Wylie out in the cold. Wylie, however, was gracious through it all, even volunteering his assistance in the transition and hinting to Becker on several occasions of his own availability in a consulting capacity to whatever future extent might be desired. Becker ignored the suggestion and instead sent Wylie packing.

By late November several changes had been made to the organizational structure. Jim Ogden remained as Executive Vice President and assisted Paige in the implementation of the new regional organization. The regional managers were all chosen by Paige, approved by Becker, and included none of the names previously selected by Wylie and Ogden in the original staffing of their plan, which had in fact been plagiarized from a report Dave Paige had authored several years earlier as a student in the Executive

Development Seminar. The personnel and facilities of Becker and Associates remained in Philadelphia, although it officially became known as the Philadelphia Branch of Elerbee Engineering. As for Paige and Becker, they were in daily contact by phone, with Becker managing to squeeze in half-day visits to Atlanta on a bi-weekly basis. Otherwise, Becker left the running of the company to Paige.

Paige had placed on full display for the new organization his intrepid management style and his typical breakneck pace. There was little time for Jim Ogden to reflect upon the incredible changes that had occurred in his reporting relationship, for Paige simply kept him far too busy. A fourteen-hour day was fast becoming the new executive standard in the corporate headquarters, and Paige himself routinely arrived at six in the morning and rarely left much before eight-thirty in the evening. It was a grind, and many of the senior managers were suddenly left to wonder about its efficacy. It came as no surprise to Paige when Ed Webb, Vice President-Marketing, along with three lesser executives, chose to resign to pursue their life's calling elsewhere rather than continue in what could only be viewed by them as an entirely unreasonable and insufferable work environment.

Revenues remained fair, even amid the worsening economy, the two successive changes in ownership, and the inevitable questions in the marketplace over Elerbee's stability. Paige was amazed that his shell-shocked troops in the branches were still left with plenty of fight. The profit picture was different, however. Profits lagged significantly behind the levels of the previous months, a fact which caused Paige no small measure of anxiety. Payroll costs were frozen simply by foregoing all new hiring, even for cream-of-the-crop, entry-level engineers. An increase in the fee schedule's hourly rates appeared to be inappropriate given the dismal economy, even though Paige knew all too well that Bob Becker had paid a premium for the firm, and that Becker justifiably expected a healthy profit in return.

For now, Elerbee Engineering was avoiding the ubiquitous process referred to as downsizing—another way of saying the firm was firing or retiring legions of employees. Paige had convinced Becker that the firm needed to become leaner and meaner, but the timing was ill-conceived for such a move because of the general state of numbness already existing in many of the Elerbee personnel. The corporate headquarters staff was another matter, though, and Paige decided that it would be reduced by a third; that branch managers, *all* managers, should become more hands-on so that many of the expensive support personnel could eventually be dropped. Altogether, the firm was eliminating only twenty-five jobs, mostly in the corporate headquarters, and accepting early retirements from another thirty—a reduction of slightly more than two percent of the total workforce.

The two successive ownership changes and the day-to-day suspicion that followed had by now pulverized the morale of many employees into a fine powder. There was skepticism everywhere, coupled with a palpable sense of foreboding and unease. Competitor firms were attempting to gain market share with a steady stream of rumors about Elerbee's instability, both financial and managerial. Elerbee's relatively few creditors kept a watchful eye on the firm's proceedings. Gone were many of the old hands, like Wylie, Collier, and Webb. There were lots of new people, new systems, new phrases, new rules, and new forms. And presiding over it all was the seemingly unruffled Dave Paige, though virtually all of his fingernails had by now been bitten off to the quick.

Larry Collier had been correct, after all. The place just wasn't the same as before.

Sherry rang Paige at his desk. "Don Burroughs is here to see you."

"Send him in," said Paige, after which he took one last sip of his morning coffee.

Burroughs opened the door to Langdon Elerbee's old office and stepped inside. He closed the door behind him and took a seat facing Paige's ominously large desk.

Paige straightened in his chair. "No need to beat around the bush, Don. You're no doubt aware of why I've called you in here."

Burroughs swallowed, and then grinned slightly. "No doubt. But I'd still prefer to hear you say it."

"And say it I shall: Don, I'm terminating your employment with Elerbee Engineering, effective immediately. You will be given three months compensation with full benefits. You may turn in all company credit cards, keys, and so forth to Jim Ogden on your way out. In return, Jim will provide you with a package that will detail all the provisions of your severance, including written confirmation of what I have just told you. Jim will also be available to answer any questions and assist where needed. Your years of service to Elerbee Engineering are appreciated, and I wish you the best of luck in finding a new position with a new employer."

Paige paused a moment, taking in the sight of the broken, beaten, perspiring Burroughs. He had a sudden subliminal image of a stricken Don Burroughs clutching his chest and falling forward, arriving graveyard dead at his temporary resting place upon Paige's office carpet. Paige blinked once, then again, and the image abruptly disappeared. He finally asked, "Do you have any questions of me?"

Burroughs took a deep breath. He clasped his trembling hands together in his lap and asked in a constricted voice, "Any particular reason?"

"Your position's being eliminated. It's part of the overall move toward a leaner, more efficient organization."

Burroughs gave a derisive snicker. "I hope you realize that you're ruining this company. Eliminating my position isn't going to make it more efficient."

"I'm sorry you feel that way," Paige said with a hard stare. "Maybe it's a stroke of good fortune for you that you won't be here to witness any more of the ruin."

"Yeah," Burroughs said, nodding. "Maybe it is, then."

Paige stood. "If there are no further questions, thank you again for your service to the firm."

Vince Kincaid, Vice President-Finance, had just been told by Dave Paige that his position would remain intact in the new structure, albeit downgraded somewhat, but that he, Kincaid, would not be the man to fill it. "You don't fit with what I'm trying to build," Paige explained to the stunned Kincaid. "And I really don't think we could ever overcome some of the things that have happened in the past, Vince. The firm's moving in a different direction, with a lot of different people. And I regret to inform you that one of those different people will be in your job."

"But I just don't understand, Dave."

"You're not the man I want on my team, Vince. It's as simple as that. And I'm appointing your replacement today. I'm sorry it has to be so sudden, but that's the way these things work sometimes. As for you, you'll have a nice severance package that you can get from Jim Ogden, who will be available to answer any questions and assist where needed."

"My God, is that all there is after almost fifteen years of service with this firm?"

Paige let out an audible sigh. "I'm afraid so."

Kincaid looked frail and hurt. "Who's gonna be my replacement?"

"Hal Mortensen."

"That goddamned kid?" said the indignant Kincaid, suddenly stiffening in his chair.

"That's the one, Vince," Paige said, standing. "If there are no further questions, then I thank you again for your service to the firm."

"Dave, Ron Steinkempf is here to see you."

The chief technical practitioner took a seat across from Paige. He was understandably ill at ease, and it showed. The word was already out that people were being carved up like sides of beef behind these same closed doors.

"I'll make this short and sweet, Ron. Is that okay with you?"

Steinkempf swallowed hard. "You're calling the shots, Dave," he answered, the strain evident in his voice. "I'm at your disposal."

"I'll get right to the point, then. I want you to know that I very badly need you on this team, that I'm counting on you to stay and see this thing through with me. I have no plans to change your job, except maybe to ask you to take on even more than you were given in the past. But my main reason for calling you in here is to reassure you that I need you, that you're my technical expert of choice. You know my values, and I know yours. And we're compatible. And I need that kind of compatibility with the person in your job. I know you'll come and tell me when you think I'm screwing up, in plain language, and I trust the sound judgment that I've come to identify with you over the years."

Paige then stopped and stared at Steinkempf for a moment, nodding and saying nothing further.

Steinkempf breathed a great sigh of relief and slumped down in his chair. The smile came back onto his face in degrees, like a PowerPoint slide in a slow, grainy transition. "Good grief, I thought I was a goner."

"Nope," Paige said, shaking his head. "You're definitely a keeper."

"Dave, Mike Petrovic is here to see you."

It was late afternoon. Paige had been behind closed doors for most of the day, and was enjoying his first unscheduled time for what seemed like weeks. Petrovic, for his part, had waited until noon to leave St. Louis after receiving Paige's early-morning summons.

"Come on in, Mike," Paige said when he saw Petrovic in the open door.

They smiled and shook hands, and then settled into their chairs in the relaxed, unpretentious manner befitting old friends.

"The air's thick enough in this building that it'd take a friggin' David Bowie knife to cut it," said Petrovic. "Everybody I've talked to assumes you're about to fire my ass, since you've gone to the trouble to send for me."

Paige smiled. "I believe it's Jim Bowie, but what the hell? As long as the knife cuts, right?"

"Hell, maybe you *are* gonna fire me. What gives, D.P.?"

"How would you like to move to Atlanta and work closely with me on running this company on a day-to-day basis?"

Petrovic chuckled. "You're getting ready to can Ogden, right?"

"Don't worry about Ogden," Paige answered, unsmiling. "I'd like to bring you in here as my assistant. I'll make you a Vice President of 'Something', Operations probably, and let you take some of the day-to-day stuff off me. You'll get a big raise and a big office and—"

"But I'm just getting settled in St. Louis. You want me to move again, so suddenly?"

"Yes. Is that a problem?"

Petrovic shrugged. "Nah, not really."

"Then get settled in Atlanta."

"Can I have Sherry as my secretary?"

"You most certainly cannot."

"Can we share her?"

"We most certainly will not."

"I'll take the job any damn way. When do we start?"

Paige began laughing at the irrepressible Petrovic. "Couple of weeks, or so. We'll have to designate a manager for the St. Louis Branch, and I'll want your advice on that. Why don't we make it effective after the holidays, say January second?"

"You got it, boss. January two it is."

"You're an easy sell, you old whore," Paige said, grinning broadly.

Petrovic leaned back in the chair with a smug look on his face as he took a deep breath and slowly shook his head. "How in God's name did you manage to swing all of this," he asked, arms outstretched.

"Pretty crazy, huh?"

"Very."

"I had some help, obviously."

"Obviously. Did it take much to get Becker on board?"

"He jumped all over it when I brought it up, almost as if he'd been thinking the same thing. But he made it all happen a lot faster than I ever thought possible. When he decides to move on something, man, does he ever move quickly."

"How did Wylie take it?"

"Stunned," Paige answered with a satisfied chuckle. "No way did he see things turning out like this."

Petrovic giggled. "Wish I could've seen his freakin' face, man."

Paige also chuckled. "I know he was thinking about all the times he should've fired me, kicking himself the entire time. And I knew that once the discussions with Halloran started, he couldn't fire me because of the 'value' that I'm sure Grace Elerbee thought I would've added to the asking price."

"What's the story with Grace Elerbee?"

"She's royally pissed at me. She told Larry Collier's wife that I'd 'duped' her, and that I was a disgrace to the Elerbee Engineering tradition of high moral and ethical conduct. She said she never wants to see me again."

Petrovic laughed loudly. "You duped her all right, just after she'd duped the world by agreeing to sell the firm in the first goddamn place."

"I suppose so. I'm certainly not a very popular person with her *or* the old Wylie crowd."

"You've rooted out most of Wylie's people, right?"

"Right, except Ogden, and he's right here where I can watch him."

"One of Ogden's old cronies in the East told me over the phone yesterday that what you're doing is the most ruthless thing he's ever seen in his entire business career. I told him that I agreed, that it was *damned* ruthless, but that the only way we'd ever rid the castle of all the rats was to stick a burning torch down every dark hole where they might be hiding," Petrovic said, starting to laugh again. "The asshole hung up on me."

Paige smiled self-consciously.

"This could turn out to be a really good thing, man," Petrovic said, turning serious. "This is the chance of a lifetime."

"I'm glad you see it that way," said Paige, nodding.

"Becker's obviously committed to the business. And with his name and resources, we should be able to build a helluva dominant operation."

"As soon as we get our house in order, we can make this company the gold standard. Everything's all set; everything's here—the talent, the territory, the cash, *everything*, Mike. All we've got to do is keep it all pointed in the right direction."

"Any chance Becker will give in and let the employees own some stock?"

Paige nodded. "We've discussed that, and he's receptive. It may take a little time, but I believe it'll happen. He sees the value of it now."

Petrovic jumped to his feet and gave Paige a high-five. "Damn, I'm pumped. Let's get started."

"Dinner tonight?"

"Absolutely. Will Diane be joining us?"

"No," Paige said, taking his seat again. "She's out of town on business. She sends her regrets, because she really wants to meet you now that she's heard so much about you."

Petrovic turned his head slightly, still eyeing Paige. "That special, this Diane Tresvant person?"

"Yeah," Paige said, grinning. "That special."

Petrovic also sat back down. "So, have you guys moved in together yet? Are you two cohabitulating?"

"No," Paige answered with a chuckle. "She still has her own place."

"Anything from Valerie lately?"

"Nope," Paige said, showing no emotion.

"Not even a whisper?"

"Not even."

There was a momentary silence. Paige could see from Petrovic's expression that further elaboration was expected.

"What the hell is this? An inquiry? I'm your friggin' boss, you know."

Petrovic gave a boyish smile. "So when are you gonna marry Diane, boss?"

"Not tonight. Tonight's reserved for you."

"Super. Gimme three Hates."

Paige gave a momentary look of annoyance, then sighed and quickly began pondering. "I hate it when room service forgets something, like the bottle opener or the soup spoon or the mustard. I hate it when the pilot comes on over the intercom just before takeoff and starts out by saying, 'Well, ladies and gentlemen . . .' because you know you're going nowhere when that happens. I hate it when some hotshot speaker uses the term 'we're excited about it' with no more genuine enthusiasm than if he were delivering a eulogy for a complete stranger."

Petrovic nodded. "Good originality for the most part, although I think you may have used the flight-announcement thing already, back in Ninety Four, as I remember. O'Brady's in Pittsburgh, the corner booth."

"I most certainly have not."

"Whatever. A nine point five."

"That's way too low. Gimme three Whys."

"Uh, why does a guy always sniff or cough when he's in the john sitting in a closed stall, and someone else walks into the bathroom? Why is it that a person can drink more beer in one sitting than any other liquid, including water, which is incidentally beer's main ingredient and the main ingredient of most everything else? Why is it that so many people are ending their sentences nowadays with the term 'as we speak'?"

"Solid," Paige said, smiling, "but not spectacular. I'll give you a nine point two."

Petrovic stood. "Too low, but that's another issue. Drinks across the street in an hour?"

"In an hour," Paige said, already looking at a stack of papers on his desk.

"I'll meet you there. Can I invite Sherry?"

"No, you may not."

"She's got some fabulous—"

"Enough. Besides, she's busy working on something for me, even as we speak."

"D.P., you're looking at this at the thirty-thousand foot level."

"Let's table this discussion."

"It's about Sherry's bosoms. You've got to wake up and smell the roses. The fence is greener on the other side. I think this can really go somewhere if we get all our ducks on the same page."

Paige laughed and shook his head. "Enough. Now get out of here."

Petrovic stood. "Sounds like a plan."

"In an hour, Mike. Now scram!"

Paige finished the last of the paperwork in just over an hour's time. He then reached for his *Paige's Laws of Business* and took out his pen.

When it's time to seize the moment, don't waste precious time gloating over successes or whining over setbacks; seize it!

Make your best judgments about people and move on. Trust your instincts.

A really grand opportunity appears all too infrequently. Make sure it gets the ceaseless effort and attention it properly deserves. Don't squander it.

Paige looked at his watch. Petrovic was no doubt into his second drink by now. He laughed softly at the thought of his free-spirited friend. Petrovic's competent leadership would be a plus for his developing staff, not to mention Petrovic's ability to provide him with honest and unfettered advice as a highly-trusted confidant. Mike would need some work, admittedly, but it would be good to have him close at hand, Paige kept thinking as he locked his desk, buttoned his collar, and reached for his jacket. Petrovic was damned good—an unpolished but rare gem—and at this point in the process, his business acumen and leadership skills had never been more greatly needed.

Ah, but to have fifty more like him, Paige thought on his way out of the office. Then he had a quick mental flash of a grinning Petrovic in the company of a bevy of wild women in the bar.

Well, maybe one or two more like him, Paige concluded.

CHAPTER TWENTY EIGHT

He tired easily, Dot explained as she and Dave Paige sat on the sofa near Larry Collier's easy chair. Collier said little, and when he did his voice was raspy and weak, as if the battery had run down. There had been an infection from the surgery, and another heart operation had been required. It had been touch-and-go for over a week, and only in the past few days had Collier's overall condition shown any improvement. He was greatly weakened, but at least now the outlook was encouraging. Paige smiled and joked with the Colliers, and admired the bravery and the compassion and the easy touch with which Dot was handling it all. But it wasn't the same Larry Collier he had known and admired for years for his expressiveness and can-do attitude. Instead, this was a tired, weary old man, whose thinning hair and liver spots now seemed all the more pronounced to Paige.

"But he's making progress every day," Dot said with pride. "Isn't that right, dear?"

Collier managed only a soft, "Uh huh."

"If he makes the kind of progress in the next few days that he's made the last few, why he'll be almost as good as new."

Paige smiled and nodded, hoping that his disbelief didn't show. "Good. I'm going to need him as a consultant as soon as he's ready to come back."

"Larry's certainly a fighter, David, that's for sure," Dot continued. "We're going to get on top of this thing. Right, dear?"

Collier nodded slowly, his eyes showing little conviction.

Paige later enjoyed coffee with Dot, and he began speaking softly when he heard Collier's light snoring and noticed that sleep had finally overtaken his good friend. Dot covered her husband with a blanket, then returned to the sofa with Paige.

"I really do appreciate your visits, David. And I know Larry does, too," Dot said with sincerity.

"I hope Larry understands about all the things that happened in New Orleans," Paige said, the words coming with difficulty. "I really wanted a chance as soon as it was over to sit down with him and talk through the entire episode, to let him know that I didn't do anything out of spite or disrespect to him. And that I agonized about telling him in advance, about whether it was the best thing to do. I sincerely hope that I explained all of it as clearly as possible," Paige said, stopping and glancing at the resting Collier, "especially now."

"He understands," Dot said soothingly.

"I hope so. If I thought that what I'd done had anything to do with this," Paige said, suddenly becoming filled with emotion, "I'd never be able to forgive myself."

Paige felt his eyes moisten, and he feared for just a moment that he might break down and weep. Every time he looked over at Collier, his mind flashed back to the Board meeting. He took a deep breath and gathered himself.

"David, he understands," Dot said with slightly more authority as she reached out and touched Paige's arm. "You're not responsible for Larry's condition. Don't burden yourself with something that was beyond your ability to control. And the fact is, if you hadn't been so considerate of Larry and told him beforehand, the result might have been far worse."

Paige took a deep breath.

"David, I'm certain the shock would have been far greater if you hadn't told him when you did."

"You don't know how much I needed to hear that, Dot," Paige said as a tear began coursing down his cheek."

"We're gonna be just fine," she said convincingly. "And so are you, David. And we'll look forward to seeing you again and hearing about all the great things happening at Elerbee Engineering."

Paige leaned across and kissed Dot on the forehead.

Collier finally stirred and opened his eyes just as Paige was about to leave. When Paige stood beside him and took his hand and wished him well, Collier offered a weak handshake and mumbled something, twice, that Paige vaguely interpreted as, "Don't forget about loyalty," though he couldn't be sure. He simply nodded and wished Collier well once again, and promised that he'd be back to give his friend an update on the happenings with the firm. Though he couldn't tell it from the handshake or hear it in his voice, Paige knew from the look in Collier's eyes that all was well.

As well as could be, given the circumstances.

Paige drove home shortly thereafter, thinking along the way of the message Collier was attempting to communicate.

Loyalty.

The sound of the word kept ringing inside his head, along with the images of a stricken man and a wonderful woman. The visit had given him another nagging sense of unease, though there was some comfort in Dot's courage and dedication to her husband. Thankfully there was someone there for Collier, to help him when he needed it most, to see him through his life's darkest moment, to give him an assurance of worth, of love, of loyalty for all the years and all the moves and the kids and the promissory notes and the trips to the beach and the hopes for a comfortable and enjoyable retirement. There *was* loyalty in this world, still, and the more Paige pondered the subject, the better he began to feel.

That is, until he thought of Jim Ogden. Then the unease returned, squared.

But maybe that was what Collier had been attempting to communicate. Maybe Collier knew that Paige now had the opportunity to settle accounts with Jim Ogden, finally, and to rid the company of Ogden's scourge. And that by doing so, he'd be ridding the company of the last of the high-level miscreants.

Maybe that was it.

Or maybe Collier was attempting to tell Paige to back off, to show some loyalty and compassion to the sole surviving member of the old Wylie cabal. Maybe Collier was advising Paige to do precisely that, to offer what he himself had never received from that same group, and would never have expected to receive had the roles been reversed. Maybe Collier was asking Paige to spare Jim Ogden out of, what?

Loyalty?

But the conventional wisdom seemed to suggest that there simply wasn't any such notion in this day and time. The iconoclastic Bob Becker scoffed at the concept, arguing that there was only necessity and convenience, not loyalty, in a business relationship. If you want loyalty, Becker would undoubtedly argue, then go buy a dog. Paige had been working on Becker, and not without some encouraging results, but even still, in matters of profit there was, for Bob Becker, only necessity and convenience.

Not loyalty. Not yet.

Paige wondered why there had to be a distinction between business relationships and personal relationships, why one necessarily involved different values, different structures, different enduring, fulfilling, cementing qualities.

There really didn't need to be any differences, he concluded as he drove along. Business relationships and personal relationships should, and most often do, mirror each other. Human qualities are the driving force behind both, so no significant differences need exist. Trust, compassion, kindness, etc., on the higher plane. Deceit, greed, dishonesty, etc., on the lower.

And loyalty.

But what about Ogden? Would it be disloyal to sever him from the new organization after all his many years of service to the old? Should loyalty to Ogden reign above all else? After all the conniving, the manipulation, all the "lower plane" stuff that seemed to characterize Ogden's relationships, business or otherwise?

Paige drove along as the images of Collier and Ogden and a dozen other faces danced around inside his head. He had already devastated the old Wylie group, and Ogden remained the last of the bunch. What would Collier do if the decision were his alone? What would Langdon Elerbee have done? What would Wylie do? Or Ogden?

Paige grinned slightly, as if a burden had suddenly been lifted. It was clear now, as clear as it had been all along.

CHAPTER TWENTY NINE

Paige arrived early at his downtown office, earlier than usual. Nobody but the graveyard-shift crew in data processing was at work when Paige turned on his office light at five-fifteen in the morning. It had all the promise of being a long day, and he wanted a running start on it before the sun came up and the scheduled unpleasantness began.

The severance package was complete. Everything was signed and in order. With the mere stroke of a pen, Ogden would disappear from the rolls of Elerbee Engineering as quickly and easily as if he had never before existed. The mere stroke of a pen. Almost nineteen years of employment for Jim Ogden would be reduced onto a single sheet of paper, signed by David Paige, wherein the necessities of corporate reorganization were resulting in the elimination of Ogden's position and, as a result, the annulment of Ogden's continued presence.

Almost nineteen years, Paige kept thinking. With the mere stroke of a pen.

When he felt a sudden, unexpected tinge of sympathy, Paige quickly reminded himself that were the roles reversed, were Ogden actually prevailing in this org-structure tsunami, then he, Paige, would have already been summarily dismissed. No less wailing and gnashing of teeth would have occurred, so it seemed altogether fitting that Ogden, by virtue of the cards he had drawn, be cast into that not-so-shining sea of displaced corporate managers.

Power struggles in the rough and tumble of the business world were inevitably a win-lose, zero-sum game. Paige knew that; Ogden understood it. If nothing else, Wylie had been made a believer only a few weeks before.

So it was deeded. Ogden would go; Elerbee would save some money; a layer of management would be removed.

And Paige would have fulfilled a promise he'd made to himself years before—that if he ever, *ever* got the chance, he would take it upon himself to forever rid the company of Jim Ogden.

Sherry was at her desk shortly before eight. Since Paige always kept her informed, she was aware of what was scheduled to happen, along with only three others in the building. Sherry had always regarded Ogden as a coarse, boorish jerk whose sexual overtures and executive arrogance had long ago placed a black hat upon his head. She had determined some time ago that she would never work directly for Ogden, even if it meant leaving the firm. She was relieved to know that Ogden would no longer be passing her in the hall, leering and perhaps even winking; staring at her breasts; turning as she passed to admire her from the rear; feasting his eyes upon her, always, as if she were some sort of trophy. She was relieved, greatly. But she was also tense and affected by the strain of the whole proceeding.

She brought fresh coffee into Paige's office, and then took a seat in a chair facing his desk. She seemed in an almost trance-like state.

Paige noticed the drained expression on her face. "You okay, Sherry?"

"Do I look that bad?"

Paige sipped the coffee and said nothing.

"Thanks heaps, Dave. I'm already a nervous wreck and now my boss tells me I look like warmed-over crap."

"C'mon, Sherry. I didn't say that."

"You didn't have to," she said, adding, "because I can read your eyes like an open book." She sighed heavily. "When will this thing with Jim Ogden happen?"

"Soon, within the hour."

Sherry had a look of utter dread on her face.

"I can read you too, you know. What is it you want to ask me?" Paige said, still observing her closely.

"Is it okay if I like, disappear for a while?"

"It's okay, yeah. Are you sure you're all right?"

"I'm sure, yes." She stood. "I'll be in the break room if you need me."

Paige nodded as Sherry turned and walked toward the door.

"Just one second," Paige called, stopping her and motioning for her to come a step closer. He grinned, his eyes twinkling. "You look terrific, Sherry. Just like always."

She smiled. "Looks can be deceiving, you know. You should see it from inside here."

Ogden sat across the desk from Paige, his legs crossed, fidgeting nervously with his purple tie. His grey suit was fresh and neatly pressed.

He even wore his jacket into the room, prompting Paige to think that he was pulling out all the stops in a last ditch effort to save himself. Or, more likely yet, he was all set to go on a job interview immediately afterwards.

Paige cleared his throat and sat up straight. "Tell me something, Jim, and give me an absolutely straight answer."

Ogden shrugged slightly. "Sure. Go ahead."

"How long did you think you'd last here after you found out about the Becker purchase?"

"Why do you ask?" Ogden said, tensing.

"Because I had hoped you'd see the writing on the wall and resign, and spare me from doing what I'm about to do."

Ogden drew a deep breath and exhaled slowly. His eyes avoided Paige, and his face registered little emotion.

"This is it, Jim. This is the end of the line. I'm cutting you loose, effective immediately. There's a one-year severance package for you, along with all the medical and dental and so forth. But today's the day, I'm afraid. I'm sorry it has to end this way, but I'm doing away with the position of Executive Vice President."

Ogden toyed with the tassel on his shoe, but otherwise seemed calm. "I see," he said, nodding slightly.

"I have to think that you knew this was coming. I would've expected it myself had the roles been reversed. I don't think I'm surprising you."

Ogden finally looked up. "You haven't surprised me yet. And this is certainly no exception."

There was a clumsy moment of silence when neither man spoke. Finally, Ogden asked, "Who knows about this?"

"I've told only Sherry, Doris in payroll, and my finance guy, Mortensen. And Bob Becker, of course. Nobody else."

Ogden nodded. "I appreciate that, especially since you've done everything you could to humiliate me these past few weeks."

Paige immediately tensed.

"I now know," Ogden said, continuing, "what it's like to lose *and* to have my nose rubbed in it. I certainly hope you're pleased with yourself."

"My being pleased with myself has nothing to do with humiliating you. I have no idea what you're talking about."

"That's bullshit and you know it. You made me hand out the severance packages and do the exit interviews on Don Burroughs and Vince Kincaid. Those guys were friends and associates, and you knew how that would degrade and embarrass me. And them, too. That was about as low as I've ever seen."

"I could've had you terminate them yourself," Paige countered after fixing Ogden in a cold stare. "Or I could've cut you loose right at the start, which I had fully intended to do, but something inside kept telling me to give you a little time to get your feet underneath you and test the market. I had heard rumors that you and your wife had split, and that your girlfriend had thrown you out of her apartment. And while that's none of my business, as I'm sure you'd be quick to tell me, I decided to let you stay longer than I'd originally intended. As it was, I did you a favor by firing those guys myself. I made you go over the severance stuff with them only so they wouldn't have to discuss it with someone else, someone they didn't know."

"You haven't done me any favors, so don't be offended when you don't get any thanks."

"I kept you on long enough for you to get some feelers out, to make some alternate plans. You knew you wouldn't last long after the Becker purchase was announced. We've already been over that."

"Again, don't expect any thanks."

"I also had to fight with Bob Becker to get you a good enough separation deal to keep you above water for up to a year. Plus, you'll have the proceeds from your Elerbee shares."

"This company's been my life," Ogden said, his emotion finally creeping through for the first time. "I've given it everything I've got. Over eighteen years. Hell, nearly half my entire life. And now you're giving me a check and telling me to get the hell out. Can you imagine what that's like?"

"I'm not interested in getting into all of that," Paige said forcefully. "Don't make this any harder than it has to be."

Ogden chuckled in a resigned sort of way. "God, I wish it were the other way around."

Paige reached into his desk drawer and retrieved a large mailing envelope, then passed it across the table to Ogden. "If you have any questions about any of this after you've read it, you can contact either Mortensen or me."

Ogden didn't bother with the contents. "Which one of you should my attorney contact?" he said, cocking his head contemptuously.

Paige looked confused. "Your attorney?"

"About unlawful discharge."

Paige stopped and glared from across the desk. "Are you threatening me, Jim?"

"Nope. Just making a simple inquiry."

"Then I would suggest that he contact the company attorneys in Philadelphia. I'm sure they'll draw it out and make it as expensive as possible," Paige said with an air of steely determination, adding, "for everyone concerned."

Ogden took another deep breath. "Well, I suppose you're through with me, then."

"Yes," said Paige, nodding slowly. "I have nothing further."

Ogden sat up straight. "I can only hope that someday the roles will be reversed."

"I'm sure."

"Because if it ever does come to pass, my preference would be to not fire you, but to see if I could theoretically and literally work you to death."

Paige's eyes narrowed. "Right. I think this has gone on plenty long enough."

Ogden stood. "So long, Paige. I hope you get everything you deserve out of this."

Paige said nothing.

They stared at one another for a long moment, as old adversaries, neither moving, neither blinking, each with a silent, malicious, contemptible farewell for the other. It had been years in the making, and it was finally coming to a bitter end.

Paige offered his hand.

Ogden declined, turning and leaving immediately.

Paige sat quietly for a moment. After a while he turned his chair around and faced the window, exhausted. The bottle of Jack Daniels that Ogden had sent to his room in New Orleans was in his credenza, still unopened. Paige had earlier decided he would return the bottle to Ogden, but he reasoned just before the start of the meeting that such a gesture would be vulgar and classless, not unlike the first time the bottle had passed between them. His mind then flittered ever so briefly across such issues as burnout and cancer and mortality and hell and freedom and contentment and happiness and obligation and responsibility and love and hate and loyalty and honor and vindictiveness and greed and wealth and power and risk and service and loyalty and God and earth and loyalty and—

"Dave?"

Paige turned to see Sherry standing in the doorway.

"Are you okay?"

"Sure," he answered quickly, though the tired, glazed-over look in his eyes hinted otherwise.

Sherry took a step closer. "Can I bring you a soft drink or something?"

"No, nothing, Sherry. Thanks."

"A neck rub?"

"No."

"Want me to just keep you company for a little while?"

"Thanks, but no. I'm fine, really."

"Should I strip down to my bra and panties and give you a table dance?"

It took a moment, but when Paige's expression finally softened and he began laughing, she knew he was mostly okay.

Afterward, Paige drew a deep breath and tried to shake his fatigue. "Any messages?"

"No," Sherry answered. "Wait, there's one."

She left for a moment, then returned and handed Paige a note that said only, "The deal's off."

"What's this?"

Sherry frowned. "I have no idea. The receptionist said the caller didn't identify himself, and then hung up after giving her the message. Weird, huh?"

Paige shrugged. "I suppose so."

Sherry took a step closer and gave Paige a measured stare. "Everything's okay, right? Everything's cool?"

"Yep," he answered quickly. "Everything's cool."

Paige left soon thereafter, grabbing his coat and telling Sherry that he was through for the day. When he got outside, he left his car in the parking lot and began walking several blocks until he got to the movie theater, the first such visit he could remember in years.

He deserved some time off, he told himself.

He had survived. Prevailed, even. And on this particular day, that alone was cause enough to celebrate.

Funny, though, but it didn't quite feel like a victory celebration.

CHAPTER THIRTY

Sherry Painter knocked softly on Paige's open door and walked into the office. Paige was busy studying financial reports and preparing for his weekly conference call with Bob Becker and others. There was also a project proposal with a top client in need of review, in addition to the update meetings he had scheduled with his own staff.

"I know you're busy," Sherry said tentatively.

"I'm suffocating, Sherry. I may turn blue and be dead in seven minutes. Does that give you an idea?"

"I'll send her away, then," Sherry said as she turned to leave.

Paige looked up from his laptop. "Who?"

"Sandra, the billing supervisor. You know her, right?"

"Sure. What does she want?"

Sherry appeared self-conscious and unsure. "She wants five minutes of your time, something about Thanksgiving turkeys and Christmas gift cards. That's all I could get from her. She wouldn't leave. She really wants to see you."

"Good grief," Paige said in exasperation. "Turkeys? Are you serious?"

"I know, Dave. I'll tell her to come back later."

Paige drew in a deep breath, exhaled slowly, and then closed his laptop. "No," he said, shaking his head. "I'll see her."

The short, conservatively dressed, middle-aged woman came into Paige's office and took a seat. She carried a notepad and pen, and she quickly glanced down at her notes.

"How can I help you, Sandra?"

"Thanks so much for seeing me, Dave. I have a couple of things and I'll get right to the point. First, I'd like to know if we'll be getting the grocery-store certificates for Thanksgiving turkeys this year. We've been doing that for years now, and everyone appreciates it. Second, I'd like to know if we'll be doing our departmental Christmas lunches again. Those always go over so well. And third, I'd like to know if we'll be getting the gift certificates for Christmas that we usually receive. The amounts aren't that big, but every little bit helps at Christmas, as you well know. I know you're terribly busy, but have you had a chance to think about any of that yet?"

Paige paused for a moment, then smiled softly. "You know, Sandra, I haven't thought about any of that yet. But thanks for reminding me. Excuse me for a second."

He got up and walked to the door. "Sherry, find Hal Mortensen and ask him to join us. And tell him to bring his briefcase with him."

Sherry winced, following with an ominous expression.

"No, Sherry, it's not *that*. I have something I need to give him."

Mortensen quickly joined them, briefcase in hand, a confused look on his face. He took a seat beside Sandra.

"We've got three items under discussion here, Hal, and we need your help. The items are: Thanksgiving turkeys, Christmas lunches by department, and Christmas gift certificates. I'd like you to find out what we've done in the past, what our policy has been. And most importantly, I want it consistently applied across all departments. But in the end, I want our people to get their customary turkeys, lunches, and gift cards. Okay? Can you work that out and get back to me?"

"Absolutely, sir," Mortensen answered without hesitation.

"Sandra? Are we good here?"

"We're good here," Sandra answered with a smile of approval.

Sandra thanked Paige, stood, and started out of the office. She stopped suddenly, turned, and came back to Paige's desk. "Can I tell you something, Dave?"

"Of course," Paige answered.

"There were a lot of sad faces here when you resigned and left, and mine was one of them. And then there were a lot of happy faces here when you came back as our leader, and mine is also one of them. You have a lot of people who want this company to be successful, and everyone I know here couldn't be happier or prouder than to have you back with us. Please understand that we'll support you in every way we can, and we wish you the best of luck."

Paige remained seated. "Thank you, Sandra," he said, feeling the lump in his throat. "I really appreciate your saying that. It means a lot."

Sandra then left, after which Paige turned to Mortensen.

"You'll take a drink. Right, Hal?"

"Sir?"

"Let me be more specific. Will you take a drink of whiskey? And just answer yes or no. This isn't a test. There is no right or wrong answer."

"Yes."

"Splendid," Paige said as he reached into his credenza and brought out the unopened bottle of whiskey that Jim Ogden had given him in New Orleans. "This was given to me as a gift, but since I'm a beer and wine guy, I'd like for you to have it. Just make sure you take it elsewhere before you open it."

Paige smiled. "Enjoy it, and remember to always drink responsibly. Now get busy on those turkeys."

They both laughed.

Sherry stood just inside Paige's doorway and said softly, "Dave, you have a visitor."

Paige glanced up from the thick proposal he was reading. "Yeah? Who?"

"Diane Tresvant would like to see you."

Paige closed the bound document and pushed it to the side. He then followed Sherry out of the office and greeted Diane, who, in business attire, stood alongside Sherry's desk.

"Hello there," he called, motioning for her to follow him into the office. "What a pleasant surprise."

"I hope I'm not disturbing you. I was just in the neighborhood and thought I'd stop in and see you."

He leaned and kissed her on the cheek once the door was closed.

"I was just thinking of you, believe it or not," he said as he took a seat behind his desk. "I'm glad you stopped in."

He immediately sensed something was wrong. Diane's smile disappeared as she took a deep breath and attempted to maintain her composure.

"Diane, what's wrong? What's happened?"

She took another deep breath, then gave an embarrassed grin and answered, "I've just been fired."

Paige's expression registered his immediate shock. "What? You're kidding, right?"

The tears had already begun to flow when she reached into her purse to retrieve a tissue. Paige quickly got up and moved to her, beside her, and took her hand in his.

"Why, Diane? For what reason?"

She sobbed, and Paige cradled her head against his shoulder and enveloped her in his arms, eventually quieting her.

"Those bastards," he muttered.

"God, what am I going to do now?" she asked in a near panic-stricken voice. "I've lost my job."

"I'll call your boss. I'll get it reversed. I swear to God, I'll—"

"He won't listen to you, Dave. And I wouldn't go back now, even if they'd take me. Not after this. Not after being humiliated like this."

She looked at him with tear-filled eyes. "I don't know *what* I'll do now."

"It's okay," he said, taking hold of her again. "You'll be fine, Diane. I promise."

"I've got bills to pay. I've got obligations. My God, I need the—"

"You're gonna be okay, Diane."

"I mean, who's gonna hire a thirty-five-year-old female who was fired because she couldn't—"

"Diane, please."

"Because she couldn't keep from—"

"Diane, stop!"

"Because she couldn't keep from falling in love with her client."

Paige drew a deep breath and kept his arms tightly around her.

"I was told," she said, still intermittently weeping, "that my project-manager job was being eliminated, that other staff positions were being trimmed, and so there wouldn't be a place for me; that it was part of a restructuring and downsizing."

"Any other project managers involved in this?"

"None that I know of, no."

"Dammit!"

"They wanted to get rid of me, Dave, and they did. They had all the reason they needed."

Jeff Wylie, Paige thought to himself. A parting gift, a small token of his sincerest disaffection. It had to be, *had* to be. The anonymous message about the deal being off; Wylie's friendship with Diane's boss; the fact that the accounting firm was no longer a client since the Becker organization used an altogether different firm.

"I'm sorry, babe," he said, gently rocking her. "I've brought all of this on you. It's all my fault. I'm the one to blame. You didn't deserve this. I'm so sorry, Diane."

"It's not your fault, Dave."

"Oh, but I'm afraid it is."

She straightened, cleared her throat, and then wiped at her reddened eyes and flushed cheeks with the tissue. She made an effort to smile, laugh even. "I should've gone straight home and spared you all of this."

"No, I'm glad you came."

He got up and went to his laptop to take a quick look at his calendar. The remainder of his afternoon was clear.

"C'mon, sweets. Let's go. Let's get out of here."

She gave a puzzled look. "Where? Why?"

"We'll get away. We'll drive up to the mountains. We'll spend some time together, breathe some fresh air. There are some things we need to discuss."

He closed his laptop, locked his desk, and walked over to the still-seated Diane. He extended his hand to her. She reached out and took it, but remained seated. He smiled, then raised her hand and kissed it, and she eventually rose from the chair.

"My God, I'm so thankful that you're here for me," she said. "I don't know what I would've done otherwise."

He squeezed her hand. "C'mon. Let's go for a drive."

CHAPTER THIRTY ONE

Paige was alone downstairs, wrapped in a white cotton robe. A ceiling fan on low speed stirred the air in the room, creating a chilly comfort as he sat in his chair amid the plants and paintings and modern furniture of his North Atlanta condo. It was three o'clock in the morning, and he was wide awake.

Upstairs, Diane Tresvant was sleeping.

It's working, Paige kept thinking. Elerbee Engineering was profitable, the company was moving forward, and a team spirit had begun to saturate and predominate—a direct result of the efforts and actions and attitudes of the top management, together with the employees' perceptions and aspirations and overall high levels of commitment.

It felt good to be winning. And it felt especially good to be in charge.

Paige sipped the red wine and enjoyed its warm path from his throat to his deep interior. He laughed softly when he considered for a moment the notion of his taking his first drink of the day just a few scant hours ahead of the leading edges of dawn. What the hell, he thought. It was Saturday.

Elerbee Engineering was conforming to his style, his direction, his leadership, just as he had hoped, and he was loving every day of it, every minute. And Diane was likewise his. Just that same week she had moved into his condominium, intent upon sharing her life with him to the fullest extent possible, short of contractually. But they had discussed it, more often in recent days, and marriage seemed a very real possibility in the not too distant future.

If that wasn't enough, Bob Becker had never seemed happier since his investment now seemed certain to pay off in spades over the long haul. The housecleaning and reshaping of headquarters had taken only two months, and had indeed been bloody—the commercial equivalent of D-Day at Omaha Beach—but the net result had been to launch the firm on an aggressive path of market-share gain. The newly constituted company was the single dominant entity in the industry, and Becker was virtually beside himself.

It was autumn in Atlanta. The summer's heat had bid good riddance, finally, and the dogwood, maple, cherry, and poplar leaves were transforming themselves into hues of brown, orange, red, and gold, draping the city in a virtual blanket of stunning natural beauty. The mild days and cool nights were refreshing and uplifting to the spirits of everyone, like the laughter of a baby.

And Elerbee Engineering, under Dave Paige's leadership, was kicking ass in the marketplace.

"Is something wrong?"

Paige turned to see Diane standing nearby, wearing a silky, light-blue gown, looking at him expectantly. Diane ran her hand through her hair and then folded her arms across her front.

"No," Paige said, smiling. "If anything, it's just the opposite. Everything's perfect."

"Perfect?"

"Yeah, baby. Perfect."

"At three o'clock in the morning?"

"At any hour of the day or night."

"Are you drunk?"

Paige laughed. "A bit mellow, maybe. But definitely not drunk."

"God, I thought for a minute that it might be me," Diane said as she crowded into the chair by mostly sitting atop him. She wrapped her arms around his neck and rested her head upon his shoulder. "That I'd driven you out of the bedroom and into the bottle at oh-dark-thirty in the morning."

"Not a chance, lady."

She knew it was true. She also knew that Dave Paige was a notoriously light sleeper, subject to bouts of insomnia, as if the considerable energy stores within his body and mind would erupt at a moment's notice and thereby void any opportunity for peaceful slumber.

"So why are you drinking so early?" she asked without looking at the glass he held away from her.

"Because it's chilly in this room, and because I couldn't sleep, and because I was thirsty, though not necessarily in that order."

Diane raised her head up and glanced at the fan.

Paige laughed. "Good catch. I made it chilly so I could use the wine as an excuse. Care to join me?"

"Are you kidding? You're more than twelve hours out of sync, sweetie. Happy hour's on the *other* side of the planet."

He chuckled and kissed her on the forehead. "I've never been more in sync in my entire life."

He kissed her on the lips and held her close, until soon she became limp and he could hear her steady, rhythmic breathing. He kept thinking of how well things were proceeding; how the profit picture had begun to develop some traction, finally; how he himself was now viewed by the other top executives in Becker International with respect, perhaps even envy; how well Mike Petrovic had developed into a first-rate corporate executive; how young Hal Mortensen had gotten his chance and quickly demonstrated that he had the right stuff; how the firm had finally rallied to Paige when the first vestiges of stability could be seen after the staffing makeover. Diane had ridden an emotional roller coaster for several weeks but she was now greatly excited by her new chief financial officer's position with a young, dynamic Atlanta biotech company.

Indeed, there would be some interesting times ahead.

Opportunities, as Becker would say.

And Paige and his people were up to it, he knew all too well. Every way, every day.

He shook Diane gently. "Let's go upstairs, sleeping beauty," he whispered.

"Okay," she said without moving.

He waited a moment before he stood, with Diane still in his arms, and started toward the bedroom.

He felt her softness and enjoyed the scent of her hair and the sense of her body's warmth. She was light in his arms, as light and buoyant as the feeling he held in his heart and soul, as light as his head sometimes felt, spinning with joy and excitement and gratitude when he realized just how fortunate he was to have someone so wonderful to love, something so meaningful and fulfilling to do, and so very much to look forward to.

At this point in his life, he concluded as he climbed the stairs, at this very moment, he was in *perfect* sync.

CHAPTER THIRTY TWO

"It's about people, Bob."

Dave Paige sat across the desk from Bob Becker in Becker's large but otherwise surprisingly modest Philadelphia office. The two of them were alone, each sipping a soft drink and each indulging a late-afternoon hunger with bags of pretzels. Along with other top executives, they had earlier that day completed a business review of the entire Becker organization, with each operating entity presenting their respective results for the quarter and year-end, and ending with a brief overview of their plans for the new year.

It was late January, 2003.

"I beg to differ, hotshot," countered Becker. "It's all about results. Results are what matter to me. You're not going to drop a load of that 'touchy-feely' crap on me, are you?"

Paige laughed. "No, of course not. And I don't disagree about results. But in the end, it's the people we've got that will produce the results we need."

"Do you think I don't know that? Is it your feeling that I fell off a turnip truck in Venezuela and hitchhiked here to get this job?"

Paige laughed again. "No, I've never identified you as a hitchhiker from Venezuela."

Becker took an outsized sip of the burning soft drink, belched and then wiped his mouth with his hand. He leaned forward, staring at Paige. "What are you trying to say here, Dave? What's on your mind? Is this about the new acquisition?"

"Yes," Paige said with a nod. "I was bothered by something you said."

Becker shifted in his chair, leaning back and pushing the soft drink can away. "Then get it out—tell me what I said that's bothering you."

Paige swallowed and took a deep breath. "This company that you're acquiring—the project-management consultant company from Denver— seems like a great addition and a natural fit. They have expertise that we can all benefit from, I'm sure."

"Right. So what's the issue?"

"Do you remember saying that we'll leave their management team in place until our own people can learn the business, then we'll decide which side of the helicopter to push them out of? Do you remember saying that?"

"Sure. It's standard practice. We know how to do acquisitions. We've been doing them for years."

"And do you remember one of your guys saying—and this got a pretty good laugh from around the table—that soon it would be another neutron bomb, where you kill all the people but leave all the buildings?"

"I remember that, yeah."

"I'd be curious to know if the same sort of thing was said when you acquired Elerbee Engineering?"

"Ah," said Becker, nodding and straightening in his chair. "Struck a nerve, huh?"

"I'm just curious, that's all."

Becker looked away for a moment, staring out the window, and after a sigh and a deep breath, returned his gaze to Paige. "Okay, fine. Yes, the same sorts of things were said when the Elerbee deal went down. There, does that make you feel better?"

"Not especially."

"Why?"

Paige shifted nervously. "The impression I got today is that the Becker model is to leave the acquired management team in place only long enough to make sure the transition doesn't belly-flop, and then perhaps for some undetermined time after that. After that, it's all hair, teeth, and eyeballs, or a freefall from a chopper. And if that's the model, I suppose I could be living on borrowed time if you've got someone else in mind to take over Elerbee Engineering at the appropriate time. There might be quite a few of us living on borrowed time if the model is to eventually blow off the Elerbee management team after a decent interval has passed."

"Do you think that's what I intend to do?"

"I don't know. That's why I'm asking."

Becker rose and walked to his door, declaring, "No calls," to his nearby assistant, and then closing the door before returning to his desk. He took another long gulp of his soda, emptying it, before loudly tossing the can into a nearby trash container.

"I'll ask you again: Do you think that's what I intend to do?" asked Becker, this time in a firmer, more deliberate tone.

"That seems to be the acquisition model, Bob. And if that's the model, and if the established practice typically involves the detonation of a neutron bomb at some point, and which, from the look of things, the key members of your team seemed to understand and accept, then yes, it would seem to me that that's exactly what you intend."

"How well do you think you know me?"

"Not as well as I thought I did, I'm afraid."

Becker grimaced. "I'm not taking that as a compliment, amigo."

"I'm not trying to insult you. I'm only trying to discover where I stand, where my operation stands. You've never been anything but supportive and straightforward with me, but I have to tell you, what I heard today about how you plan to deal with the Denver company, which you're telling me now is standard procedure, is like a sudden kick in the gut. I didn't see it coming, and from my own experience with you and your team it was such a huge departure that it stunned me, to say the least. I suppose it's safe to say I was knocked off balance with that much variation over what I had experienced before and with what I heard in that conference room today. Do you understand what I'm trying to say?"

"I understand exactly what you're trying to say."

Becker got up and walked to the closet in the rear of the office. Inside, there was a small refrigerator from which he removed two bottles of beer. Paige heard the bottles clink together before Becker returned and handed him a brew.

"Cheers," Becker offered as he sat down and twisted off the cap.

"Cheers," replied Paige.

"I've spoken to you about my background, about how I view things," said Becker. "We've had those discussions, right?"

"Right."

"I grew up in the construction trades, like my father, like most of my top guys," said Becker. "It's a demanding, unforgiving, cutthroat environment, hard and mean and nasty—and that's when it's going *well*— and the business tends to attract and keep people who can work in such an atmosphere and still keep some semblance of sanity about them. It's a hard business that attracts hard people, *demands* hard people, and I suppose I'm a bit of a poster boy for the sort of person who ends up getting in, and staying in, this lunacy. I would venture to say that it's unlike anything you've ever experienced in your working career. Not to say that it's better or worse, but that it's different, very different. Would you agree?"

"Yes, of course."

"When I got my M.B.A., I was taught a boatload of technical and analytical concepts that gave me an insight into the workings of business that I'd never had before, especially the high-level, strategic training, like the specific financial strains that growth imposes upon a company. I've used that knowledge to grow this company far beyond what my father could have imagined—hell, beyond what I could have imagined when I first became the president. And we've developed a model for organic growth, along with a model for acquisitions. We plan for each, and we know what the mix needs to be to hit our overall objectives. We'll buy 'em and integrate 'em. And sometimes we'll acquire one that's flawed and undervalued, make it a shining star, and end up selling it off for a bunch of cash that enables us to go and do something else. We're always open to those sorts of windfalls."

Becker took two more gulps of his beer, draining it. "Of all the useful things that grad school taught me, and there were many, do you know what it failed to teach me?"

Paige turned his head slightly and thought for a moment before answering, "No."

"I wasn't taught anything about business ethics. There was no more discussion of ethics than there was about the Reformation. It was all science and no art. I don't consider myself an unethical person, mind you, but ethics isn't something I find myself thinking about very often. I spend more time thinking about my bodily functions than I do about ethics."

Paige chuckled. "So it's all a bunch of shit?"

"I didn't say that," Becker countered, raising a finger in the air. "I just meant that it wasn't high on the list of things that hold my daily attention. And that, sir, is where you come in."

Paige gave a confused look. "Oh? How so?"

"Do you remember on the golf course in Florida when I asked you if you considered yourself an ethical person? Do you remember that conversation?"

"I remember it, yes."

"I was told by a number of people that you were an ethical person, a man of integrity, a man who could be counted upon to live up to his word. We share several clients with Elerbee, as you know, and every one of those clients I talked to told me you were a man they could trust to do what he said he would do, without exception. Your peers in the industry hold you in high regard, and in the time that I've gotten to know you and work with you and observe you closely, I can see that it's justified, no question about it. I've watched you very closely, my friend, much more closely than I typically pay attention to managers from an acquired company, and probably much more closely than you've realized. And I've had my people watch you very carefully, and their opinion of you is consistent with my own, which is not surprising. Do you have any idea why I've had you under such scrutiny?"

"I can only guess, Bob," Paige said with a shrug.

"Then give me your guess, please."

Paige took a quick sip of beer to moisten his suddenly dry mouth. "I'm not sure how to say this, and I'm afraid I'm going to put my foot in my mouth in my attempt to say it."

"Say it anyway. I'll extract your damned foot if it gets stuck."

Paige took a breath before saying, "Okay, I'll just go ahead and put it out there. Based on what you've shared with me tonight, what more I've learned about you, you may be keeping me around to provide you with an example of something you don't have."

Becker quickly pushed back from his chair and stood. Paige froze until he saw Becker heading back to the refrigerator, whereupon he pulled out two more beers. He gave one to Paige and then returned to his desk where he opened the bottle, took a sip, and stared at Paige for what seemed an eternity. Paige could feel his heartbeat in his temples, and his mouth became dry again.

"Bingo," Becker finally said. "You got it, pal."

Paige remained silent.

"I will continue to observe you, Dave. I will learn from you. I will use you as a resource and seek your counsel about matters that sometimes may fall outside your specific areas of responsibility. You will not only make this organization better, but you will make me better, both professionally and personally. I will demand that you provide me with results, always, and I will challenge you and hold you to your numbers just like I do everyone else on my team, but I haven't seen anything thus far that gives me reason to think you won't be up to it. Am I coming through loud and clear?"

"You are, indeed. And I'm honored that you view me as you do."

"And you should be," Becker said, pausing before saying, "and I want to address the 'neutron bomb' thing that got you sideways with me."

Becker glanced out the window and collected his thoughts. "How long do you think I would've left Jeff Wylie and his crew in charge of Elerbee Engineering if you hadn't been in the picture?"

"Only as long as it would've taken to get your own handpicked people in place."

"And would you consider yourself a handpicked person?"

"Yes," Paige said with a nod. "I had a moment of doubt earlier, but no more."

"Bingo, again. The reason we didn't blow everything up in the beginning is because we had you there. You were my guy all along, and I suppose it's my fault for not making sure there was zero confusion on your part. Is that clear now?"

"Yes, thanks."

"Earlier in this conversation, I got the impression you might be struggling and having second thoughts about being part of this company, and about working for me. Am I right?"

"Honestly, yes. I have to confess there was a moment of doubt."

"Still there?"

"No."

"Are you sure?"

"I'm sure."

"Because if you're going to have second thoughts about being a part of this organization, or about me, then you should leave. Tonight, and without delay. The demands on you will be heavy, as you can already see, and if your heart's not in it, then I damn sure don't need the rest of you. You won't do me any goddamn good, and you'll end up wrecking your own friggin' health. It happens all the time. I will not let that happen here. Loud and clear?"

"Loud and clear."

"I should make it clear that neither you nor anyone else in Elerbee Engineering has a lifetime contract. You know what I've said about results. I should also point out that Elerbee Engineering is guaranteed absolutely nothing as far as being an ongoing part of this organization for infinity. It doesn't work that way. Nothing is sacred; nobody is sainted. Are we clear on this?"

"We're clear."

"Then are you in or out?"

"I'm in, Bob. Let there be no confusion about that."

Becker stared at Paige before nodding and grinning slightly. "I'm certainly glad to hear that, and I'm glad we've had a chance to clear the air. But you've not had much to say, pilgrim. Anything you want to add? Any questions, comments, bitches, ultimatums?"

Paige laughed. "No, none of those."

"Okay," said Becker, shrugging. "Then teach me something."

"Beg your pardon?"

"That's right. You heard me tell you that I wanted to learn from you. So teach me something."

"About what?"

"About how I can make this a better company, for starters."

Paige stood. "Another beer?"

Becker laughed loudly. "Yes, grab us another one."

Paige distributed two more bottles and took his seat.

"I'm waiting," said Becker after a sip. "And you should be as direct with me as I was with you. Those are the only ground rules."

"Then for God's sake stop referring to changing a company's management as 'blowing them up.' And get rid of that neutron-bomb bullshit. You're giving the impression that there is absolutely zero loyalty in this company, and that's not quite accurate. You and your top guys have been together a long time, and there is a strong bond between you. You're all tough businessmen, and that's fine, but you don't want to be seen by the newly acquired company as heartless, condescending bastards in an impenetrable little clique, all knowing and all to yourselves. You're professionals, not thugs, and your language and behavior should reflect that. You should've outgrown that by now."

Becker recoiled, and seemed ready to respond.

"Do you want it straight, or not?" asked Paige in an authoritative tone.

Becker threw up his hands in mock surrender.

"I know we've talked about loyalty before, about how someone should buy a dog if they want loyalty, about how you've scoffed at the whole concept, saying conclusively and even proudly that there is no such thing as loyalty in business anymore. I find that not only inaccurate, but also ignorant. I've seen how you and your closest managers interact. I know enough about the history of this company to know that there were many, many people loyal to your father, and then loyal to you, as this company grew and prospered. And I have to believe that that loyalty was returned. I also know that you're married, and from everything I can gather, very happily married. And my sense is that loyalty plays a role in both the quality and the longevity of your marriage. I spent three years as an officer in the Marine Corps, and loyalty is a fixed cornerstone in what is easily the finest, most overachieving organization on this planet, bar none. And that's loyalty up and down, to be specific. When the loyalty of the managers and employees started breaking down at Elerbee Engineering after our founder's death, the company began a downward spiral that would have morphed into a death spiral if not corrected. Am I reaching you loud and clear?"

Becker smiled. "Loud and clear."

"And, to your credit, the downward spiral was corrected when you stepped up and purchased the firm. Our morale is good, our people are motivated, our managers are excited. Do you think those descriptions would apply if the Elerbee employees knew their top parent-company executives were laughing and talking about turning a neutron bomb loose on them? And you don't have to respond; I already know the answer. I know the answer because I know them, because I'm one of them."

Paige paused, nodding at Becker. "Come to Atlanta next week, Bob. Sit in with my staff and me. Talk to some of our employees. Ask them how they feel about their company, and why. Let them tell you about the sense of family we've developed, and how we're still working at it. Let them tell you about our culture and our traditions, about our respect for one another, about Thanksgiving turkeys and monthly birthday cakes and quarterly all-hands meetings where anything and everything goes. Come to Atlanta and get a sense of something other than the P&L and the projects list."

Paige nodded and took a sip of beer. "That's it. That's all I've got."

Becker sat back and relaxed, his hands clasped behind his head. "Are you sure, honcho?"

"I'm sure, yes. I've probably said enough already to get my ass fired twice over, so I'll stop."

"I'll be in Atlanta next week. Then I want you to go with me to Denver and meet with our newest addition. And I want you to spend some time with their executive team. And at some point I'll want you to provide your impressions and observations on them to my staff here in Philly. Can do?"

"Can do."

"Listen, Dave, I'm sure as hell glad you're a member of my team. I can't tell you how pleased I am to have you with us. You're going to do great things here, I know it."

"So I'm not fired."

Becker laughed and held his beer in the air. "You're not only not fired, but Sally and I are treating you and your beautiful daughter to dinner tonight."

Paige smiled broadly. "In that case, I thank you, Sara thanks you, and the Atlanta jeweler where I'm about to buy a diamond engagement ring thanks you."

Becker stood and moved toward Paige, reaching for his hand and offering an enthusiastic handshake. "Well now, congratulations, my man," he said. "Now *that*'s the best news I've heard all day."

CHAPTER THIRTY THREE

They had come all the way from Frankfurt—five in all—to cold, damp Philadelphia. They represented one of Germany's largest engineering conglomerates, flush with cash and determined to use those resources to grab a large slice of American market share.

It was November, 2003.

Bob Becker had been skeptical at first when his old friend Peter Halloran had called from Boston and advised him of the Germans' keen interest. It seemed especially odd, now that everything had finally settled so nicely into place. But, Halloran had quickly added, these guys were rich and powerful and had made it abundantly clear that they would spare no expense to get what they wanted. And Becker knew from experience that the timing wouldn't always be ideal when an opportunity so suddenly materialized out of the clear blue.

So, Becker had agreed to listen.

There were interpreters to assist with the language difficulties, though all but one of the Germans in the negotiating party spoke passable English when they weren't pecking away at the laptops they each carried. There was an attorney in each group, but most of the talking was done by the business principals. Halloran was also there, serving as a go-between from his friendships and previous dealings with the German executives.

The session lasted ten hours on the first day, eleven on the second, and four on the third. By the time it was completed, the German firm had offered Bob Becker the equivalent of more than twice what he had invested in Elerbee Engineering.

Becker wanted assurances of employment continuity for the key members of Elerbee's top management. The Germans countered that such an arrangement would only impede their ability to administer the business as they saw fit. They might indeed retain several of the Elerbee executives, perhaps even more, but that decision would need to rest solely with the purchaser, argued the Germans. Becker insisted upon some sort of stipulation; the Germans resisted and offered in its place an even higher price.

It went that way, back and forth.

Until finally the Germans were ready to call.

Halloran advised Becker that all of the chips brought from Frankfurt were now squarely on the table. It was time to take it or leave it, to "make whoopee or make tracks," as Halloran so deftly characterized it. When Becker's Senior Vice President of Finance looked over the details of the final German offer, he waited until he and Becker were alone before he uttered an expletive and gave a look of astonishment.

The simple question thus became: Did Becker want to continue in the engineering-consulting business in a big way? Or, might the proceeds of what would amount to a sizeable cash windfall be used more productively elsewhere, as in the predominant and core Becker International segment, the contracting business? And there was the issue of the Elerbee team of executives, especially Dave Paige, who had done such a sensational job in bringing the company up to speed so quickly, and then keeping its performance at a high level. What of them? Leaving them unprotected was distasteful, yet there was always the possibility that the German firm might indeed retain many of them. Generous exit packages had already been baked into the purchase price.

It was the cash that so tempted Becker. It seemed too much to walk away from; just too damned much. Everything and everybody had a price, and the boys from Deutschland were thinking among themselves that they had found it with regard to Robert Becker and Elerbee Engineering.

Becker needed a break to clear his head, so he abruptly left the building and went outside in a strong, biting wind for a short walk on the city streets.

And Halloran? He was quietly detached, but he was clearly the one who had brought the Germans to Philadelphia in the first place, and he just as clearly wanted to broker another lucrative deal for Bob Becker and another handsome fee for himself.

Becker passed a deli and, realizing that he had worked through lunch, stopped in for a beer and a steak-and-cheese. It was noisy inside, bustling with nearby shop owners and harried businessmen eating on the fly. The tables and booths were all occupied, so he squeezed onto a stool at the counter. As soon as his order had been placed, his mind shifted involuntarily to the crucial business decision that awaited him at his office. He went over once more the fact that, even though he had exactly what he wanted with Elerbee Engineering and Dave Paige, the financial model validated what was all too obvious: That the amount of cash on the table was simply too much to ignore; that an offer of this magnitude should be seized before the other party gained its senses and rescinded it; that the potential uses of the cash boon should displace any hesitation or emotion or loyalty he felt to his Atlanta group, or to anyone else.

Or should it?

He was the one with the judgment and the brain of a human being, not a model.

But when he contemplated the ridiculous sum the cocky Germans were offering, and the many productive uses to which it could be put, he seemed uncharacteristically overwhelmed. He stared at his sandwich for a moment, shook his head, and then began to laugh out loud.

And he could clearly see the dollar sign through the laughter.

And the many digits that followed.

And what the infusion of that much cash could mean to his organization.

When it finally hit him in its full measure, like the inhalation of an anesthetic agent, it momentarily stunned him.

"What the hell's going on here?" he suddenly blurted out, drawing mid-bite stares from several of his lunchtime neighbors.

"Have another sip o'suds and it'll all make sense," called an unkempt, grizzled old-timer nearby at the counter, dining on beer and soup.

Becker smiled. "You're probably right, pop," he said as he relaxed and heeded the advice. "A glass of water for me, please. And while you're at it, freshen the glass of my friend here, and give me his check."

He returned to his office and took a seat, glancing quickly at a report from Dave Paige on several opportunities for improved market share for Elerbee Engineering. He thought about Paige, and about the enthusiasm he had sensed from the Elerbee employees he had met and talked to on his visits to the Atlanta headquarters and their far-flung branches over the course of the past year. Even the people in the Philly office, the former Becker and Associates, whose excitement over the purchase and consolidation had initially been tempered, were now highly supportive and enthusiastic over what they had seen and heard from Paige and his top-flight management team.

Becker thought about the team-building sessions, creatively developed and deftly facilitated by the talented Paula Markham, that Paige had initiated with his Elerbee group with such success that the same training was now working its way through several other Becker International entities.

He thought about the many conversations he had enjoyed with the insightful Paige, whose opinions mattered greatly to him and whose counsel he had come to value as much as anyone he knew, anyone he had *ever* known, apart from his own father. The newly married Paige was growing in his executive role, and would soon be prepared for even greater responsibilities, of that Becker was certain. And Becker had grown as well in the past year, his softer skills becoming more polished through the practice he now conscientiously applied. He was still the analytical, demanding, hard-driving alpha leader he had always been, but perhaps now with a bit more introspection, a bit more awareness of his influence upon those close to him, a bit more mindful of the impressions that others came away with after being in his arresting presence. He knew in so many ways he was still a work-in-progress, and always would be, but he had never before been as comfortable with himself as he now was.

Becker swiveled his chair around and stared out the window at the Philadelphia skyline for maybe a minute, maybe two. The world seemed to slow, then pause, allowing the swirling mass of issues inside his head to move to the center, slowly, as if drawn there by magnetic force, and then to stabilize into a discernible, comprehensible order. It all then seemed to crystallize, clearly and suddenly, and he nodded and turned his chair around to face a world that he knew would not wait on him indefinitely. He nodded and smiled, knowing that he was probably imprudent, probably foolish, perhaps even slipshod, but otherwise altogether comfortable with his decision.

Becker summoned his finance guy from the meeting room, drew a deep breath, and declared gruffly, "Decline the bastards' offer and kill the negotiations. Tell 'em I'm staying with what I've got because I've got what I want, and who I want. It's as simple as that."

The finance executive looked at Becker disbelievingly, as if the perceptive, opportunistic, hardnosed boss he knew so well was under the influence of some sort of mind-altering drug.

"Are you sure, Bob?"

"Damn right I'm sure. Tell our Frankfurt friends thanks and so long, and be sure to advise Pete Halloran that Elerbee Engineering is here to stay, and with me."

THE END

EPILOGUE

Paige's Laws of Business:

*When things seem so bad that they can't possibly get any worse, expect another short dose of agony before things start to turn around and the rain finally stops, the sun shines, and the skies are blue.

*When things seem so good that they can't possibly get any better, expect another short dose of ecstasy before things start to turn around and the sky turns dark, the wind blows, and the rains begin.

*Charisma can open the door; character will keep you in the room; competency will open successive doors.

*Look, listen, and learn, now and forever more. And take the time to enjoy a laugh with a friend.

*There really is such a thing as loyalty. I see it every day.

AUTHOR'S NOTE

My strongly held belief reflected in this novel is that business is an honorable and worthwhile profession. Every vocation has its share of charlatans, and business is certainly no exception. The highly publicized misdeeds of a few have been costly to many, and most often the malefactors have rightly been convicted and sent away to prison. But the business profession is populated by an overwhelming majority of good people who behave responsibly and ethically, who care about and look after their stakeholders, and who provide opportunities for those who seek success. I know. I saw them, knew them, and worked with them. For years, I was one of them.

The American system of free enterprise has provided countless millions with economic prosperity, upward mobility, and the dignity that comes with honest effort and accomplishment. Business leaders and innovators have provided our society with astonishing advancements in transportation, communications, manufacturing, medicine, and information, to name a few. American business has helped this nation win world wars, reduce poverty, and achieve a standard of living that is unparalleled in human history. Business executives have created charitable foundations, financed museums, libraries, and aquariums, and donated billions toward making the lives of others better.

I sincerely hope that the business profession will continue to attract ambitious young men and women of integrity, with high standards of ethics and professionalism, and in so doing help to crowd out those of dubious character. Like it or not, the extent to which business can successfully and convincingly regulate itself will go a long way in determining the levels of regulation that will be imposed upon it externally.

— **Gerald Gillis**
Marietta, GA

ABOUT THE AUTHOR

Gerald Gillis is an award-winning author who had a successful career in the medical-devices industry before becoming a full-time novelist. He holds business degrees from the University of Georgia and the University of Tampa. After college, Gerald spent three years as an officer in the U.S. Marine Corps. He and his wife reside in the Atlanta area. *Dare Not Blink* is Gerald's third novel.

OTHER BOOKS BY GERALD GILLIS

Bent, But Not Broken

Mike Billingsley volunteered for officer training and combat duty in Vietnam with the U.S. Marine Corps. Billingsley led his men through the jungles and the rice paddies, discovering along the way that men are built of more than blood and bone. He discovered that he could be bent, but not broken, by the rigors of warfare and the emotional strain of the Vietnam War

ISBN: 9780878440658

Shall Never See So Much

U.S. Marine Lieutenant Tom Flanagan is serving as an infantry platoon leader in Vietnam during the 1968 Tet Offensive. Meanwhile, on the other side of the world, his sister Kate works on the staff of Senator Robert F. Kennedy, as RFK begins his ill-fated quest for the presidency. The brother and sister are estranged and their reconciliation, along with Tom's own survival in combat, becomes uncertain. *Shall Never See So Much* is a story of heroism, tragedy, and triumph.

ISBN: 9781609101312